PLUG IN

The Guide to Music on the Net

Ted Gurley

W.T. Pfefferle Ph.D.

Prentice Hall P T R
Upper Saddle River, NJ 07458

For book and bookstore information

http://www.prenhall.com

Library of Congress Cataloging-in-Publication Data

```
Gurley, Ted.
     Plug in : the guide to music on the net / Ted Gurley
  W.T. Pfefferle
       p.  cm.
     Includes index.
     ISBN 0-13-241050-8
     1. Music—Computer network resources. 2. Internet (Computer network)
  I. Pfefferle, W.T.  II. Title.
  ML74.7.G87 1996                            95-33741
  025.06'78—dc20                                  CIP
```

Editorial/Production Supervision
   and Interior Formatting: ***Ann Sullivan***
Interior Design and Formatting: ***Gail Cocker-Bogusz***
Cover Design: ***DeMarco Designs***
Manufacturing Manager: ***Alexis R. Heydt***
Acquisitions Editor: ***Mark L. Taub***
Editorial Assistant and Copyeditor: ***Dori Steinhauff***

©1996 by Prentice Hall PTR
Prentice-Hall, Inc.
A Division of Simon & Schuster
Upper Saddle River, NJ 07458

The publisher offers discounts on this book when ordered in bulk quantities.
For more information, contact:

   Corporate Sales Department
   Prentice Hall PTR
   1 Lake Street
   Upper Saddle River, NJ 07458

   Phone: 800-382-3419
   Fax: 201-236-7141
   email: corpsales@prenhall.com

All product names mentioned herein are the trademarks of their respective owners.

Printed in the United States of America

10 9 8 7 6 5 4 3 2 1

ISBN 0-13-241050-8

Prentice-Hall International (UK) Limited, *London*
Prentice-Hall of Australia Pty. Limited, *Sydney*
Prentice-Hall Canada Inc., *Toronto*
Prentice-Hall Hispanoamericana, S.A., *Mexico*
Prentice-Hall of India Private Limited, *New Delhi*
Prentice-Hall of Japan, Inc., *Tokyo*
Simon & Schuster Asia Pte. Ltd., *Singapore*
Editora Prentice-Hall do Brasil, Ltda., *Rio de Janeiro*

Contents

A Basic System Checklist and Additional Resources

2 The Fan

B Fan Newsgroups

C Fan Mailing Lists

D Newsgroups About Music Styles

E Mailing Lists for Music Styles

F Mailing Lists for Record Labels

3 MIDI

5 For Dreamers 275

Foreword

So one night a party you get into this discussion with a bunch of other music buffs about whether Jimmy Buffett ever really lived in Montana, and, if so, why did he leave? You say he did, but left to get away from a bad marriage. They say you are wrong. Now you have to prove yourself.

You could spend most of the next day reading the liner notes off of all Jimmy's old album covers but there is a better way: The Internet. A most amazing information resource for anyone interested in anything.

Whether you are a musicologist, DJ, musician, promoter or just a "big fan," the Internet is the playground that has previously existed only in your mind. It is a bottomless cup of facts, trivia, history, song lyrics, artist bios, itineraries, fan clubs and that's just for starters. Each day, new and exciting pages are being added to the web. Newsgroups and bulletin boards where you can discuss specific topics with others who share your interest are springing up all over. And it's just beginning.

Users of the Net are not only talking music, they are making music, sharing sounds and ideas with others around the world. The dawning of the interactive age has given away to a bright new way of exchanging information. Thoughts are being transformed to sound and immediately made accessible to millions.

It is utterly amazing.

But amazing as the Internet is, it is still a tough place to find your way around; that is why this book is so important. With PLUG IN: THE GUIDE TO MUSIC ON THE NET, Ted Gurley and W.T. Pfefferle have created a dazzling roadmap to the musical resources on the Internet. This is a highway they have been traveling daily for years. They have seen it grow from a dirt path to a big eight-laner. They can steer you away from the bumps and construction zones and help you avoid a few toll booths. So if your obsession is sound, fasten your guitar strap, the long, (and sometimes strange) trip is about to begin!

ROBERT A. LINDQUIST
Editor-In-Chief: *Mobile Beat: The DJ Magazine*

About the Authors

TED GURLEY

Ted Gurley has worked in the broadcasting and entertainment industry for over 15 years. His main gig is negotiating advertising time for Katz National Television's client stations. He also writes for "Mobile Beat" magazine and spins for Sound Associates, a mobile DJ company in Dallas, TX.

W.T. PFEFFERLE Ph.D.

W.T. Pfefferle, Ph.D. teaches English and writes in Dallas, Texas. He's been playing music for over 15 years and favors Fender products. He runs Moonguy Management, a multi-faceted music and production company.

ABOUT THE ILLUSTRATOR

Marc Borms

Marc Borms is a 30 something guy from Belgium, married with 3 lovin' children. Programming is his job. Illustrating and blues are his passions. He met up with W.T. and Ted somewhere on the Net.

Acknowledgments

We'd like to thank Mark Taub for seeing the potential in this book. This project could not have been completed without the herculean efforts of Dori Steinhauff and Ann Sullivan. Gail Cocker-Bogusz made everything inside look pretty. We thank all those folks at Prentice Hall for their unending support.

We also want to thank our cool drawing friend Marc Borms for bringing "Pluggy" to life, and Gene Confrey for supplying great MIDI information.

We'd also like to thank our reviewers, Frederick Barthelme and Bob Lindquist, and our friends and families. We also want to thank our hundreds of Net friends who corresponded with us over our months of research.

Introduction

ELVIS SURFED

Being a musician is a lot like working for a really cool moving company. Most of your time is spent moving amps, guitars, drums, and PA equipment from place to place and every once in a while you can plug in and play. Being a music fan is like working in a very cool warehouse. You're always in the process of completing your CD collection, making tapes, storing old albums, shopping for that hard to find piece of product, and searching grocery stores for last month's issue of *Guitar Player*.

Musicians and music fans are obsessed with stuff. How do we get it? Where do we find it? What do we do with it when we've got it? It's an overload of information that at its worst begins to suck some of the joy out of just playing or listening to our favorite music. So, when someone says they're going to give you even more stuff, it's easy to want to run away.

But that's what this book is about, in part. We've got more information for you than you've ever seen. We're going to take you, both musicians and fans, to a world of information. But we're not just loading you up for no reason. We're doing all of it because over these past months we've discovered that the Internet, the international network of computer servers, is the most amazing place. There are resources here that simply make the job and the joy of being involved in music more gratifying.

And the book is for everyone, from the basic, rabid fan of a single band like Pearl Jam; to the fan of a genre, like the blues; to the working musician; to the club owner; to the recording industry professional. But obviously this slim volume is only one part of this multi-media package.

- *Think of this book as your sampler. It's where we give you a taste of some of the best and most heavily trafficked areas online.*

- *The CD ROM contains software demos to introduce you to a world of musical expression.*

- *And finally, we've built a little home for all of us on the Internet; it's what we call a website. What we'll be doing on the website is updating this book and all the info in it on a regular basis. We all know how quickly computer information goes out of date, but we're going to fight to keep you up to speed with the latest stuff we find.*

Nowhere else has the Internet and its music services been opened up like this. We've done the work; we've spent the time. Now it's time for you to have fun. This book and the accompanying CD ROM will take you (literally) to places you never believed were possible. We'll do everything from telling you where on the Internet you can find the lyrics to your favorite Hank Williams' song, to explaining where you can find that hard to locate poster of KC and the Sunshine Band. We'll tell you how to use the Internet to get your band heard by music executives. We'll show you how to set up your own homepage, or just visit the homepages of your favorite stars.

And because music is something we like to share with others, we will introduce you to a world of people behind the Internet: people like you who know the words to every Bruce Springsteen song; people who know exactly when and where Blues Traveler will next tour your area; people who can help you find a bootleg of that concert you went to in 1982 in Denver, Colorado; people from Denmark who once met Jimi Hendrix in a club and played his guitar. Get ready for a journey, a ride, a breathtaking trip into a world of information unlike any you've ever seen.

The book is broken down into chapters that in many ways stand completely alone. If you're new to computing, or even just new to the Internet, we think Chapter 1--Getting Online--will be imperative. There you will find everything you need to know to get involved: What kind of computer do I need? What kind of hardware? Software? Programs? Monitor? RAM, ROM? All those abbreviations and acronyms and seemingly pointless jargon gets stripped away as we show you how to put together an honest to goodness system, or just get your current system ready to rock.

If you are a music fan, then Chapter 2 will be a godsend. In this chapter we sort out the sometimes confusing and widespread world of newsgroups, mailing lists, and World Wide Web homepages. These locations are part of the essential lifeblood of many artists worldwide, and we'll show you how you can be a part of the dialogue, discussion and fun that comes only to those people in the know. We also try to introduce you to fundamental sources of information about styles of music. If you're looking to get introduced to the blues or bluegrass, zydeco or rap, techno or Texas swing, we'll send you to places where you can get the history and the background.

In Chapter 3 we begin helping musicians. The world of MIDI (Musical Instrument Digital Interface) has been discussed in thousands of books, but never like it is here. Again, we try to cut through the morass of jargon and technical overload and instead get you up and running in the shortest amount of time with the smallest investment of time and money. We'll not only help you get situated with the right equipment (keyboards, drum machines, etc.), we'll also help you choose the right software. Then, when your system is ready to go, we'll plunge into the vast resources of the Net to show you how a world of information is going to help you make, create, shape and play music like never before.

Chapter 4 is for audio professionals; whether you're a musician; DJ; recording studio owner, producer or engineer. Even if you have your own home studio. In this chapter we talk about maximizing your chances at business success. We talk about equipment and where to get it online. We provide directories of record companies online. We help you find business software. Being online means easier and more immediate contact with record companies, artists and equipment supply companies. Being online means no more waiting.

Finally, we'll do a little crystal ball thing. We let you in on the future of music on the Net in Chapter 5. The field is expanding and growing almost exponentially, so we've found a way to keep you up to date. We'll update the book at our Plug In website.

Anyway. It's time to start having fun. It's important to remember that while Elvis lived long before the information superhighway got rolling, that he definitely did surf. We think he'd approve. Let's get online!

I have always been into singing songs with the radio and at church, believe it or not. (You have to admit the Baptists have some pretty rockin' tunes!) and then I started playing guitar. I discovered Ozzy Osbourne and the Beatles at about age nine...from then on, music has become my passion, my love, and my life. You feel like part of a big family of sorts...it kinda lets you know that you aren't always alone in the world.

Shannon D. Darst
sdarst@acad.stedwards.edu

Getting Online 1

Okay, let's go. Getting "Plugged-In" is painless if you have the right equipment, the right software, and you know where to call. This chapter will focus on the basics of gaining access to music online. We will look at the hardware and software setup needed to:

1. go online
2. connect to bulletin board systems (BBS) and commercial services
3. hook into the Internet resources directly

This chapter will provide you with a foundation for plugging into the world of music and point you to detailed specialty resources for learning more about a specific topic.

THE EQUIPMENT

First you need a computer and a modem, the device that allows your computer to communicate through the phone lines with other computers and networks.

The computer itself is relatively unimportant in making online connections on commercial services and BBSs. A hand-me-down 286 or 386-PC or yesterday's Mac can make the connection to these type of services. To connect directly to the Internet use a top-line PC or Mac system.

> ## Platforms? Windows vs. Mac
>
> There's a lot of talk and concern about Windows vs. Mac. Of course this debate goes back in time among any faithful users of machines. (We've had lots of friends who still swear by their old Commodores, Apple IIes, and Amigas.) This debate, however, goes away once you're on the Internet. All the different platforms are equal, so whether you're on an Unix-based Vax, Sun or Sparc workstation connection at your office or university, or state of the art Windows or Mac system, you all move around on the Net in the same way.

Modems are defined by speed, the amount of data that can be received and transmitted in a second. You can plug in and access data with any speed modem; however, the faster the connection, the faster you can enjoy the music or files you are trying to transfer. The local BBSs and commercial services usually allow connections at speeds up to 28.8 kbps. Most new machines today are being shipped with a 28.8 kbps modem (meaning that 28,800 bits per second can be transmitted and received. However, a 28.8 pushes the limits of the current analog telephone system. In the near future, faster connection will be possible with digital phone lines and cable connections (check out chapter five for more details about this).

Your modem needs a communications package that gives you an interface to "speak" with other computer systems. If you're not yet using the latest 32 bit version of Windows and its built-in communications package, get a program like Qualcomm, Telix, Procomm or Crosstalk to allow you to connect to the Bulletin Board Systems. Most of the commercial services provide special software free-of-charge to interface with their service.

At the end of this chapter, after you read about the various services available, you will find a checklist of the basic setup you need.

THE WORLD ONLINE

There are three types of online connections you will want to consider: bulletin board systems, commercial online services and a direct Internet connection. We'll contrast the three and give you some criteria to decide which connection to the world of music you want to plug into.

Bulletin Board Systems (BBSs) tend to be specialized in nature. If you are only interested in the world of MIDI or communicating with other musicians or fans with the same interest as you, a bulletin board may be the only online source you need.

The commercial services like AOL, Prodigy and CompuServe tend to be helpful especially for beginners by pointing the way to information and entertainment you might be interested in. Additionally, for the new user, the pleasant and easy graphical interface of the major servers makes for a fairly easy entry into the online world. Even with a moderate amount of Windows experience, for example, you will find AOL to be a dream. Big clear buttons to click on. Colorful headers to direct you around the space. Originally, with the commercial services you were confined to the service you had dialed into; however, with the addition of the World Wide Web access you can now use the commercial service simply as a starting point.

Direct connection to the Net provides the most flexibility to the online user. It is usually a flat fee based system with unlimited access to all resources of the Internet. Most services that offer direct connection also provide custom services for bands, businesses, or anyone that needs more than just simply a connection.

The following chart will help you compare connection choices:

Services	BBSs	Commercial Services	Direct Connection (SLIP/PPP)
Flat Fee	Sometimes	Usually	Yes (except for users who get accounts at school or at work)
High Speed Connection (28.8 and above)	Sometimes	Depending on Location	Yes
World Wide Web	Rarely	Yes	Yes
Internet E-mail	Sometimes	Yes	Yes
Newsgroups	Sometimes	Yes	Yes
Custom Services (website design)	Rarely	No	Yes
All Internet Tools (archie, telnet, gopher, etc.)	Sometimes	No	Yes
All Internet Access (full access to Usenet)	No	No	Yes
Free Software	No	Yes	Yes

The type of connection you select is based on your needs. Each connection has strong merits depending on your interests.

Bulletin Board Systems (BBSs)

BBSs have been around since the first microcomputer appeared on the scene. The idea is simple. A computer is set up with both a modem and a phone line to act as a central point for information exchange. Many of the BBSs far exceed the hobbyist level and add multiple phone lines and multiple CD ROM drives to provide specialty information. Most BBSs charge a fee for access and you also incur any long distance charges. There are several BBSs dedicated to music that we will refer you to in later chapters.

For the most part, BBSs are connected using the basic communications software we discussed in the equipment section above. Every major city in the U.S. has hundreds of localized BBSs. Usually lists of local boards can be found in regional or local computer newspapers. To keep up with the BBS scene look for a magazine called, *Boardwatch*.

The Commercial Services

The commercial services are one of the best places for the beginning user to start. Each one has a wealth of information for someone interested in music. All of these services provide music news and information groups you can plug into, and also Internet E-mail and newsgroup access.

Each service has added Internet World Wide Web access to allow the user to venture outside of the commercial site. The World Wide Web (WWW) is the graphical network that contains websites dedicated to one topic, person, or company. These locations are known as homepages and allow seamless jumping to other locations on the Internet (see Internet section later in this chapter.)

The costs for commercial services start at under ten bucks a month; however, be sure you understand the per hour charges. Here is a thumbnail sketch of each of the major services.

• *CompuServe 1-800-848-8199*

CompuServe is the oldest of the online providers. More than three million subscribers worldwide use CompuServe's special interface, which is available for both Mac and Windows users. It has more than 2,500 databases available for user access. Many people consider this one of the best research services available online.

The basic service is a flat fee that allows unlimited access to more than 100 services. Extended service incurs a pay-as-you-go charge.

CompuServe provides Internet web access through its partnership with SPRY. Connection is accessed within CompuServe with the command GO INTERNET. This command will access the NetLauncher and its two components: SPRY Mosaic and the CompuServe Internet Dialer. The dialer provides local call access to the World Wide Web for 92% of the United States and allows the use of any browser. Net-Launcher software can be downloaded free of charge from the information service.

CompuServe offers user discussion areas called forums. There are forums focusing on all aspects of music. Several music oriented businesses are also online, offering vendor support for various products. Here's just a handful of the music oriented businesses and areas you'll find on CompuServe:

Some CompuServe Music Resources

All Music Guide (GO ALLMUSIC)

The popular All Music Guide is the complete reference to all styles of music. There is a discussion forum that is linked to the AMG on Compuserve.

BMG Music Club (GO CD)

Compuserve has cornered the market on the music clubs; not only do they have Rolling Stone magazine, but all inserts that go inside.

Columbia House (GO FREECD)

Our old friend. We used Columbia House to build our music collections back in the 70s.

Creative Labs (GO BLASTER)

Anything you want to know about Sound Blaster cards is here.

Entertainment Encyclopedia (GO HHL-249)

Includes a ton of music references like an A-Z listing of rock oriented music groups.

Fan Clubs (GO FANCLUB)

You'll find all the fan clubs here.

MIDI Vendors (GO MIDI)

Software and hardware for the musician.

Music/Arts Forum (GO MUSICARTS)

This is a catch all area. You might find folk or bluegrass discussions here.

Music Collectables (GO COLLECTORS FORUM)

How much is that Beatles LP with the butcher cover really worth?

Music Hall (GO MUSIC)

This is the entry point to all the music topics on CompuServe.

Recording Industry Forum (GO RECORD)

This is the area for all the record companies.

RockNet Forum (GO ROCKNET)

This is where you will find discussion about your favorite artists.

Rolling Stone Online (GO RSONLINE)

The magazine we all know and love is here with Random Notes and a discussion area.

• America Online (AOL) 1-800-827-6364

America Online is the number one commercial online service in the US. AOL provides its own interface software that is available in Windows, Mac and DOS formats and is free of charge from the 800 number. (It can also be found bundled in numerous magazines; you might have the software laying around right now.) AOL's software is a bit more graphical than the CompuServe software.

AOL houses a huge collection of software; it boasts that it has more than 40,000 free software and shareware programs online for the taking. (A piece of shareware software is an evaluation copy. You can try the program out and if it suits your needs, you can purchase a full-featured version of the same program. Shareware is extremely common.)

Like CompuServe, it also provides user forums that focus on all aspects of music. It has an extremely busy Grateful Dead forum. AOL also has a specialized music section called Music Space; you'll see a graphic of it on the following page. Within Music Space you can connect to almost anything oriented to music. You will find music-oriented magazines online like *Spin* and *Stereo Review*. If you like classical music then you will want to read the latest reviews from *Saturday*

Review. Also in Music Space, you will find MTV Online, tour information from popular bands and connections to musical sites on the World Wide Web.

AOL is accessible at 14.4 kbps through the AOLnet and, in certain parts of the U.S., it can be accessed at 28.8 kbps. AOL provides Internet Mail, Usenet newsgroups, and the Web.

A Sampling of AOL Music Resources *(we've listed the keyword in quotes)*

Advanced Gravis Sound Cards: "gravis"

Here are some tips for the sound card.

Chat: "centerstage"

Center Stage houses live AOL events like interviews and discussions. Check out the "archives" to see previous guests like Mick Jagger.

Comptons Encyclopedia on Rock & Roll: "Compton Rocks"

An encyclopedic entry for important players in the history of rock music.

Grateful Dead: "dead"

Of course, the Grateful Dead forum.

House of Blues: "blues"

The club is online with sound samples and schedules.

Interviews: "rock interviews"

An archive of interviews.

MTV: "MTV Online"

MTV's home on America Online.

Music News: "entertainment news"

The entertainment headlines.

Music Trivia: "rock and roll -> more -> NTN Rock Trivia"

We like this area; it's just like playing one of those trivia games at a bar or restaurant. If you see one of us on here, watch out!

New York Times Music News: "times music"

Rocklink: "Rocklink"

Here's where you will find some reviews.

Spin Magazine: "Spin"

The magazine online.

Stereo Review Magazine: "Stereo"

You can check out some really neat gear here.

Tower Records: "Tower"

A virtual store where you can browse or buy.

Tribute to Rock & Roll: "Rock and Roll"

Warner Records: "Warner"

You can see the new releases here.

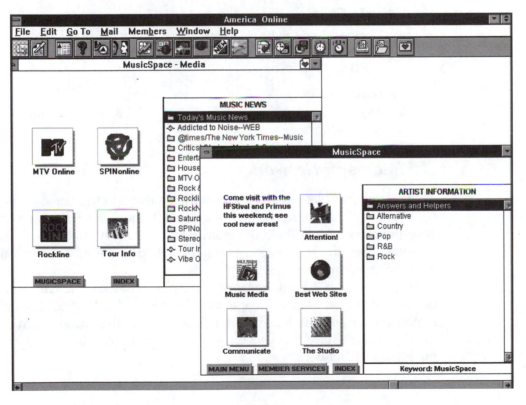

• Prodigy 1-800-776-3449

Prodigy is even more graphical than AOL; it also has its own software. Prodigy provides five hours of access a month for $9.95.

It was the first commercial online provider to offer World Wide Web access through its own software.

A Few Music Resources on Prodigy

Music 1 Bulletin Board

This is a message area that focuses on rock music and alternative music. You reach this board by using jump "music 1bb."

Music 2 Bulletin Board

This is the message area that features jazz, folk, classical, contemporary, reggae, blues and any other discussion thread not covered in Music 1. You reach this one by jumping with "music 2 bb."

Music Chat

Chatting seems to be popular with a lot of Prodigy members. To reach a music chat room, use the jump word "chat" and then select the "music" room.

Music Charts

Several categories of Billboard music charts are online, use the jump words "music charts."

• Microsoft Network

The Microsoft Network (MSN) is available through the latest version of Windows. The program offers seamless Internet connection and has advertising partners to help underwrite the cost of the network. It will definitely keep the big three commercial networks (AOL, Prodigy and CompuServe) on their toes.

Every user who installs the latest version of Windows will have Internet and Microsoft Network capability. By the end of 1996, it is estimated by analysts at International Data Corp. that more than 65 million PCs will have this version and will be a mouse click away from the Microsoft Network.

Music Resources on the Microsoft Network

Guitar Network

Information about products, repair, interviews and articles.

Jazz, Blues, Folk and World Music Forum

A place to find out information and discuss these styles.

Music Central

This is a link to a very useful Microsoft product. It is a database that includes music reviews, sound and video clips and discography information.

MIDI and Electronic Music Forum

You can download music and get technical assistance.

Mr. Showbiz

CD reviews and entertainment news.

The Music Resource Forum

Dedicated to music education. It has online guitar and bass lessons, music theory lessons, and music related Internet links.

Rock Net

A live chat area and rock music newswire.

INTERNET 101

Here's how to get connected directly to the Internet. In this section we'll tell you how to get connected and introduce you to the tools you need to navigate the network and find all kinds of music resources.

Direct Internet Connection

Anyone can get access to the Internet using a local service provider. Service providers sell several different kinds of Internet access at different speeds and with different features. As with buying a stereo system, you have to know what features you want and what you want to pay, then shop for the best deal. (Nearly every primer on the Internet fills up pages with lists of providers for all areas. One of the best sources is

Internet CD, a Prentice Hall book by Vivian Neou. We would also recommend you look in the business section of your local paper, or ask friends who have computers to get tips for the best providers in your area.)

Before you invest in a service provider, find out if you are already connected through your company or school. If you don't know, go to the computer center or the MIS department and ask around. If you are already connected through your school or company, this is almost always a better service than you can buy from a local provider.

Grades of Service

If you don't already have Internet access, here is a summary of some of the types of services available.

• *Dedicated Access*

Dedicated access is the most flexible and expensive of the Internet connections. Caution, this is a labor intensive approach. Recording studios and record labels might want to consider this type of access. This connection gives you full access to the Internet. A service provider will help you lease a dedicated high speed phone line (the faster the more expensive), then install a special routing computer at your location known as a server. All the computers at your location will be connected through a network to the server and will be full-fledged Internet computers. The Prentice Hall book, *Internetworking with TCP/IP, v.1*, can help you with a dedicated setup.

• *SLIP and PPP*

SLIP and PPP is the perfect solution for connecting at your home. This is the way to put a record store, band, or yourself on the Net. In most major cities, providers are popping up everyday, and many of them can give you "almost dedicated access" for a fraction of the cost. You use specialized Internet software to dial into a network when you want access. Once connected you are actually on the Internet, you are not just using someone else's computer. Typically, these services run $20-$40 a month for unlimited access. You will need the special software that is either available commercially or as shareware, a high speed modem (28.8 kbps), and a top of the line PC or Mac.

Be sure to comparison shop the features of the service provider. Some providers have someone available around the clock for customer support. Strong support is key since you will be running specialized software and may encounter some problems that you need a real "geek" to solve. Find out the speed of the incoming modems at the service provider. This will limit your access speed. Again, the faster the better. Find out if the provider subscribes to all of the Usenet newsgroups available. Also, ask the provider if server storage space is available for creating your own site on the World Wide Web.

THE INTERNET TOOLKIT

The tools and resources of the Internet are vast for the musician and music enthusiast. The following is a guide to the features of the Net. Each tool has an icon next to it, these will be used later in the book to make sure you are using the right feature. You will want to refer to this section as you read through our guide. If you need additional help pick up *Zen and the Art of the Internet*, 3rd edition; or *The Internet Passport*, 5th edition; both published by Prentice Hall.

Stuff to Read

• *E-mail*

E-mail is the most basic and widely used form of Net communications. Every system on the Net supports some sort of mail service. Users who are not connected to the Internet can also receive and send mail originating on the Net.

Mail finds its way to your mailbox by using the Internet address. Addresses have two parts that are separated by the @ sign. The first part before the @ sign is the mailbox, which is the name you use on the network. The second part refers to the computer you use to access the network and is called the domain. You can see how this works by looking at our E-mail addresses: tgurley@onramp.net and bobhate@airmail.net.

Sending and receiving mail is easy. If you are actually on the Net, you send and receive E-mail by starting up the E-mail software that came with your Internet software package or a shareware version like Eudora. The E-mail program connects to your server and retrieves all the mail with "your name" at that address. You can send messages to anyone in the world via Internet E-mail. All you need is to know the address of the person you are sending to.

Commercial services and BBSs have a mail area that guides the user through the mail process. Be sure you know if the service you are on charges you for incoming as well as outgoing mail.

• *Mailing Lists*

One of the most common things to do with E-mail is to subscribe to mailing lists about topics you are interested in. There are hundreds of lists for musicians and music fans on the Net ranging from lists for fans of specific groups to specialty lists for harmonica players. All you have to do is subscribe to the list and soon you'll have a mailbox full of mail about a topic you are interested in. At the end of each section you'll see a list of mailing lists you might be interested in.

Small lists are usually maintained manually by a person at the other end. This can be a list that sends out the monthly calendar for a local band. Later in the book we'll show you the music related lists; a good rule of thumb is if you see the word "request" in the address, it is probably handled by a real person and all you need to do is simply send a polite note request to the address and ask to be added to the mailing list.

As lists grow, often they automate and have software manage the mailing list. These lists automatically send out messages posted by the members of the list to every member. This can happen almost instantly. One of the most common types of automated lists is a Bitnet list. This is a network within the Internet that automatically processes and sends mail directed to a specific mailing list. To work with Bitnet lists you need to have a basic understanding of listserv. Listserv is a software system on IBM mainframes that automates the list. One listserv list we subscribe to generates between 70 and 120 E-mail messages each day.

Listserv, the Mail List Manager

Listserv is the automatic mailer for IBM based mainframes. The automatic mailer can handle thousands of mail addresses efficiently.

Suppose that your name is Bob Smith you want to join the Blues-L, the Bitnet blues list, which lives at @brownvm.brown.edu.

JOINING A LIST:

Send message to LISTSERV@brownvm.brown.edu that contains this line:

SUB BLUES-L Bob Smith

You don't have to have anything in the subject area. After you send this message you should get two messages back:

A short welcoming message with a description of Listserv commands.

A technical message telling you how hard the system worked for you.

Then the messages will start flying.

POSTING A MESSAGE:

To send to the list, mail to the list name at the same machine for example:

BLUES-L@brownvm.

In your message be sure to include a brief summary of the subject since many people get 100s of messages every day.

GETTING OFF THE LIST:

Send message to LISTSERV@brownvm.brown.edu with the line:

SIGNOFF Blues-L

STOPPING MAIL FOR AWHILE:

If you go on vacation or on a business trip and you don't want to come back to a full mailbox. Send:

SET BLUES-L NO MAIL

It will stop sending blues-l messages. To turn it back on send:

SET BLUES-L MAIL

The mail will resume.

GETTING HELP:

Listserv can do a lot of different things. To see the list send a message containing:

HELP

and you'll get the list.

• *Newsgroups*

As lists grow, they often become public accessible newsgroups as well. Newsgroups are similar to the lists that you subscribe to except the newsgroup is available for anyone to read. Newsgroups are distributed by the Usenet network. This is not an automatic feature of the Internet; Internet providers, commercial services, and BBSs must pay a fee to subscribe to all or part of the Usenet, and to offer the newsgroups to its users. Every site ships all the articles it gets several times a day to all of the computers connected to the Usenet. The Usenet newsgroups can basically be thought of as a giant bulletin board with each message being placed in an appropriate area. Each day more than 50,000 articles in more than 20,000 newsgroups are distributed over the Net.

There are hundreds of music related groups. They are arranged in hierarchical groups; for example, the alt group (alt is short for alternative) contains: alt.fan.madonna, alt.music.ska, and hundreds of others. The rec (short for recreational) area also contains a lot of music related groups like rec.music.indian.classical. The following page has a listing of the articles available in the alt.music.ska newsgroup as seen with the Winvn news reader. (Winvn is one of several excellent newsgroup readers available as shareware.)

Newsgroups are read with SLIP or PPP connection through a news reader program that is packaged with your software. On the commercial services, you use the built in software. To add a new group to your news reader, simply download the current list or view the current list and type in the name of the newsgroup. All the current messages in the subscribed group will be made available to you. To find out more about the newsgroups you can refer to Prentice Hall's *USENET: Netnews for Everyone* by Jenny Fristrup.

```
                              alt.music.ska (71 articles)
Articles   Sort   Search
>17379 05/31 el9m3@cc uou e9u      23 MODEL CITIZEN tour dates HELP!
n17380 06/02 tan4               6 Scopalomine- come back!!!
n17381 06/02 Madrus            13 Re: Boston shows???
n17382 06/02 Madrus            10 Skaville Vol. 2
n17411 06/03 Mike Toole        37  .
n17423 06/03 Moon Records       3    .
n17416 06/03 Madrus             5      .
n17383 06/02 maxson            28 stop shouting:Re: Date Rape Song
n17384 06/02 Terry Dwyer       15 Test
n17385 06/02 Terry Dwyer        4 Bim on Friday, Bim w/ Steady on Sat.
n17393 06/02 Kevin Mayer -Goldman  29  .
n17386 06/02 Ivan Falalang     81 Re: SKA! In the midwest!
n17387 06/02 Mike Marvis       67 FREE! music journal. Subscribe here
n17388 06/02 Michael Feldgarden 19 shows in CT-NY
n17389 06/02 Dale Delcosamto   29 Re: LA area shows, June 15th-19th!
n17390 06/02 Moon Records       4 Re: Toasters Tour Dates?
n17391 06/02 Richard Dennis Fer 23 Re: MIDWEST SKA!!
n17392 06/02 Liam A Angeles     5 Re: LA area shows, June 15th-19th!
n17394 06/02 Robert Reville    25 NE Old School Ska Party
n17449 06/04 Robert Reville    30  .
n17395 06/02 SKAVENGERS         2 Let's Go Bowling & Skavengers
n17396 06/02 Anne Goulet        8 Boston shows???
n17397 06/01 Dennis Higgins    13 Re: old school on CD?
n17398 06/02 Lady I             4 PLEASE PLAY DENVER 6/23!!!
n17422 06/03 Matthew Pusicha   17  .
n17425 06/03 Jeff Bosco Biafore 13  .
n17443 06/04 Lady I             6  .
n17399 06/02 Pinky Tuscadero   27 Re: MN ska
n17400 06/03 Stewart J Dickson 18 New York Citizens
n17429 06/04 MockTBaup          1  .
n17401 06/02 Da Colonel        28 Re: SKA! In the midwest!
n17402 06/02 Da Colonel        17 Re: Bouncing Souls...
n17403 06/02 Maiye              2 Re: NO DOUBT (SKA)
n17404 06/02 Maiye              1 Out Of Order
n17424 06/03 Jeff Bosco Biafore 10  .
n17420 06/03 Maiye              4    .
n17405 06/02 Alan and matt Rubi 8 SKA SKA SKA
n17406 06/02 Da Colonel        55 elbows and knees playlist for 6/2/95
n17407 06/02 The Checkered Cabs 16 DC SKA!
n17408 06/02 Gregory Pazmides  19 Lookin' for Music Lovers
n17409 06/03 acme@webbe.com     3 Re: !#!#!#! INSATIABLE! Live In June !#!#!#!
n17410 06/03 acme@webbe.com     7 Re: Ska: The Third Wave
n17417 06/03 Madrus             4  .
```

FTP: Moving Files

As you move around the Net, you will find files and documents that you want to view or save on your own system. You've found, for example, the guitar chording for U2's song, "One" and you want to try it with your band. Or you found the complete discography of Fleetwood Mac, and you want to take it with you to the CD store. In each case, you need to copy the file to your system. That tool is FTP. You can see in the following graphic, a basic FTP session with guitar link, which is a repository of guitar chording and notation.

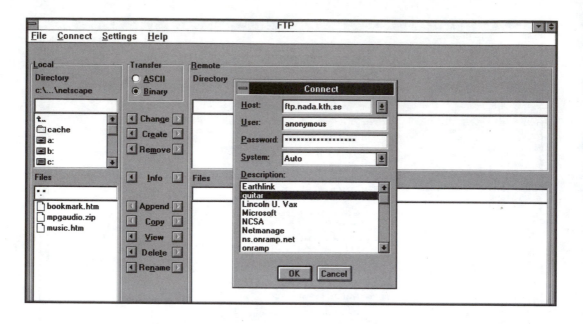

FTP is File Transfer Protocol. It is the way to log onto a system and retrieve software or files from another computer. With FTP you can load MIDI files on your system or download the biography of Robert Johnson and read about his pact with the devil at the crossroads. FTP also allows you to upload text, data, or programs to another computer.

Public files on systems are usually accessed using anonymous FTP. Most systems require passwords to log in. If a file is public, no password is required. If you start FTP and connect to a remote computer, and use "anonymous" as the log in name; no password is mandatory, however, it is considered common courtesy to give your E-mail address as the password so that the system manager knows who is connecting to the system.

Telnet

Most systems on the Net let you actually log onto the system computer and use it just like you are there. The Internet tool for getting on another computer is called Telnetting. You can Telnet to a system in the same building or halfway around the world.

Telnet tools are included with most Internet software. You can telnet to CD Stores and search the inventory. Or you can do music research by telnetting to major libraries around the world. As you can see in the following graphic, you can use Telnet to log into services like CD Now, an online CD store.

```
                                    Telnet - cdnow.com                              ▾ ▴
File   Edit   Disconnect   Settings   Script   Network   Help

                        cdnow

- - - - - - - - - - - - - - - - - - - - - - - - - - - - - - - - - - - -
                        Welcome to CDnow!
                     The Internet Music Store

      CCCC  DDDD
     CCC   DD  DDD
     CC    DD    DD    NN      N    0000    WW            WW   !!
    CC            DD    NNN     N   00   00  WW            WW   !!
    CC            DD    NN N    N   00     00 WW      W     WW   !!
    CC            DD    NN N   N   00     00 WW   W W    WW   !!
    CC            DD    NN   N N   00     00  W  W    W  W   !!
     CC           DD    NN    N N  00     00  W W     W W
     CC    DD    DD    NN      NN   0000    WWW        WWW   (tm)
      CCC   DD  DDD
       CCCC  DDDD       ------------------------------------------
                        The Internet Music Store   (c) 1994
                     Every Album. Discount Prices. Fast Delivery.
--Enter for more (q to skip)-- █




Ready                                                           VT100        NUM   22, 32
```

The most important thing to remember when you Telnet is that you are a guest on another computer. Watch for instructions as you first get logged in. Sometimes the instructions through telnet connections are full of shortcuts that long-time users have already figured out. One of the key things to look for is the exit or escape command. Usually as you log on you'll see it shown. Normally if you get stuck, type "quit" or "exit."

Search Tools

• *Archie*

If you are searching for software or downloadable files use Archie. Archie is a search utility that is provided with most Internet software packages. Archie cruises around the Net and will check database after database by searching for files or the type of file you describe.

Log onto an Archie server that is close to your Internet server site. Enter the string (or subject) that you want to find i.e. "springsteen;" the server does not recognize upper or lowercase letters. Next, set the number of hits; this determines how many matches the search utility tries to find. With Springsteen it turned up seven matches, notice the graphic of the Springsteen search below.

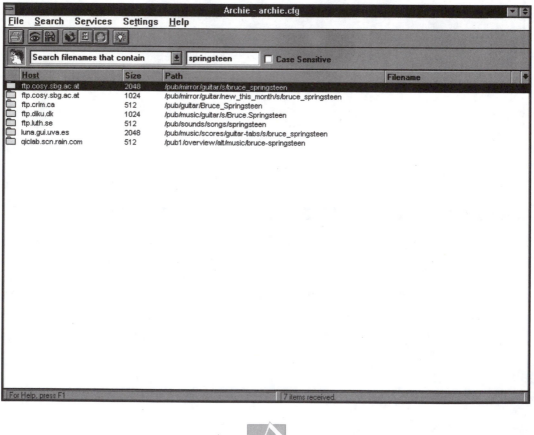

Archie has become such a popular resource that each server is often handling multiple requests from several users at one time. Try to log on during the early morning or late at night.

• *Gopher*

Gopher is a text-based search tool that displays nearly everything in a menu format. It displays Internet resources much like the directory display on your computer. Searching gopher space is usually the fastest way to find information on the Net.

Gopher is a stand alone software that is part of most Internet software packages. It is also available as shareware.

To use Gopher you log onto a computer's gopher server and you will be presented with a hierarchical display of places to go all over "gopher space." The Gopher tool also has a search utility called Veronica that can search all of the gophers in the world by key words. Below you'll see a Veronica search of the word blues.

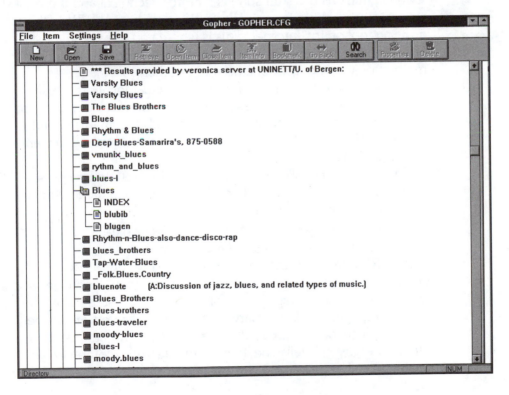

World Wide Web

If you think all this stuff sounds a bit too technical and there must be an easier way, there is. The World Wide Web or WWW is the fastest growing tool on the Internet. This is where you will spend most of your time surfing for entertainment or information. It is an effortless method of jumping from one area to another.

The Web is actually a method not an actual location; it uses hyper-text technology. The process allows you to travel though graphical "links" along the Internet from one related document, sound file, or picture to the next. You choose where to go and when you want to go to the next location.

These links are called URL's, Universal Resource Locators. A URL is simply the address of the site of the resource you are looking for. For example here are our URLs:

http://rampages.onramp.net/~tgurley/index.htm

http://web2.airmail.net/bhate/index.htm

All URLs start with the "http" prefix; this tells the software that the document is written in hypertext transfer protocol language. A colon and two forward slashes always follow the "http" statement. The next part "rampages," tells the server (the computer you are logged into) where to look on a site called "onramp.net." The final portion of the URL, "/~tgurley," tells the host computer (the computer you have contacted) what page you want to see.

Hypertext

Hypertext is the key to the engine that will drive you through the Web. Think about the last time you were in a record store and went looking for a style of music you knew only a bit about. You look through the blues section and some things look familiar like Muddy Waters, but others like Skip James really don't. Is Skip like Muddy or like Stevie Ray Vaughan? So you keep searching trying to find links. Hypertext technology provides those links.

Imagine if the same record store was hypertexted online. In the following graphic you can see a page from the "Blue Highway" web site, as you look at the artist, you see a photo of Muddy Waters. You click on Muddy's photo and it tells you that Muddy is part of the "Chicago sound." Next you can check out Muddy Water's "roots" or see other "Chicago Sound Players."

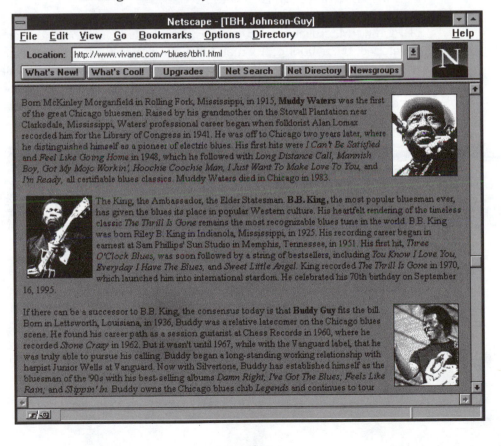

Next you click on Muddy's "roots" and discover that his style developed from the "Delta sound" made famous by Robert Johnson. Then you notice that Skip James was a contemporary of Robert Johnson. Now you've got it! Skip is a traditional Delta player who was playing a bit earlier than Muddy Waters.

The Browser

Different servers have created Internet WWW browsing programs. It was created at the European Center for Particle Physics as a text-based system for scientists to exchange data. The forerunner of today's graphical browsers was "Mosaic," which was developed for mainframes and work stations by the National Center for Super Computing Applications (NCSA). A Windows version was developed, but the general impression was that for the home user it was too slow for dealing with the large graphics files on the Web.

The current browser of choice is the "Netscape" browser. Over 85% of PC and Mac users are currently using Netscape. The browser was developed by a young, former employee of NCSA (the makers of Mosaic, the granddaddy of web browsers) who realized the potential of creating a program that kept the speed limitations of the home user in mind. Evaluation copies are currently available by FTP on the Net.

• *World Wide Web Search Tools and Indexes*

The Web is growing at such a fast pace, you could spend days trying to locate one specific site. If you can't find the music resource or band information by using this book, or the Plug In website, fortunately there are search engines and indexes to help you out.

The Web contains dozens of online directories, indexes, databases, and search tools to help you find things quickly. Some of these are very broad searches and others are music specific lists.

Also, in your web browsing package or on the commercial services you will find bookmark lists and hot lists to get you started.

General Lists and Search Engines

You will quickly find that *everyone* is trying to build a better mouse-trap as it comes to finding information. Obviously like any kind of mousetrap, some will be better and some worse. You can probably find 50-100 different search engines online somewhere, but why bother? We've taken a spin on nearly everything out there, and we swear by the ones listed below.

CUI W3 Catalog

http://cuiwww.unige.ch/w3catalog

A searchable database of several Net catalogs. This site is in Switzerland, but is mirrored at several locations around the globe.

TradeWave Galaxy

http://www.einet.net/galaxy.html

A collection of lists. Including a large number of music oriented lists.

Harvest Information Discovery and Access System

http://harvest.cs.colorado.edu/

This site contains a lot of specialized search engines called brokers that conduct a search based on criteria you input.

InfoSeek

http://www.infoseek.com

The full featured version is a subscription based search tool to the Web. You can do a free search only yielding 100 hits. It's also available as a preset button on Netscape.

Jump Station

http://js.stir.ac.uk/jsbin/js

This site uses robots to sniff out sites on the web. It is somewhat slow from the U.S.

Lycos

http://lycos.cs.cmu.edu

One of the easiest search engines to use. Input a topic and a list of sites containing that topic are returned.

Webcrawler

http://webcrawler.com/Webcrawler/WebQuery.html

Another good searchable database. It responds fast.

World Wide Web Worm

http://www.cs.colorado.edu/home/mcbryan/wwww.html

This is another searchable database that has over 3,000,000 World Wide Web locations and is serving over 2,000,000 searchers every month.

Yahoo

http://www.yahoo.com/

This is the most popular combination list and search tool. It has tons of music related stuff.

Alta Vista

http://www.altavista.digital.com/cgi-bin/query

Yet another search engine, but because it's coupled with an equally easy to use newsgroup searcher (that's a little better in our estimation than the one in Deja News), it's a good all purpose unit.

Open Text Index

http://www.opentest.com/omw/f-omw.html

Talk about a search! Open Text claims that their engine actually searches every word on the WWW. This claim is big, but we believe it. The downside is that to really do a decent search, your jumping off point should be pretty clean. Don't spell anything wrong; don't get words in the wrong order. It's a terrific search, but it's a little unforgiving for those of us who may be a little vague.

PLUG IN For More Info!
Browse to the website at
http://www.prenhall.com/~plugin

• *Music Specific WWW Search Tools*

Global Electronic Music Marketplace

http://192.215.9.13/Flirt/GEMM/gemmhome.html

This is an interesting place. It contains a search engine that allows you to type in an artist name or a style and you get a listing of both new and used items for sale and resources on the Net that might be of interest. For example, a search for Muddy Waters discovered a couple of web links and several collectable records for sale. After the search you are given the option to subscribe or to make this a permanent search, in other words, every time something pertaining to Muddy Waters shows up the service will send you a mail message.

The Ultimate Band List

http://american.recordings.com/wwwofmusic/ubl/shtml

This engine tends to be heavily oriented to popular and rock music. The same Muddy Waters search that we used in the Global Electric Music Marketplace turned up no matches. More about this site in the Fan section.

WWW Music Database

http://www.cs.uit.no/Music/

This is a Norway based site that allows searches by artist or group or album title. There are over 800 artists listed with links to albums and reviews. This site is independently maintained.

NOW YOU'RE READY TO PLUG IN!

So now you are ready. You've seen some rock information, some blues and roots music. Now, we'll show you where to find the music you are interested in.

With these tools of the Internet, you now have everything you need to start discovering the world of music on the Net. If you need more help look at our basic system setup and additional resources to help you out. Or, turn to a section that interests you and start a musical journey around the world.

Basic System Checklist and Additional Resources A

Here is a basic system for any fan or musician who wants to take full advantage of the music resources on the Net. You can still access the Net using systems smaller or less powerful than the versions below. However, if you're starting out or ready to upgrade, we'd heartily recommend you shoot for the levels listed below.

THE HARDWARE

	PC	Mac
Processor	Pentium 75 or better	Power PC chip 75 MHz
Memory	Minimum of 16 MB RAM	16 MB RAM
Hard Drive	At least 1 Gigabyte	Gigabyte
Modem	28.8	28.8
Add-ons	Soundcard and Speakers (Soundblaster compatible) CD ROM (at least Quad speed)	CD ROM (at least Quad)

THE CONNECTION

The first choice is to sign up with a local service provider that you can talk to and who can help you with problems. Normally you will pay less than $30 a month for a PPP connection. If you don't have access to a local provider, consider AOL. Also, look at adding a separate phone line to access the online world, this will keep your family or roommates happy.

SOFTWARE

To connect to your service provider, you'll need SLIP or PPP software. Your provider will usually give you shareware versions or you can buy a commercial package. In several of the Prentice Hall resources listed below you will find software bundled with the book to get you started at low or no cost.

You will also need to collect sound file players to allow your system to decode several of the sound files on the Net. You see, sound files can be created for Mac, PC, or UNIX based systems and each format requires a different decoding package. These can be found once you get up and running on the Net itself.

The Ultimate Collection of Winsock Software

http://www.tucows.com/

Like the name says, when you need Winsock software, this is the place to head.

PRENTICE HALL INTERNET RESOURCES

Single copies of these books can be ordered at 1-800-947-7700 in the U.S. or via E-mail: orders@prenhall.com.

Basic Guides:

Zen & the Art of the Internet. This is the basic primer to all the terms and network basics of the Internet.

The Internet Book—subtitled "Everything you need to know about computer networking and how the Internet works."

Connectivity

Instant Internet with WebSurfer. This is a one-stop connection source to getting online.

Internet CD. A collection of Internet tools described in detail in the book and distributed on a CD.

Internet Anywhere. This package is designed for the small business or the home user to be able to get online fast and get moving with E-mail and newsgroups. It also comes with software.

Resources

Usenet: Netnews for Everyone. A guide to newsgroups and where to find them.

Internet Mailing List Navigator. This is for Windows users and includes software and extensive details about all the mailing lists.

The Downloader's Companion for Windows. Another great resource that includes handy software for viewing, transferring, and decoding files.

HTML

HTML for Fun and Profit. A guide for setting up HTML pages on the web and includes HoTMetaL an editor for this language.

Security

Protect Your Privacy. This is a guide to security on the Net and includes a copy of PGP, Pretty Good Privacy software.

PERIODICALS

Boardwatch

As we mentioned earlier, this is the best reference for keeping current with the nuts and bolts of the BBS scene and the Internet.

Net Guide

A monthly that will keep you current with web sites, newsgroups, and the latest techniques for web page design.

Wired

A great magazine for getting a glimpse of what the future may bring for the Net community. The magazine focuses on the big picture of the Net and its impact on our society.

The Fan **2**

Quite simply, the Net brings people together. My favorite musician, a folk-rock singer/songwriter named Harry Chapin, died in 1981 in a car accident on the Long Island Expressway. I felt that his music and his message had long been forgotten by most people, until a friend and I created alt.music.harry-chapin. Without even advertising the group, hundreds of people have found it and have shared similar feelings towards the man and his music. The Internet has that unique ability to bring people with similar interests and feelings together.

Brian Bieluch
bribieluch@aol.com

Regardless of your tastes, there is a home for you online. Whether you have single artists you're interested in, or a whole genre of music, the Internet features hundreds of newsgroups where fans trade info, criticism, breaking news, concert info, tapes and CDs. You can chat with another Grateful Dead fan, or trade one of your Pearl Jam concert tapes with someone in another country. You can read the newest issue of *Spin* magazine or order the newest CD by Green Day. Your options range all over the Internet, including the major commercial servers.

This chapter is a little unwieldy, so here's a quickie guide to what's coming up:

- Newsgroups - Usenet groups where single artists are discussed.
- Mailing Lists - Lists for artists that will be sent to your E-mail address.
- Music Styles - A guide to all kinds of music, blues to classical to world, etc.
- Artist Webpages - World Wide Websites for some major Net powers, and for an esoteric collection of others.

NEWSGROUPS

There are two primary ways in which to correspond with fans: 1) the Usenet newsgroups (see chapter 1 for more details) and 2) mailing lists.

Perhaps the greatest boon of the Internet are the newsgroups. These groups—really like bulletin boards—feature comments, ideas, reports, questions, gripes, criticism, love notes and the like over nearly every artist. Big or small, from Presley to, say...Primus, there is likely a group available to you.

Regardless of software, most Usenet viewers look a bit like the following one, the very popular Winvn. This is a sample group page, showing some of the groups available.

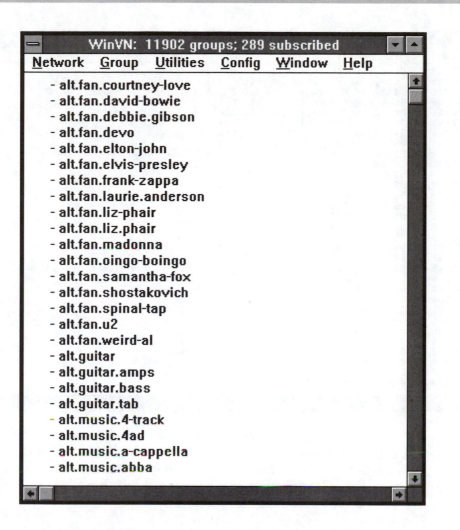

Once you've scanned these, you might want to pick a particular one. Let's see what folks are saying about Madonna!

```
 —                        alt.fan.madonna (99 articles)              ▼ ▲
 Articles   Sort   Search
 n12837 06/04 MCross#755          1 madonna's homepage                   ▲
 n12853 06/05 Jan Arild Lindstre 10   ▮
 n12841 06/04 Marty Robinson     16 Re: % Intruder at Madonna's! %
 n12866 06/05 William McBrine    10   ▮
 n12842 06/04 Oliver Maxwell Irv 10 Looking for a M. doll
 n12865 06/05 William McBrine    10   ▮
 n12844 06/04 superfly@RTD COM   28 Diana Ross Vs. Madonna, Liz Taylor, Stre
 n12856 06/05 Jan Arild Lindstre 35   ▮
 n12879 06/05 superfly@RTD COM   40     ▮
 n12885 06/05 CHUCKRAF            7       ▮
 n12881 06/05 Michael Rivas      12     ▮
 n12859 06/05 CHUCKRAF            5   ▮
 n12880 06/05 superfly@RTD COM   26     ▮
 n12867 06/05 Sean Kinnell       28     ▮
 n12878 06/05 superfly@RTD COM   36     ▮
 n12888 06/05 parlo@yvax bvu edu 27   ▮
 n12900 06/06 superfly@RTD COM   82     ▮
 n12907 06/06 FAZ                36       ▮
 n12845 06/04 LONE WIERDO         1 test..ignore...
 n12848 06/05 Deanne Eleanor Ver 13 Re: 15 Least Favorite List—LTTWM
 n12849 06/05    none             3 Re: Madonna on Dave?????
 n12850 06/04 Robert Alonso Jr   17 I'll Remember
 n12882 06/05 Michael Rivas      21   ▮
 n12851 06/05 Sonya Walker        3 Madonna Web Page
 n12855 06/05 Jan Arild Lindstre 19   ▮
 n12896 06/06 Sonya Walker        8   ▮
 n12854 06/03 Rick Wilcox        11 Re: TOP 15 FAVORITE MADON
 n12857 06/04 Jordan Redner       2 Test Posting, please disregard
 n12858 06/04 superfly@RTD COM    8 Re: Madonna AIDS?
 n12877 06/05 puente@ids net     17   ▮
 n12883 06/05 Michael Rivas      22   ▮                                  ▼
 ◄                                                                      ►
```

You can see the names and/or E-mail addresses of the different posters; you can see the size of their articles (# of lines), and the title or "header" for their piece. (Whenever you see the little blocks ▮, that denotes a "thread," or a number of posts all about the same topic.) So you decide to read one particular post.

Once you read it, you find you've got something to say in response so you decide to fire off your own note.

The size and frequency of posts varies considerably in these groups, but in the section that follows we've covered groups that are both heavily traveled (upwards of 100 posts a day and more!) and/or exceptionally worthy. You'll quickly find out that a few stellar posters in a worldwide newsgroup will make the time you spend reading all worthwhile.

The heart of the Net is information. Sharing and exchanging information is why people use and love the Net. For me the music newsgroups are useful and entertaining. The exchange of information concerning new releases, bootlegs, and imports travels so fast, you always hear stuff on the Internet before reading it in a newspaper or magazine.

Joshua S. Jacob
JoshuaSJ@aol.com

The mailing lists may have a different format, but they are the equal of the newsgroups in every way and maybe even better than the groups because they are moderated more carefully and usually contain just the best of the info submitted. We'll look at newsgroups first and then mailing lists second.

Be forewarned that the list below is not intended to be comprehensive. It is merely a sample of some of the best and the brightest. We've tried to compile a representative list of newsgroups. These are healthy, lively, and offer some real opportunities to involve yourself in your own choice of fandom. Of course, as you read this, groups are coming in and going out of favor. It's important to be creative in your own searches. This is a nice little list to use as a starter. Don't be afraid. Lurk. Post. Get involved.

> **PLUG IN For More Info!**
> **Browse to the website at**
> **http://www.prenhall.com/~plugin**

Keep in mind that the boxed sections are representative samples of posts right off the newsgroups themselves. They're written by fans and the sections are prone to inaccuracies and spelling errors and moments of both tremendous insanity and terrific brilliance. They're here to show you the level and the reach of the groups themselves. Enjoy. You are officially "lurking."

Special Note

The newsgroups are the most sociologically interesting parts of the Net. The types and scope of conversations here are far ranging, fascinating, infuriating and mind-boggling at all times. Music has such a powerful effect on fans that when they are given the chance to speak about it, the results are often beautiful and harrowing.

---

alt.fan.barry-manilow (20/day)

Okay, go ahead and make a joke. All right, done? Anyway, Manilow is an adult contemporary giant and the level of discussion here is quite high. It's true there are quite a few "My wife kissed Barry in Vegas" stories, but there's also time for the fans to get together a petition to Barry's record label asking for a more speedy CD release of some older albums.

○   OK...here's more fuel for the discussion of singing at a Manilow concerts...How can one compare singing with a CD of Manilow, than singing with him LIVE? It is a dream of mine to sing with the man, one I know will never come true, and the only way I could even come close to fulfilling this dream is by singing along with him at the shows. Beside, I think Barry likes it when we sing along...I think it makes him feel well loved (he already knows this...but it still feels good) wouldn't it be amazing to hear 10,000 people singing at the same time? What an experience that would be! Especially if Barry started us off...I can almost picture it......Barry starts his a cappella "One voice," and in the true spirit of the song, his backups join in by the second verse, and then more and more of the crowd starts singing with Barry, until everyone present is singing "one voice" all started by BARRY!!! Wouldn't this be incredible? Does not every Barry fan dream this of happening? At the end of the song we're all singing....

"And Every....one.....will....siiiiiiing............."

ztyler@mcl.ucsb.edu

---

alt.fan.courtney-love (30/day)

Ms. Love has made her presence known on the Net as much as any contemporary artist. Her appearances on this newsgroup and on the AOL chatlines are well known. This group is a particularly good example of a good newsgroup. There are the right amounts of fawning fandom and criticism. It's lively and very current. While there's always a certain amount of sociological discussion on groups, Courtney seems to get more than her share of advice concerning her health. A recent and lengthy battle over a discussion concerning "Heroin / Beer" took up several months of space. It will be interesting to watch how the group ebbs and flows along with Ms. Love's mercurial career. In addition to comments about her, the group also features plenty of thoughts about her late husband Kurt Cobain and her band, Hole.

○   I don't know about you, but all of this Courtney Love bashing is getting more tired than an 87 year old man in a whore house. I wade in through endless posts that bash her over and over again. And, these posts are always the same thing: what a whore, slut; unfit mother, junkie bitch, publicity seeker, etc. to ad infinitum.

My...how dull your lives are to live for this.

I would like to discuss her music, but that ain't happening here. Seems like this (as well as other use groups) have degenerated into cyber screaming matches that rival a rerun of Geraldo. It is so easy to sit and point figures at a public personality. There we can pin our blames and hatreds on them. Their faults, thanks to sleazy magazines who have found it's better to create a controversy and cover it, than to talk realistically about issues that face us, are so easy to see under the blare of flashbulbs. The bottom line: Hole plays wickedly great songs, with great hooks catchy lyrics and more soul than a thousand grab bag alternative bands of the month. What she does with her life is her business. Not mine, yours or anyone else's. So, maybe you people who love slagging Love should start alt.hate.courtney-love base and flame away. Just pray that your life never becomes so circumspect. Maybe one day you'll be famous and we'll have an alt.hate.your-name-here base. Now, would you all kindly shut up?

jimmis@cpcn.com

alt.fan.david-bowie (20/day)

One of our all time favorite discussions took place here in the middle of 1995. An original post asked fans what Bowie songs people had played or had played at weddings and/or funerals. The posts went on for months, everything from the sublime to the ridiculous. Overall the group is rather orderly, with responses sticking to the point of the initial question, for example, and over time nearly all the regulars make an appearance on any one item.

> ○ Last night (to be precise in the early morning) I sat down with a pair of headphones and listened through the whole album for the first time in at least 5 years. It was really a pleasurable surprise! The whole album sounded so fresh and new. I think it has hardly dated at all. For example when I first heard "Zoo Station" by U2 I immediately thought of "Beauty and the Beast", I thought it sounded like a 90s update. (Of course the lyrics are not very similar; I am thinking of the sound and mood of the music.) I think if I heard these two songs now for the first time, I would have great difficulty in deciding which came first. "Joe the Lion" I have never really enjoyed before, but now I have come to realize what a Bowie-classic it is; so much intense desperation. Has anyone noticed that Bowie sings almost exactly like on his earliest songs ("Rubber Band" for example) in "The Sons of the Silent Age"? Has anyone got a clue what this song is really about? I tend to think that the instrumentals are not quite as good as the rest.
>
> richard@matstat.unit.no

alt.fan.frank-zappa   (80/day)

Zappa inspired a devoted, manic following and the group is a great testimony to his own fervor. This is not a group for a casual fan, however, as the discussions run very deep. Since Zappa played with so many terrific musicians, this group also has a fairly broad coverage of important former band members (Steve Vai, etc.). His rather recent death increased usage of the group considerably and continues to this day. Additionally, Zappa's huge catalog of recordings is rather unmanageable for any fan. Many members of the group exchange healthy reviews and tips for others completing their collections. Also, here's a little newsgroup tip for you. The first section below comes from the Frank Zappa FAQ (frequently asked questions). Almost every group has some kind of moderator (fan, really) who over time compiles and posts a list of the most commonly asked questions. (This saves the group lots of time, because as new members join the family, they can simply be directed to the FAQ to catch up on things they don't know.) So, the question about Zappa's favorite records comes right out of there.

○ What were Zappa's favorite records?

KCRW in Santa Monica aired a tribute to Frank Zappa which included comments by Nicolas Slonimsky, Zappa music, and a re-broadcast of a 1989 program called Castaway's Choice, hosted by John McNally. This program contained interesting dialogue between Zappa and McNally, interspersed with excerpts from Frank's ten records he'd take to a desert island, and his reasons why. Frank said "Back in the days when I had recreational listening time these are the things I would actually listen to."

1. Octandre by Edgar Varese
2. The Royal March from L'Histoire du Soldat by Igor Stravinsky
3. The Rite of Spring by Igor Stravinsky
4. Third Piano Concerto, first movement by Bela Bartok. Zappa: "I think it is one of the most beautiful melodies ever written."
5. Stolen Moments by Oliver Nelson
6. Three Hours Past Midnight by Johnny Guitar Watson
7. Can I Come Over Tonight by The Velours
8. Bagatelles for String Quartet by Anton Webern
9. The Anton Webern Symphony, Opus 21 by Anton Webern
10. Piano Concerto in G by Maurice Ravel

When asked if he could only keep one of the above, FZ chose Three Hours Past Midnight.

Incidentally, I recall that Frank was once a guest on the Dick Cavett Show in 1980 (or thereabouts) and in terms of contemporary popular music, Frank stated that he was particularly fond of Lucky Number by Lene Lovich.

dmanno@hsc.usc.edu

alt.fan.madonna (85/day)

Madonna qualifies as one of the most important cultural figures of the past twenty years and her iconography is debated daily on this very active group. Sure there are a healthy number of dissenting opinions, but for the most part Madonna remains queen of the world here. Unlike most artists, Madonna's fans support both a very healthy news-group (this one) and a satisfying mailing list. Usually it's feast and famine. (Springsteen for example, a similarly sized icon, only generates enough posts in the mailing list format.) Naturally because of her over one decade long and controversial career, a lot of this group focuses on the phenomena of MADONNA. There's still time for the music, but a good deal of the time is given to fans responding to a flame like the recent: "Madonna is a Pig."

> ○ The "Great Alfonso" on this newsgroup posted a response to my response about "Cute Guy", with deals with the dancer Luca. GA felt offended about what I said concerning Luca's sexuality and states his disgust in a follow-up in the thread. I stated that he "probably" is gay and that this is "good." To begin, it was merely my opinion that the dancer MIGHT be gay. Seeing that Madonna happily works with many gays and lesbians, I do not feel that by me saying that I am being stereotypical or judgmental. The guy who originally posted the letter asked if anyone had any ideas if he is gay, straight, or bi. Thus, I gave my opinion. If the Great Alfonso has a problem with people giving his or her opinion about a question posed, then too bad for him.
>
> erotica@bu.edu

alt.fan.u2 & alt.music.u2 (25/day & 30/day)

More than any group that we've seen, U2 generates the most "hate" mail. Singer Bono comes under constant attack here, and even with a continuing support from the faithful, he takes hit after hit. (Many U2 fans in fact don't seem to like him.) So, much of the group is taken up with personalities. There's the regular info available: hard to find disks, etc. But this group wastes a lot of focus on whether Bonehead (his apparent Net nickname) is worth anything or not. [Note: At some point these groups will likely merge. As it stands now there is a lot of cross-posting—messages sent to both—so you won't miss much on either one. Since these groups are oftentimes put together by individuals, there's no particular checking procedure to make sure this doesn't happen.]

○   I'm not sure if "Dancing Queen" is a B-side anywhere, but they did an acoustic version of the ABBA song which is on the "Zoo TV: Live from the Mixing Desk" CD set. It was recorded in Berlin, I believe. Great sound quality, BTW.

It's a really funny performance, about midway through the song, Bono forgets the words and starts singing, "...something, something, something, you're in the mood for a dance." They completely broke down in the middle of the song. After the song, Bono said, "It's finally happened. We're shit." It's cool to see a band as good as U2 completely screw up a song.

rlg@metronet.com

alt.music.amy-grant (20/day)

While most newsgroups aren't officially moderated, it's very clear at times that someone is watching out for the best interests of the group. In many cases one member will be responsible for the FAQ (discussed above). In the Amy Grant newsgroup, that duty falls to Pradeep Bhatia. An example of the good feelings on this group is a long letter sent through most of the regular members where everyone posted: "Thanks Pradeep," or some variation. Friendly and comfy and very heavy on Amy Grant concerts upcoming and the Christian element in her career. In the past several months though, no single post from any newsgroup has made us smile more than this next one. In tracking it down in fact, we were able to talk to Ruth McGinnis, Amy's personal trainer, who was frankly a little astonished that we wanted to publish the recipes. Anyway, you decide.

○ You may be gratified to know that Amy is writing upon the June issue of the FOA newsletter even now. Our families spent a nice, relaxed morning together watching the kids all play in the pool. When we left, she was hoping to put Sarah down for a nap and do a little writing for us. I hope I can contain it all in less than novel size...

For your holiday enjoyment, I am reprinting here some tips given by Ruth McGinnis, fitness expert and Amy's personal fitness trainer. Ruth appeared on a local TV program yesterday (Talk of The Town) and gave some wonderfully practical tips about making it through the holiday in healthier form.

This will also serve as a preview for you for upcoming issues of the newsletter. Ruth has graciously offered to write for the newsletter and I asked her if we could just make her contributions a new feature. Beginning with June - that's just what we'll get! As Ruth said, "For whatever reason, being a part of Amy's life also makes me feel like a part of her ministry and I just want to give something back."

Let me say that providing this sort of encouragement really fits in with Amy's own priorities and care for other's well being. First - it will hopefully balance out the message that is sent by virtue of her beautiful images being broadcast from magazines to billboards to tours. ("Don't just try to be "skinny", but be healthy and you will look your best.") Second - good health is a priority in her life and she does all she can to encourage those around her by giving them a gift of fitness sessions, inviting some out to workout in their home gym, etc. I'm rather home-bound with kids, so she gave me an exercise bike. We all hope you will find something practical and improving in this information!

The Traditional Memorial Day meal contains between 1500 and 2000 calories, but with some slight modifications, all the essentials can be enjoyed without all the fat.

Grilled Chicken Breasts:
Conventional: 253 Calories, 10.9 fat grams
MOD: Remove the skin: 197 calories, 4.5 fat grams

Potato Salad
Traditional: 1 Cup - 320 calories, 19 fat grams
MOD: 1/3 Cup potato salad + 2/3 Cup steamed or baked potato, mix well. 182 calories, 6 fat grams

(cont.)

Cole Slaw
With Mayonnaise: 1 Cup - 150 calories, 3.5 fat grams
MOD: no mayo, vinegar or no-fat dressing. 120 calories, 0 fat grams

Baked Beans
With bacon and sugar: 1/2 Cup - 170 calories, 3 fat grams
MOD: no bacon, no sugar: 1/2 Cup - 130 calories, 0 fat grams

Homemade Ice Cream
1 Cup - 540 calories, 36 fat grams
MOD: 1/2 Cup ice cream + 1/2 Cup fresh fruit - 325 calories, 18 fat grams

COMPARE:

Traditional Meal -
Total calories: 1433 (3 days worth!)
Total fat grams: 72

Modified Meal -
Total calories: 954
total fat grams: 28.5

Adding activity to the weekend will also help. Here is the calorie-burning value of 30 minutes worth of the following activities:

Brisk walk (4 mph) = 156
Swim (crawl) = 230
Badminton = 130
Softball = 120
Basketball = 174

alt.music.beastie-boys   (50/day)

Beastie fans speak their own special language and the group then becomes a pretty friendly place for the initiated. A lot of time is spent also talking about the various business enterprises of the band: the X-Large clothing stores, and the Grande Royale record label and magazine. If you need tickets for an upcoming show you'll find someone who can hook you up here, or at least someone who will want to go with you!

Depending on your software, you most likely will have an option about "quoting" others' words when responding to a newsgroup. The example below shows that. The top paragraph is marked with > marks. That means the section is being quoted from another poster. The second section is the response.

○   beastiefan@dump.com says:

>bad faith...get these newbies outta here

>wouldn't know illin' from fillin' bellies.

>coulda, woulda, shoulda, didna...

>Peace 2 the True Beasties!!

I suppose this is futile since the debate may never end, but why do people constantly insist on some kind of 'scale' for fans?

why should it matter whether you own every album or none, whether you've been 'down' (whatever *that* means) since 1852 or last week, whether you can recite all the lyrics by heart or you just love the bassline you heard on the radio once yesterday?

are we beastie fans or 'beastie-trivia-and-memorabilia-and-who-has-the-biggest-dick' fans?

people talk like there's something *wrong* with folks who just learned of beastie magic recently. yet I'll bet these are the same people who just became fans of groove holmes or chuck chillout or frontline or any one of a million other musical doors that beastie music can open for you.

We're *all* new to this at some point. we should be celebrating that people are discovering and enjoying beastie boys and not posturing and trying to preen our feathers at those who might have a higher number on their ticket from the beastie deli.

david.sklar@yale.edu

http://www.cis.yale.edu/~sklar/

alt.music.billy-joel (15/day)

Billy Joel fans seem to have three major interests: the meaning of his lyrics to their and other fans' lives; the current status of his ex-wife Christie Brinkley and daughter Alexa Ray; and whether or not the "Piano Man" is smoking cigarettes or not. Recently a number of folks have been writing about the recently published list of "40 Worst Albums/40 Worst Artists." If you hadn't heard. Billy "won" worst artist of all time. Naturally the newsgroup was abuzz about this travesty.

○   Hey guys! I have some really exciting news for you all!... well most of you. I have been approved to have my own Billy Joel scrap book on AOL. First, I guess I should explain what a scrap book is. Basically, there is this thing on AOL (that's America Online for those of you that don't know) that allows users to make up their own "area." Each of these new areas is called a scrap book. You need to apply and get interviews and I have done all of that and I have permission to have a Billy Joel one!

They are very strict about not violating any copyright laws so I can't post album covers or lyrics. However, other things they said would be perfectly fine. So, I envision a place where YOU GUYS, the fans, can put stuff that you have done. Some possibilities would be: pictures that YOU have taken, poetry about Billy that you've written, albums, reviews, stories, drawings, artwork, parodies of songs, etc. All stuff that you or a friend has written or done. Anything that YOU have made. And of course I will grant you any credit that you want. Any suggestions are welcome and appreciated. I also plan to maybe do polls and contests. Perhaps biweekly we can have a different question. (and of course I can also post the question to the message board, mailing list and newsgroup.)

So, if you have anything that you would like to include PLEASE send it to me. I would LOVE to add it!

freshseth@aol.com

alt.music.blues-traveler (115/day)

Blues Traveler is one of the unknown kings of the Net. Like their psychic and musical brethren, the Grateful Dead and Phish, much of their popularity bubbles underneath the mainstream media, and therefore fans find alternate ways to keep the faithful together. And like many underground acts, the fans spend a lot of their time trading tapes. The tape trading phenomenon is associated often times with bootlegs, but different groups have different tolerances about this. (The Grateful Dead, of course, set aside certain areas of their concert halls specifically so tapers could set up their equipment.)

○   A totally different "use of the Net" I have found is in the trading of live tapes of a whole slew of small, relatively unknown bands around the country who allow and encourage taping of their concerts. By far the biggest one would be the band Phish, whose popularity is largely the result of the prolific distribution of their live tapes, and the distribution of their tapes has been abetted exponentially by their Internet newsgroup, where among various fascinating discussions/analyses/critiques of their music and their performances, thousands of people exchange tapes of their shows, and new fans can get in on the trading scene. For many other small, as of yet unknown bands, the tape distribution possibilities provided by "tape trees" on the Net have, and will continue to help them get exposure and gain new fans in ways that they traditionally never could. Providing people with a sample of their music, instead of a potentially limited and misguiding description of it, and doing this on the scale made possible by the Internet, allows a band from Albany who's never played outside of NY to come to Alabama and fill up a fairly good sized club. That's pretty significant, IMO.

Rob Walker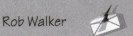

rgw@dukebar.crml.uab.edu

alt.music.enya (15/day)

The dreamy Enya has a lightly trafficked group, but like many adult contemporary artists, her fans are fawning and loyal.

○ Out of curiosity, I started looking through my world atlas for the locales in "Orinoco Flow." I found nearly all of them. If anyone is interested, here are my findings:

"Orinoco" — River in Venezuela

"Tripoli" — City in Northwest Libya

"Yellow Sea" — Between China and Korean Peninsula

"Bissau" — City in Guinea-Bissau (On Africa's far western tip)

"Palau" — City in Sardinia (West of Italy, South of Corsica)

"Avalon" — French Town, about 200 km. Southeast of Paris

"Fiji" — Polynesian Island, North of New Zealand

"Tiree" — Island off West coast of Scotland

"The Isles of Ebony" —?????????

"Peru" — Country in South America

"Cebu" — Island in Philippines

"Babylon" — Site of Hanging Gardens

"Bali" — Island just East of Java

"Cali" — City in Western Colombia

"Coral Sea" — Off Eastern coasts of Northern Australia and New Guinea

"Ebudae" — Island in Ariosto's "Orlando Furioso" (Geographical location unknown)

"Khartoum" — City in Northeast Sudan

"Sea of Clouds" — One of the Lowlands (Maria or "seas") of the moon (another Sea of Clouds on Earth?)

"Island of the Moon" — Metaphor for celestial body containing the Sea of Clouds(?)

DaveH47@delphi.com

alt.music.genesis (15/day)

Formerly progressive rockers, and for the past decade, popsters, Genesis garners an interesting mix of newsgroup participants. Singer Phil Collins doesn't get much play here, except for the odd comment about his acting career. Instead the fans seem to be from the band's earlier incarnation with Peter Gabriel still at the helm. The current discussions center on typical newsgroups topics like "Best Album," etc., but there's also heavy discussion about Tony Banks and Mike Rutherford, the two lesser known current members of the band. The group was also instrumental in the release of former member Steve Hackett's solo project. One group member was in contact with the guitarist's record label and in fact was asked to spread the word about a possible forthcoming album. Fans had a chance to respond to label questions about song, song order, etc., and were given first crack at the record when it came out.

○   I just finished speaking with the ever diligent Alan Hewitt of The Waiting Room magazine and there is some good information to pass along.

First is news on the box set. According to the individual who is "organizing" the box set (as opposed to Nick Davis, who is engineering it) they hope to have it out some time in November. The latest on its contents is as follows:

Disc 1- Entirely made up of live Lamb material.

Disc 2- Entirely filled with unreleased tracks and b-sides. Apparently they have even gotten some tapes from before the first album which should be included.

Discs 2 and 3- Will contain a mixture of unreleased material, b-sides, and live material from other tours (definitely including the Selling England tour)

Here's the frosting on the cake. It sounds like they will not fill up any space with already available album tracks!!   Good news that.

They are expecting to have a single from Tony's new one released (at least in the UK) some time in July.

billbrink@mail.utexas.edu

alt.music.jethro-tull (20/day)

This is one of those bands that was made for the Internet. Its fans are mostly middle to upper middle class (one of the current principal demographics of the Net.) While this traffic doesn't seem extraordinarily high, for a band that is virtually out of the media mainstream, it's quite busy.

○ I found the Toronto Divinities concert to be quite uplifting. Ian was in a great mood, joking with and reacting to the audience. The sound quality was fantastic. They played, gave meaning and verve to all of Divinities. They played a near-dream set of acoustic Tull pieces (well, there were only three acoustic instruments - Ian's voice, his guitar and his flutes, the rest of the instruments were synthetic (including the voice in the last chorus to Heavy Horses, where tape was used to embellish Ian's singing).

My wife and I took my 8-year old son along - this was his first concert. I learned something from him - he takes Suzuki piano lessons, where the secret is to listen to the music long before you attempt it. I did this with Divinities - played it for my son and myself at every chance during the weeks leading up to the concert. He's been listening to Nirvana and Offspring lately, but thought that Divinities was "cool" and wasn't bored by the concert in the least (at his age, I would have been whining after the first song :-). His evening was topped off by the fact that we waited outside of the Stage Doors (for 1.5 hours) and finally got autographs from all of the band members (except the violinist who had managed to vanish). Giddings was extremely friendly and made a friend for life (not me!) by suggesting that we take our son to McDonald's as a reward for sitting through the concert. Anderson paid my wife an offhand complement by suggesting that our son was her "little brother." [I will forever kick myself for not asking Giddings for hints on how to play the piano part for Wond'ring Aloud :-].

tarvydas@turing.toronto.edu

alt.music.led-zeppelin (40/day)

Obviously the recent Page/Plant tours have brightened this group up considerably. Still, a good amount of newsgroup action chronicles the real period of the band (up to 1980). This group does contain an inordinate amount of tape traders (both audio and video), not only of the 1995 tour, but of old Led Zep as well. Much discussion centers on the quality of various bootlegs. This is a real goldmine for someone looking to exchange or find favorite concerts.

○   Hi. I'm trying to identify a bootleg, all the info it has on it is California '75. A major clue however is Robert sings "...Can you tell me Long Beach..." in the middle of Sick Again which narrows it down to 11/03/1975 or 12/03/1975, Civic Arena, Long Beach, California and the track listing is

Rock & Roll

Sick Again

Over the Hills

In My Time of Dying

The Song Remains

The Rain Song

Kashmir

No Quarter

Whole Lotta Love

Black Dog

Trampled Underfoot

Stairway to Heaven

galvinr@ee-wp.bham.ac.uk

alt.music.monkees (40/day)

We swear this isn't a misprint. The Monkees' faithful keep this group rocking day after day. The fact that members Mickey Dolenz and Mike Nesmith have both made the Net a part of their own lives helps a lot. There's a real friendly atmosphere here; in fact there's a large number of posters who identify themselves as "2nd Generation" Monkees fans, fans born after the band had already broken up. Conversations here feature not just the music but the members' lives since the 70s and the TV shows as well (in constant syndication somewhere.)

> ❍   (Maybe this should be added to the list of questions for newcomers)
>
> In your record or CD collection, what artists/albums come immediately before and after "Monkees"? And yes, EVERYTHING counts, whether you bought it when you were 10, got it for a nickel, were given it as a gift, or your roommate stuck it in there as a joke (mine actually does this.) You may EXPLAIN why they are there, but you MUST NOT FUDGE in any way!
>
> I'll start:
>
> LPs - Molly Hatchet "Flirtin' With Disaster" (God, how awkward! - bought for 50¢ at garage sale years ago) —
>
> [Monkees] -- Eric Idle and Neil Innes (filed under "Monty Python") "Rutland Weekend Television."
>
> CDs - completely out of order now, but if you people play the game, I'll sort them and post later. It should be more respectable than the LPs list.
>
> Dancing@Auschron.com

alt.music.nin (450/day!!)

This is the one. Trent Reznor and his band, Nine Inch Nails, generates more posts day-in and day-out than all other music newsgroups. It's prone, of course like all the others, to a certain ratio of "NiN rules!" and "NiN sucks!", but like any newsgroup you will find correspondents and posters who are well worth your time.

○ I am soooo pissed off.....I picked up the latest copy of the Village Voice today, when what to my wondering eyes should appear but a front page blurb that read "Blood Brothers: Trent Reznor and Tim McVeigh." Okay, I figured this had to be something very sarcastic and tongue in cheek about blaming musicians for the ills of the world, but the author (R. J. Smith) spends the first four long paragraphs making fun of Trent's method of expression and the videos he puts out (specifically Hurt). A choice quote: "Suddenly we realize hell isn't other people, it's this one guy, the tormented soul mingling his agony with a ton of Time-Life documentary footage, his well-toned forearms eclipsing the scrawny girls of Belsen."

Then the fifth paragraph starts outlining the connection to Tim McVeigh. I only got to "McVeigh is a major Nine Inch Nails fan." Then it says "continued on page 132," with one major disadvantage: there is no page 132. Mind you, this article is advertised on the front page, as well as having a little black and white still to illustrate it in the Table of Contents. My first response? COWARDS. They can't even finish the article that rang the alarm bell. Could the folks at the Voice be cashing in on Rush Limbaugh, for once in their liberal lives? (I'm not liberal bashing, I'm very left of center. I just hate propaganda tactics like this one.)

So folks, I don't know how many of you are in NYC or how many have access to the Voice, but I'm writing in and complaining. The *least* they could do is finish the damn article so that I can write a decent critique of what the author is saying. The only thing I can come up with now is "Of course Timothy McVeigh listens to Nine Inch Nails. There are very few bands that allow their audience to express their pain and anger in such a direct manner. Someone like McVeigh has to have immense amounts of repressed rage in order to do something like he did, and listening to NiN was probably an avenue to let off some of that steam until it became too much. Nine Inch Nails fans aren't all sociopaths with a bomb in their pockets. Some of us are just very angry people with better things to do."

What do you think? I'm incredibly angry and could say a lot more, but I've already spent far too much post time. Thanks for reading.

serraya@aol.com

alt.music.nirvana (150/day)

After Kurt Cobain's death the traffic here greatly increased. And naturally the discussions moved away from the normal fan/music axis to the band's relevance, significance, and historical place in rock music.

○ First of all, NIRVANA is NOT dead... as long as people like it, have the tapes.. as long as even one single copy of any nirvana song is still good, then NIRVANA is NOT dead...

Second of all, NIRVANA was NOT Kurt Cobain... so stop all your fucking whining, and stop buying kurt cobain t-shirts.. because NIRVANA was more than Cobain.. Nirvana Was Dave, Krist, Kurt and all the others.. NIRVANA couldn't have been with kurt cobain only... So stop being so cobain fanatic and be Nirvana fanatic.

In a small overall conclusion to this setting straight... If you have started listening to nirvana AFTER his death because you thought it would get to be worth something someday, then FUCK YOU... If you bought a KURT COBAIN T-shirt without possessing a Dave Grohl T-shirt or a Krist Novoselic T-shirt then screw you.. Nirvana was meant to be nirvana and will always be, in my opinion, NIRVANA!!! Long live the true music!

ce651@FreeNet.Carleton.CA

alt.music.pearl-jam (120/day)

Even after Pearl Jam's seemingly endless trouble with Ticketmaster, a lot of this group is given over to discussing when and where Eddie and the boys might be seen somewhere. Also a fair amount of discussion is given over to the relative merits of most recent drummer Jack Irons versus Dave Abruzzese from the earlier incarnation of the band.

○   I was just thinking about the way Pearl Jam seems to be going downhill. From all polls I've seen, the vast majority of people loved TEN, liked VS, and then kinda bought Vitalogy hoping. Don't get me wrong, there are some great songs on both VS and Vitalogy, but it just isn't TEN. IMHO, Ten is the best cd of all time. It flows (rather evenly). You can just put it into the cd player and jam. It is the best cd made for using that nifty little repeat function. I mean, it is awesome how the end of the cd fades back into the beginning.

Here's a few reasons I think Pearl Jam has changed...

They aren't focusing on the music as much. On Ten, the great songs were instrumentals first (the music had to be good enough to stand on its own) for quite some time. Now I think that they rely on Ed a little much to carry the songs to grandeur (yes, they're still jammy, but just not breath-taking).

Ed's life has changed. He doesn't cope well and now he's writing more songs about issues I personally don't care about (fame, etc.). Back in the good old days, the songs were more universal and personal.

Well, I thought I'd speak up and please don't be overly hostile.

Anyone else consider Candlebox to be Pearl Jam's "real" second album?

jbond@iti2.net

alt.music.pink-floyd (250/day)

Naturally enough this is a busy place. The band, which ranks among the top two or three tours, year-in and year-out, is a discussion-making machine. The fans are obsessed with the work of being a Floyd-head. Their discussions about how the P.U.L.S.E. version of "Comfortably Numb" is different from one of the other 500 live versions are always detailed, well-written, and passionate.

○   I've noticed a lot of people complaining about how Pink Floyd has released another double live album after only one studio album. All I can say is that I wish they had released a double live album after EVERY studio album! Maybe they're just trying to make up for the fact that the only "official" live material released up to now was the first half of Ummagumma (only 45 min or so at that). Personally, I'd love to have live versions of the Wall, Animals, Meddle, Piper... just about any album, really. Even experimental stuff that never made it to the studio.

The thing that really bugs me about Pulse is the fact that the noises they played before the concert were put on the tape, but not the CD. I was really hoping some of that would be on the CD, that stuff really got me psyched up at the concert. Hey Dave (or the record company folks), how about a limited edition 3rd Pulse CD with that stuff on it, along with OoTD, Marooned, Take it Back, Terminal Frost & Echos (from the last tour) and anything else you have lying around? I'd buy it. How about a live Floyd Boxed Set (assuming there's that much material available)? How about doing what Frank Zappa did and cleaning up some bootlegs and re-releasing them as official product? Nah, I'm just dreamin'...

PS - are the "opening noises" on the Pulse video?

robert_eichler@fmso.navy.mil

alt.music.primus (20/day)

Les Claypool's bass driven band is an emerging force not only in alternative music, but also as a player among newsgroups. Primus is one of those bands that seem to grow larger through a cultish appeal than because of any particular musical growth. (Exactly like Wall of Voodoo, for you fans of 80s music.)

> ○ What are you trying to say? That Les should be just like Paul McCartney; just play ordinary bass lines, albeit melodic ones? That would suck. Les does the slap-pop thing because it gives his band a unique sound. I'm willing to guess that originality is more important to Primus, and especially to us- the listeners of Primus, than is ordinary done-a-million-times-before "melodic basslines." Tiresome is hearing the same sort of music from every single half-wit band out there. Tiresome is being able to predict when the next change is going to occur every time you hear a "new" song. Tiresome is the various musicians doing exactly what every other musician with the same instrument in the entire world is doing. Tiresome is not being able to listen to a song repeatedly and always being able to pick something new out of it.
>
> Paul may be a more experienced bass player than Les, but Les has more unique creativity in his bait box than Paul has in his multi-million dollar estate.
>
> jamb0002@gold.tc.umn.edu

alt.music.prince (85/day)

There's quite a bit of discussion about the name thing, but like the Madonna newsgroup, this is a fairly reverential bunch. It seems like icons get more protection than run-of-the-mill superstars. You can be sure to be "flamed" viciously if you suggest the Purple One has lost any of his genius.

○   I get an E-mail early on Thursday Morning, saying that Prince
0-+> played a short set at Paisley park, late Wed Nite (actually
Thurs. Morning). So after a few phone calls, me and 2 of my boys
are on the road from Chicago to MPLS at 4pm Thurs. afternoon.
We get to Paisley Park around 1 am, and already there is a crowd
in the parking lot, after meeting a few friends, I am told that
2nite's party is Invite only, but not to worry, as that is probably
just to keep the crowd size low.

At about 2am, the lights are turned off, and the party begins, no
one has been let into the studio, except for a few technicians.
Sometime after 2am, 0-+>'s main bodyguard opens the door and
announces "Alright, we are letting the ladies in first, so fellas
please move to the side or step outside." About 70 ladies are let
in, and the doors are closed again. This leaves about the same
amount of men waiting outside or in the atrium.

Now the bodyguard opens the door and jokes, "OK now we are
gonna let some ugly men in" and picks like 5 or so fellas to join
the party. After a good 20 minutes of no Men getting inside
things started to get really ugly. Fights were going to break out,
including one guy who kept on shoving his elbow into my boys
chest, seems like some ass was going to have to get kicked.

Around 3am, we can hear the ladies inside, screaming, and we
knew that 0-+> was about to take the stage. Not many men,
maybe only 10 had been let in, and after a song or two, a different
bodyguard came outside and said "that's it, no one else is
getting in."

 I've been told by a friend in MPLS, who is in the know, with various
doings of 0-+>, that he told his bodyguards NOT TO LET ANY
MEN IN. The only guys who got in, were buddies of the
bodyguards. If this is true, this is an awful thing to do, and
totally makes me think, if anything besides musical notes are in
0-+>'s head. This Boy/Girl thing has been a way of letting people
into the Paisley Parties for about 2 months, I'm told. So if this is
true, I don't know if I can really forgive 0-+> for some really sexist
shit. If this was a party that only Men were allowed in, I would still
be upset.

alt.music.queen (50/day)

Fairly typical group: bootlegs, top ten lists, "I saw Brian May at Guitar World," and so forth. But regardless of group, regardless of artist, the love of fans is always apparent. Amidst the more ordinary and normal posts, there are always a few like the following.

> ○   I will never forget November 24th, 1991
>
> Saturday night (the 23rd), I had thrown my first party......stayed up til 3am talking with a friend.....Sunday afternoon when I woke up.........
>
> I had been dating someone for four years, and we knew it was ending......While he was on his way over, I curled up in corner listing to Love of My Life and crying.......We were both big Queen fans, so after we had decided to break up.....after we had made love.....he told me he had heard the announcement on the radio that Freddie had AIDS. I knew this already....but it was devastating to get confirmation from the media. I stayed up most of the night sobbing.......in the morning, I heard the news that Freddie had died.
>
> In one day, I lost the two most important men in my life.
>
> egl@halcyon.com

alt.music.rush (90/day)

Canadian progressive rockers embraced technology early in their career and their complex and dense music seems to attract folks who would one day find themselves on the Net. So this is a busy group with rather intense discussions of the music. (In some ways, a lot like the Zappa newsgroup.)

Why do critics hate RUSH? IMHO, critics aren't critics any more. I honestly believe that they have succumbed to the masses of what's "in" or what's "out." Perhaps, it RUSH's musical complexities that frustrate critics and the mainstream fans of "rock music." The way I see it, that's were the genius of RUSH lies, their complexities, and how beautifully they are interwoven in to the music. What I can't get over, is the fact that the Canadian Music Industry FINALLY admitted RUSH into the Canadian Music Hall of Fame last year. Long overdue, and (surprisingly) the few critics who dare to write about RUSH finally agreed. As far as I'm concerned, the boy's from RUSH deserve a huge apology from the Canadian Music Industry for being overlooked all these years. Did RUSH get admitted into the Hall of Fame (or "Hall of Farts" as Alex's son Justin called it), because the Music Industry couldn't think of any other group. I think without an apology, the admission of RUSH into the Hall of Fame is nothing short of a slap in the face for RUSH, coming from the Industry and the general public. Still, RUSH is used to criticism, and as Geddy once said about bad critics, and criticisms: "You just slug it back at them, and say 'Ah, what do they know, anyway'...."

Geddy, you couldn't have said it any better.

mgowin@tibalt.supernet.ab.ca

alt.music.smash-pumpkins (20/day)

A light group considering the relative popularity of this Chicago band. Billy Corgan gets most of the play here, understandably.

O   Excuse for sounding so damn naive, but I'm too lazy to go searching for the ages of Iha, D'Arcy, Chamberlain, and Corgan so someone please fill me in. It's just one of those little quirkish inquiries I developed during my status quo daily living.

daho@u.washington.edu

rec.music.dylan (15/day)

The bard of all rock music has an extremely literate newsgroup devoted to his work. Dylan's constant touring makes him a prime candidate for bootlegs and tape trading, and so naturally this group features a lot of that. However, like other older artists, there is also a fair amount of play given to retrospectives of his work. "Best CD from the 80s," versus "Best LP from the 60s" and so forth. His multiple faiths often come into question as well. A great source of info about concerts and hard to find product.

○ I assume that according to your perversely narrow theology, the Jews who went to their deaths at Auschwitz with the Shma ("Hear O Israel, the Lord, our G-d, the Lord is one") on their lips were all, including the children, delivered from one Hell into another.

It would be a unthinkably perverse deity that would yoke His people to a "Law" (more properly translated as "the way) that could not possibly maintain only so that He

Himself could come to earth and redeem them through a human sacrifice that was anathema to them and flew in the face of everything they had been taught. But then maybe you believe in two G-ds, one who enslaves and one who redeems.

You may think you are acting in the Name of G-d when you judge others so harshly, but, in fact, you are merely acting the bigot. BTW, it isn't my intention here to "bash Christianity." Some of my best friends are Christians. (This is an example of irony -- if you didn't catch it.)

My intention is to bash you.

Thank G-d most Christians (some of them, granted, don't believe in biblical errors) don't share your bigotry.

P.S. I am reminded of that great theologian, Jimmy Swaggart, who said the Jews had endured the Holocaust because they were not under the protection of Our Lord, Jesus Christ. Up yours, friend.

rec.music.gdead (300/day)

After the death of Jerry Garcia, mainstream America had one of its first chances to understand the power of the Net. Newspapers reported nationwide the "wildfire" of information that was disseminated among Dead fans through this and other newsgroups. In the first few *hours* after Garcia's death was announced, over 700 posts were made to this newsgroup from around the world. In the first 12 hours, seven new homepages were created; devoted to his work both solo and with the Dead, lyric archives, photo archives, etc. This was a seminal moment in Net development because all the major media outlets (*USA Today*, *Time*, CNN, etc.) reported how the Dead fans were sharing their grief online. The loss of a great artist like Garcia allowed the personal and emotional side of the Net to be shown.

Like we've already covered, the Dead have a major fan support base on the Net. Not only is the newsgroup active, but it's well written as well. Since so much of being a Deadhead is sociological (the clothes, the time period, etc.), the group focuses on the experience of Dead shows, etc.

○ Has it already been three whole weeks- I feel like it was yesterday- August 9th so etched on my mind. Everywhere I go (except my "home town"), I see little articles, displays in store windows, magazine covers all dedicated to Jerry. (In my desperation to validate my grief, I tried to start a gathering announcing the place on the radio, faithfully placing roses & odd bits of memorabilia every night for a week. A few friends showed up one night, but after finding my roses cut & chopped into mulch by the village mowers, I got lonely & turned to writing to folks on the "Net." Actually sent some stuff to the local paper to print.)

All my closest friends and family (very few of them Deadheads) have accepted my remorse, sending articles from SF, Boston & NY Times on every facet of "The Deadhead Phenomena." I know more about Jerry's personal life & artwork than I'd ever care to know. Finally got sick of sifting through the tripe for something REAL about the man and his music. Sick of being called a Deadhead, everyone assuming I was some sort of lost soul now that my guru was gone.

(cont.)

No, it's not the end of the world. But I still don't feel okay. A big part of my life is missing. Don't know if I would've been better off living near a gathering place, like SF or NYC. I like to think that some how I'm better off living here- but I'd better give up my fantasy of putting up the Dead in my home for now and just get on with living & loving life. Thanks to all of you for your kind words & shared memories- Let's all stay in touch and keep on trading!

Peace!

O   SueBee

Bob 'n' Me

I was fifteen years old, my best friend and I rebelling against FM radio in a shithole town by browsing the only good record store for stuff with cool covers. Hüsker Dü? Flip Your Wig? What the hell? By the third listen, I was completely hooked, and for the last decade, Bob Mould has been the soundtrack for my life. Depression was accompanied by "Too Far Down" or "The Slim", anger by the Zen Arcade album, happy times by "These Important Years."

As I progressed along into my adult years and became a professional computer geek, I was submerged into the Internet. Usenet provided areas for me to talk about some of my passions, including the pro-wrestling business, and electronic mail let me have further, private discussions on any topic under the sun. A little over a year ago, I discovered there was a mailing list on the computer systems at Cal-Berkeley, dealing with all things Bob, Grant & Greg. Sugar, Hüsker Dü, solo material, everything and anything. Excellent. People who are as passionate about the music as I am.

One day I get an E-mail, with the subject "A STRANGE CROSS-REFERENCE," talking about how I must be the only other person who posts to the pro-wrestling UseNet group and the Sugar mailing list. It's Bob! Bob Mould! Sending me E-mail! Yeah, right. He'd just volunteer to come in out of the blue and say "Howdy."

(cont.)

So I started putting it together. Bob's been a wrestling fan forever, even to the point of wearing a "Cage Match" sweatshirt for the cover photo of one of the Hüsker Dü singles. He's been involved with getting the band Sugar, and Rykodisc, involved with the Internet. So, in all confidence, I send back mail saying "Are you kidding me?! Is this some kind of joke?!"

Well, since that time, we've sent mail back and forth, talked on the phone a little bit, even got together for a wrestling show in Dallas. And you know something? I met quite a few musicians when I worked as a disc jockey in college, and most of them were a let-down. When you hold some in as high of regard as I hold Bob Mould, and he lives up to the expectations, and then some, it's a relief. I'm thrilled to know him and consider him a friend. All thanks to the music, the wacky and wonderful business of wrestling, and electrons on a wire.

Paul Herzog
pdherzog@hooter.aud.alcatel.com

MAILING LISTS

These work differently than newsgroups. Rather than you going in search of them and their information, they come straight to you, via E-mail. Newsgroups are more plentiful and free-wheeling but often times the mailing lists are moderated, therefore much of the dreck and the dross of the newsgroups gets filtered out before it reaches you. (None of that "Bruce rules," "Bruce sucks" thing.) The downside is that some of the groups do not come in digest form. Instead you get individual E-mails of every document that goes to the list. If you're not actually checking mail several times a day—like some of us nuts—then you'll definitely want to ask about digest forms. (You might want to check out the Listserver sidebar in Chapter One.)

The following is a sample page from one of the lists we subscribe to, the Steely Dan digest. It comes to our E-mail address just like a piece of mail. We can read it, respond to it, file it, print it, like any ordinary piece of mail.

```
┌─────────────────────────────────────────────────────────────┐
│ ═                        Eudora                      ▼ ◆     │
├─────────────────────────────────────────────────────────────┤
│ File  Edit  Mailbox  Message  Transfer  Special  Window  Help│
├─────────────────────────────────────────────────────────────┤
│ ═     Jim McKay, 06:26 PM 6/5/95 , Steely Fan Digest for Jun 3 - │ ▼ ▲ │
├─────────────────────────────────────────────────────────────┤
│ [Normal]  ± │ Subject: │ Steely Fan Digest for Jun 3 - 5      │
├─────────────────────────────────────────────────────────────┤
```

In article <199506041425.AA11231@ux1.cso.uiuc.edu>, apasulka@ux1.cso.uiuc.edu [Andy Pasulka] writes...
> [Very interesting quote deleted for brevity]
>
>Of course, he wouldn't put *us* in that category, but really, off the top
>of my sleepy head, I can't really think of a truly sci-fi/futuristic lyric
>from any of the SD albums. However, I do detect that rapid-fire, beatnik
>jazz style in Gibson that Fagen and Becker dig so much. Any specific
>citations I'm missing?

"Have you heard about the boom on Mizar-5?"

[Mizar is a 2nd-magnitude star in Ursa Major; according to the usual science-fiction convention, Mizar-5 would be the 5th planet out in that solar system.]

The rest of "Sign in Stranger" is chock-full of lyrics that would suggest a world very similar to those in Gibson's stories.

Tim. [shoppa@krl.caltech.edu]
_____

PRETZEL LOGIC

At the end of this chapter you'll find a list of the major mailing lists. Next to each artists' name is some sort of instruction about getting subscribed. Usually you send some E-mail off to the address listed with the word "subscribe" either in the subject line of your E-mail or all by itself in the body of your document. If the list requires a different kind of method, we've noted it for you in Appendix C, at the end of this chapter.

Music is the most basic form of communication and the most vivid form of expression. With music, you can see anything, touch anything you can hear. And no one hears the same sights, smells and sounds as anyone else. Yet there's a common thread that runs through all music. We all hear it - that's why my grandfather can tap his foot to "Rock and Roll" by Zeppelin, and my head bobs to "Take the A Train." It's why Ugandans smile to Russian folks songs, and Germans clap to Indian beats.....

Frank Lafone
hflafone@mailbox.syr.edu

MUSIC STYLES ON THE NET

Remember the magic of discovering a new type of music? When we were younger we would go to friends' homes with stacks of albums that we had found at garage sales, in our parents closet, and at the neighborhood record store.

We would hang out by the big wood-grain Zenith console hi-fi and trade music. In other words, we would take turns playing DJ and getting or offering feedback about what was being played. One sound led to another. From the pop of Chicago to the strange sounds of Mile Davis then to Jefferson Airplane, we traveled through all styles.

The music wove a patchwork of sound that always led us to more questions than answers: "What is jazz fusion?" "What is improvisation?" "Who else is part of the San Francisco sound?" We would try as hard as we could to learn more and answer these questions about different styles of music by going to the library and talking to other people, but we always felt that we were missing something that we should be hearing. For every Southern California band you'd play, I had an obscure Canadian power pop group for you to hear.

With today's tools of the Internet, the music listener is fortunate. With a few keystrokes, you can have a dialogue with experts about any style of music. Some of these people may be teachers or historians, others may be professional musicians, and others may just specialize in one small aspect of the music style that you are interested in.

If you are trying to build a library of South American Indian music or a basic bluegrass collection or learn more about the Opera, the resources and the people on the Net will lead you down the right track. Music is as varied as people's unique tastes and opinions. You will see that the Internet isn't a sterile computerized environment, but a dynamic open area with a continuing dialogue about music.

In this section we'll take an in-depth look at five different styles of music. We'll show you the some resources available for each of these styles of music and conclude with an exhaustive list of resources for almost any style of music.

Blues

Before we show you some blues sites, you might want to pick up some tunes. Start this journey with a stop at Metaverse, http://metaverse.com/vibe/ab.html, and pick up the latest version of "American Blues." "American Blues" is a 30 minute Internet radio program that can be heard instantly with "Real Audio" software (see the following boxed information) without waiting for it to download on your hard drive. The show features contemporary blues music and has an Internet DJ hosting the program. It is updated every two or three weeks.

> ### RealAudio
>
> RealAudio lets the Internet user listen to music and radio programs at anytime. The software allows the music to be listened to as it downloads (not after); this cuts out a lot of time.
>
> RealAudio is a service from Seattle-based Progressive concepts. It requires a connection to the World Wide Web and sound-player software, which is distributed free.
>
> All you do is call up a menu and click on the program you want to hear. The software cues up the program and plays it back on the computer. Depending on your system, you can go back to work on a spreadsheet or word processor, or simply continue web surfing with the music or the program playing in the background.
>
> The player is currently available free in an attempt to set the market standard and is available in Macintosh and Windows formats. To get the software go to Progressive Networks' World Wide Web site, http://www.realaudio.com.

• Blues Mailing Lists and Newsgroups

What is the best John Lee Hooker recording? Is there a bootleg version of Stevie Ray Vaughan's last concert? Is Eric Clapton truly a blues artist? The discussion groups and mailing lists handle these questions and debates everyday.

Birthday Wishes to Blues-L: The Blues Mailing List

I would like to add my Birthday reminiscences to the ether. I've only been here for about a year. I found this joint the same day I learned what a "Veronica Search" was. My very first search was on the word BLUES. I got hundreds of "hits" the vast majority of which, much to my disappointment, had nothing to do with the Blues but with The Blues Brothers. I did see a reference to Blues-L and downloaded the FAQ. I immediately knew I had found what I was looking for. I don't know if I can adequately describe how important Blues-l is to me. It is, surely, only a PART of my life,

(cont.)

but it's a part I can't imagine doing without. I generally go to the E-mailbox every day at about 5 AM (when I usually get up), and again around 6 or 7 PM when I get home. When I have a musical gig, I am usually forced to skip the evening session. If something goes wrong with my Internet access for even a few hours I start to panic. I pay big bucks for a SLIP connection, and I'd say it's largely to satisfy my need for a Blues connection. Despite how we often seem to feel when we are together here, we are a VERY small minority. We make up for that in passion, but we are very small segment of the music loving public. It is perhaps because of that passionate aspect of being a Blues lover, that we need each other so much. Blues-L is like food to me.

I feel as though I have a globe-wide group of about a thousand good friends here. Friends I wouldn't dare to name for fear I'd leave someone out. Some of my friends still manage to upset me now and then, particularly with their youthful intolerance, but I have a very sincere love for all of you.

Happy Birthday Blues-L

BTW, my web page started as a whim. Something I thought would be cool. The response has been so great, with so many people asking to buy my non-existent album, that it has convinced me to record one.

P.W. Fenton
E-mail: pwfenton@gate.net
http://www.gate.net/~pwfenton/

Blues-L is the bitnet mailing list dedicated to blues music. It has over 1,000 active participants from all over the world. Usual traffic is between 60 to 80 messages every day. Several of the members of this list are nationally known musicians and have been active in the blues scene for many years. Blues historians are also on the list to keep the subscribers on the right track. Blues DJs also hang out on the list posting their weekly play list. The list members take the music seriously.

Once you subscribe to the list your mail box will begin to pop with tributes to musicians, producers, and anyone that has had anything to do with blues. There are ongoing discussions that cover mundane matters like new releases, or more difficult topics. One question that has been endlessly debated over the past few years is, "What are the blues?" The question never fully gets answered on this mailing list, the consensus of the group is that blues music is always evolving and changing.

The list is a community in almost every sense. Cassette tapes are often made available to list members. Some of the musicians on the list put together tapes of jam sessions they've performed and use traditional mail to send them to anyone that wants one. Every week important blues musicians' birthdays and deaths are posted to the list. Members actually travel to meet other members and get together for an informal gathering of playing, listening, and talking about the blues. List members also get together at major blues festivals and at small ones around the world.

To subscribe to the list, send a subscription request to listserv@brown.vm.brown.edu. The list is also available as a newsgroup bit.listserv.blues-L.

• *rec.music.bluenote.blues*

Rec.music.bluenote.blues is a newsgroup that attracts a bit different discussion than blues-L. Ideas are traded about the essential blues recordings. Reviews are posted to the group pretty fast after a new release comes out. Aspiring musicians ask questions about amps, guitars, strings and harmonicas. The group is a great place to get quick answers to questions about the blues.

• *Starting Points for the Blues on The World Wide Web*

The Blue Highway

http://www.vivanet.com/~blues/

Comments from the Author of The Blue Highway

I've always enjoyed the blues in a general sense, but it wasn't until I subscribed to Blues-L (the blues mailing list) on a lark a few years ago that I really began to appreciate the depth of the music and the culture that spawned it.

By the time I got my first real Internet account in January, 1995, I was a full-blown blues addict. I had no trouble deciding what I was going to do with my web space. I'd seen enough "me and my dog" web sites to know that WASN'T what I wanted, and I knew that others would appreciate sharing my love for the blues.

I didn't realize at the time how The Blue Highway would change my life. It has become my cause to try to paint a picture of the lives and times of the great blues makers. I'd like everyone to come to understand not just the music but its social context. It's a very moving tale.

I'm amazed daily at the response, particularly from visitors outside the United States. They know the blues, demonstrating that the emotions it generates are indeed universal. I've seen the accesses grow from 20 or 30 a day to upwards of 500. Right now, The Blue Highway is averaging about 7,000 visitors a month, and the number seems to be growing by 1,000 a month. I am remarkably satisfied, and the gratitude expressed by so many makes me much less blue.

Curtis Hewston
curtis@magicnet.net The Blue Highway

From site to site the blues are woven on the web. One of the best starting points is a site put together by Curtis Hewston. The "Blue Highway" spins the tale of blues music with graphics, great pictures, and audio for downloading samples of specific blues artists and blues styles.

When you first hit the introduction and dedication of the "Blue Highway," you can see that it is going to be different. The site begins with a brief cultural history of the blues and its position as part of African-American culture. It suggests that to really learn about the blues, we ought to look at the history of African-Americans as well as the musicians. From the same screen you can also enter a virtual chat room called Muddy's cabin.

The actual "Blue Highway," jumps right into the blues musicians covering over a dozen musicians, such as Robert Johnson, Mississippi John Hurt, Bessie Smith, BB King, Muddy Waters and Buddy Guy; who are all given coverage in the first section. Each entry has enough information to give the reader a feel for the style, a small sound sample and a photo of the artist. Below you will see the entry for Robert Johnson.

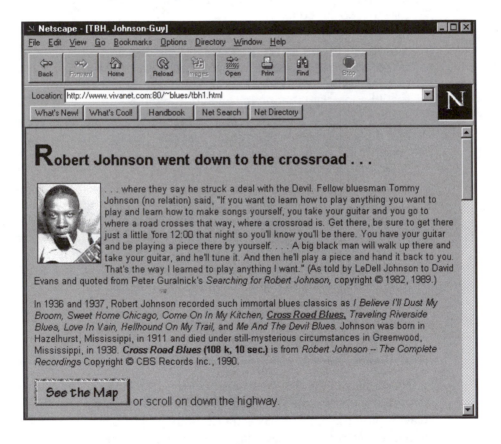

The site also features a map of the Mississippi Delta area punctuated by the two real blue highway's US 61 and US 49. Also the site has a blues news section for a look at current events. Announcements like a tribute and a fund raiser taking place for famous blues man, Johnny Clyde Copeland, who has heart problems and no health insurance, was recently in the news section.

Ziggy's Blues Home Page

http://ivory.lm.com/~davidsr/

Ziggy's Blues Home Page, is a collection of interviews with blues artists conducted by David Rubenstein. On Ziggy's page, David interviews B.B. King, John Lee Hooker, Lil' Ed Williams, Charlie Musellwhite, David "Honeyboy" Edwards and several others.

Blues Net

http://dragon.acadiau.ca/~rob/blues/blues.html

The "Blues Net" is a spin-off from the Blue-L mailing list and the Blues-L FAQ. The site maintained by Rob Hutton can be found at http://dragon.acadiau.ca/~rob/blues/blues.html. The site features several blues biographies and listings of important CDs by each artists. It also features a section called mentors which is a listing of blues artists and people who can help a researcher or beginning fan with information about each one of the artists. Original photographs from blues festivals and concerts are also displayed here.

Blues WEB

http://nanaimo.island.net/~blues/

If you're looking for a lot of music and pictures check out the Blues WEB. Gary Jones has put together a highly graphical summary of blues music with a peppering of his own commentary about the blues between features on the musicians. It features music samples and profiles and pictures from the greats. The screen shot on the next page is the page featuring harmonica player Sonny Boy Williamson II.

The goal of the site is to really focus on the musicians and expose blues music to people who might not have much experience with the blues. Some of the musicians featured are: The Paul Butterfield Blues Band with the "Walking Blues," Percy Mayfield, Little Walter, B.B. King, Slim Harpo and many others. SPOTlight is a neat part of the Blues WEB; it's an area that focuses the spotlight on an unsung blues musician who has been around for awhile, but hasn't gotten much recognition. The Blues WEB is a jumping point for the online blues magazine "The Delta Snake Blues."

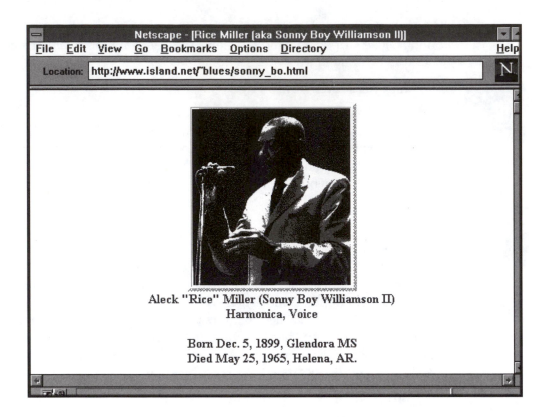

Aleck "Rice" Miller (Sonny Boy Williamson II)
Harmonica, Voice

Born Dec. 5, 1899, Glendora MS
Died May 25, 1965, Helena, AR.

• *Blues Publications*

All of the major blues magazines can be accessed or reached online. *Blues Access*, edited by the affable Cary Wolfson, has been experimenting by putting its complete issue online on a web site. For their current location, E-mail roosterman@aol.com. The site has typically featured reviews, stories about the artists, festival reviews and every issue has a survey of the blues scene in various regions of the country. You can see the online version on the following page.

Ole Miss University publishes, *Living Blues*. Back issues and subscriptions can be placed online at the Center of Southern Culture at http://imp.cssc.olemiss.edu/blues.html.

Blues Revue is reachable by E-mail at: bluesrevue@aol.com and is active in the two major newsgroups. They plan to have a web site in the near future.

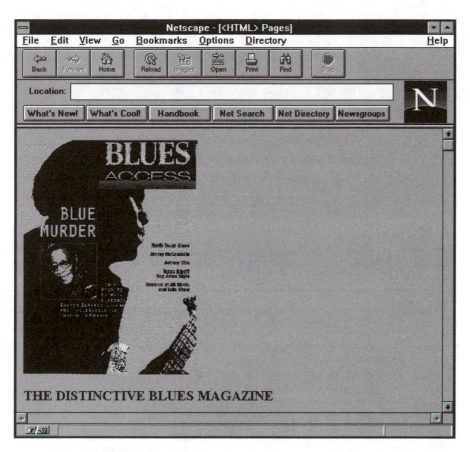

• *Blues Festivals*

Blues fans often come together at blues festivals. There are hundreds of festivals around the world every year. Two of the biggest festivals in the United States are online as well as several of the smaller ones.

The New Orleans Jazz and Heritage festival is a celebration of New Orleans music and includes a lot of blues music. The festival takes place over the last weekend of April and the first weekend of May. Information about the Jazzfest is available at: http://www.wisdom.com/la/jfinfo.html. Here you'll find pictures, schedules, and other information about the festival, compiled by Mike Perry.

The Chicago Blues festival is the largest free blues festival in the U.S. It takes place in June each year. Information about the Chicago Blues festival is available at: http://www.ci.chi.il.us/

• *The Roots of the Blues*

If the story of blues music makes you want to find out more about the history of African-American music and the history of the American south, the World Wide Web can take you there. The United States Library of Congress has a very detailed exhibit of the history of the African-American peoples focusing on the migration from the south to Chicago, the north, Kansas City, and all major hubs of blues music.

The Discovery Channel also has a web site that focuses on the migration of African-Americans from the south to Chicago. "The Promised Land" can be reached at: http://ericir.syr.edu/Discovery/Promise/Welcome/welcomepage2.html.

Classical Music

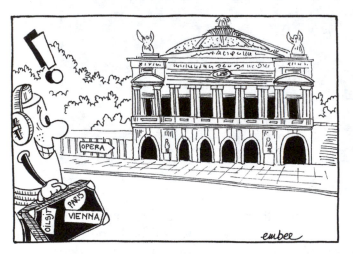

The plugged in world provides a concise overview of serious or classical music. In fact you can think of the Internet as your guide to Music 101. The Internet not only provides "just the facts" that would be covered in an Introduction to Music course in college, but a lot of personal opinions are also brought into the discussion of serious music through the newsgroups and the mailing lists.

• *The Basics of Classical Music (Music 101)*

Traditional music appreciation courses cover the basics of music: the history, composers, and performers. Typically study is presented in a lecture format with listening exercises. The Internet has the resources to give the student or just someone interested in classical music the basics and more.

Classics World

http://www.classicalmus.com/bmgclassics/index.html

Classics World has put a lot of work in its World Wide Web site. It combines the resources of BMG and RCA to create a monster resource for classical music lovers. By clicking on "The Idiots Guide," you'll be taken to a basic introduction to classical music. It includes the history of classical music and a handy glossary of music terms online. You'll see the introduction page below; each period from early music to contemporary music is discussed in its own section. By clicking on the word Romantic, a new screen fades in with some art from the period and a Tchaikovsky sound sample of the style. Next you will see brief history of the period with a listing of several of the important composers of this period.

Classics World has searchable indexes for all classical composers that features a basic biography and a listing of important recordings. The index is searchable by name or by period. A search on Romantic composers had over 35 listings. You can see the opening screen of the search below.

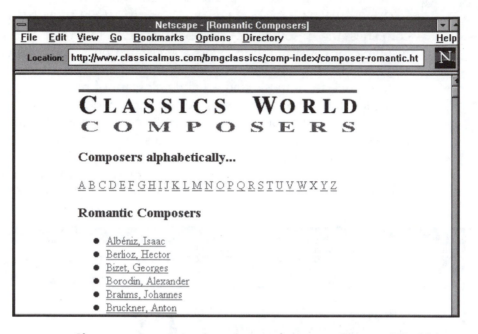

If you are interested in the performers, Classics World has a database for this as well. Van Cliburn's page in the database has a picture with a sound sample followed by his biography and some recommended recordings. The Cliburn screen is shown below.

Each screen on the BMG site has a link to the CD Catalog. When this is clicked you get whisked away to a searchable database for the recordings that BMG has to offer. There are over 350 composers and 1200 individual artists featured in the online catalog.

• *The Music*

Collecting and purchasing classical recordings can be a huge project. How do you judge what the best recording is with over two dozen versions of most of the popular works. There are several resources to help you out. One of the best starting points of course is the ongoing discussions in the classical newsgroups. Here are a few points on the Web to get you started building your library.

Building a Classical Library

http://www.ncsa.uiuc.edu/SDG/People/marca/barker-beethoven.html

Canadian DJ Deryk Barker, along with some of the other Classical DJ's at radio station CFUV, has put together an ongoing project aptly titled, "Building a Library: A Collector's Guide." The first part of this project focuses on the Beethoven symphonies.

A Basic Repertoire List

http://www.webcom.com/~music/rep/top.html

Dave Lampson, the classical editor for *The All-Music Guide*, has also posted a guide to the basic repertoire of classical music. The purpose of the guide according to the introduction is to, "...help and encourage people in the exploration of the abundance of recorded classical music...."

The guide is a basic foundation for building a music collection that includes all periods and styles of Western classical music. The list indicates with an asterisk recordings that can be considered as starting point of periods and composers, as you can see on the following page.

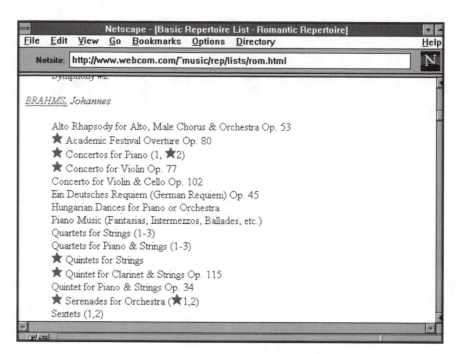

Netscape - [Basic Repertoire List - Romantic Repertoire]

File Edit View Go Bookmarks Options Directory   Help

Netsite: http://www.webcom.com/~music/rep/lists/rom.html   N

Symphony #2

BRAHMS, Johannes

Alto Rhapsody for Alto, Male Chorus & Orchestra Op. 53
★ Academic Festival Overture Op. 80
★ Concertos for Piano (1, ★2)
★ Concerto for Violin Op. 77
Concerto for Violin & Cello Op. 102
Ein Deutsches Requiem (German Requiem) Op. 45
Hungarian Dances for Piano or Orchestra
Piano Music (Fantasias, Intermezzos, Ballades, etc.)
Quartets for Strings (1-3)
Quartets for Piano & Strings (1-3)
★ Quintets for Strings
★ Quintet for Clarinet & Strings Op. 115
Quintet for Piano & Strings Op. 34
★ Serenades for Orchestra (★1,2)
Sextets (1,2)

[Lampson suggests that works from the Classical and Romantic periods might be the most accessible to the novice since they have been featured in movies and commercials.

• *Classical Discussions in the Newsgroups*

Rec.music.classical

Lisa talks about rec.music.classical

"The Net is rapidly becoming one of my primary music discussion sites! I am a violinist / violist, 25, in graduate school (but not in music). I'm not sure whether or not I'm an "amateur" or "professional"; I gigged my way through college with a couple of two-bit symphonies and a quartet. At the moment I'm just playing in our University symphony."

"I do not have a violin teacher at present, and the Net has allowed me to pose questions that would be normally directed at a teacher to a wide audience. Most times I have gotten answers from folks who, in real life, would probably never give me the time of day–members of VERY professional orchestras. I have gotten advice...from a bassist in the Finnish

(cont.)

National Opera Orchestra and advice about instrument appraisal from the principal bassist of the New Zealand Symphony (lots of bassists on the Net)."

"Also, I love to discuss music with other players, and one does not uninvitedly approach another player and ask, "wow, are you having trouble with that weird arpeggiated section in the overture?" I have met some "cyberpals" over this discussion group with which I can do exactly that–including one in my hometown whom I did not know when I lived there! Another very neat aspect of the Net is that I have gotten in touch with many people whom I had considered "permanently lost" before. I found out that one of my mom's old school buddies had just accepted a Principal post in the Philadelphia Orchestra, and my husband's bass teacher noticed my name on a mailing list and got in touch with me to find out how he was."

"The Net has been great for me as a way to continue learning and keep up with music topics that I love in a (musically, at least) somewhat isolated situation. If I was regularly gigging and had a quartet and as many music pals as I had before starting grad school, I might not need it as much. But I am the only musician in my research group (the group of people I spend 99% of my time with), and the orchestra doesn't rehearse that often. So the Net has become my surrogate violin section."

Lisa S. Boffa
bholly@polysci.umass.edu
Polymer Science Dept.
University of Massachusetts at Amherst

For the lover of classical music and those with questions, the newsgroup rec.music.classical is a perfect newsgroup to start with. This is a general interest newsgroup. The newsgroup has a heavy daily volume; almost 100 messages are posted here every day. Discussion ranges from opinions of different classical pieces, to conductors' styles, to the stories of some of the great composers. This group appeals to both beginners, musicians and experienced lovers of classical music.

rec.music.classical.performing

This group has been around since 1993. Its traffic centers on topics of interest to performers and people interested in performing classical music. Vocal and instrumental performers both carry on discussions here. According to the FAQ, the newsgroup focuses on all aspects of performance including: anxiety, technique and conducting.

rec.music.classical.recordings

This newsgroup is dedicated to discussing classical recordings. The questions you may have about what recording is the best or what is the worst is appropriate here. Recording techniques of various LPs and CDs can also be directed to this group.

rec.music.early

If you are curious about music written before what is really considered truly classical, before 1685 i.e. pre-Baroque, this is the place for you. This group tends to be somewhat academic in nature.

rec.music.opera

This is the discussion group for all topics dealing with opera.

rec.music.compose

This group is not completely oriented to classical music; however, a large percent of the articles here tend to lean towards the classical music writer. Any topic about composition, harmony, orchestration, and writing techniques is appropriate here.

• Classical Music Mailing Lists

There are five lists that cover the classical music professional and the listener. In addition to these lists there are separate lists for musicians that focus on a specific instrument. These lists are outlined in the musician chapter.

Choralist

listproc@lists.colorado.edu
   Message body: Subscribe Choralist "your name"

This list is targeted to practicing choral conductors. It is open to anyone, but is oriented towards the choral conducting professional.

Classical Music

listserv@brownvm.brown.edu
   Message body: Subscribe CLASSICAL MUSIC
Discussion list for all aspects of classical music.

Early Music

listserv@aearn.edvz.univie.ac.at

This list is linked to the early music Usenet group covering pre-baroque music.

Orchestralist

listproc@hubcap.clemson.edu
   Message body: Subscribe Orchestralist "your name"

A mailing list targeted to the professional needs of conductors, composers, managers, and others in the orchestral business.

Post Classical Music

post-classical-request@cs.uwp.edu

This list is for the discussion of artists (and their works) who are outside the classical genre, but who use classical components in the musical piece. It also focuses on experimental artists like John Cage and Edgar Varese.

World Music

Today's popular music is a combination of many styles and influences. Popular artists like Paul Simon, Peter Gabriel, and David Byrne have rhythms and instrumentation based on world music in their recordings. Zydeco and roots music can be heard in John Mellencamp songs. Music listeners and musicians are discovering that knowledge and respect of differing music traditions and styles leads to increased enjoyment and creativity.

The plugged-in network is an outpost for world and roots music. With the whole world connected, the Internet is the perfect environment for discovering and investigating world music. For the purpose of this section, we'll use the terms "roots music" and "world music" to refer to music growing out of tradition and made by people who feel strong ties to the music they create.

• *General World Music Information*

Global Music Outlet

http://www.iuma.com/GMO

The Global Music Outlet (GMO) is designed to be a link between the musician and the music listener. It is on the Internet Underground Music Archive (IUMA) server. It currently has a great section of African music housed in the African Archive. In this section there are over 300 African music titles.

The GMO has big plans to move from the static and passive web pages most sites have, to a more interactive style with video and online music. There will be a song searcher called, CustoMusic. Tony Stonefield, the founder of GMO describes it as a database "...to help Western ears find sweet ethnic music." Web radio is also being used to broadcast live from South Africa. Here's the opening page from GMO.

Global Music Outlet is an electron bridge between music makers and music lovers who seek global communion within the aesthetic realm. **GMO** is dedicated to providing musical diversity. GMO's aim is to help build integrity into cybermusic so that it may provide exotic bazaars where artists may peddle their wares.

RootsWorld

http://www.rootsworld.com/rw/rw.html

Another good starting point to get a feel for world music is RootsWorld; it is run by Cliff Furnald who is featured on the air at WPKN radio in Bridgeport, Connecticut. He also writes for several music magazines. He has created the site to bring some of the music of the world to the masses.

This site takes a minimalist approach that less is more. RootsWorld is the home to several labels and artists; it is also the home of *Dirty Linen*, a magazine that focuses on folk, roots and world music.

RootsWorld focuses on music ranging from African to Middle Eastern to Finnish music. As you can see from the intro page below, there is something for everyone on this site. Cliff has also put an extensive collection of reviews of African music on the page. In addition, there is an online music magazine called *Hollow Ear* at the site.

Welcome to RootsWorld, the world of jazz, roots, rock, folk, world music and other unique sounds from great <u>artists</u> and <u>labels</u> not in the mainstream. You can get more information <u>about RootsWorld</u>. If you would like to make comments and suggestions, (I love those!) drop a note to <u>cliff@rootsworld.com</u>. If you want to know who runs this place, you can <u>find out</u>.

<u>Before You Ask Me For A Link!</u>

News Musical and Not (updated November 30)

- Christina Roden contributes a remembrance of Senegalese singer <u>Pape Seck</u> who died earlier this year.
- New Sections: Special featured reviews every month, usually with sound samples, from both <u>RootsWorld</u> and <u>Hollow Ear</u>
- <u>Special Feature: Drums and Dust</u>
  Musician Warren Senders takes us to the Ganapati Festival in Pune, India.
- Read the latest edition of <u>Global Link</u> from *Music of the World*

---

alt.music.world

Alt.music.world is an active group focusing on the general topic of world music. Anything goes here as long as it covers roots, traditional and folk world music. Discussion of new releases, music resources, world music questions, and concert reviews all take place in this group. Articles are posted dealing with all types of general questions and comments about world music. This is a good place to get started.

• Country Specific Information

Africa-L

Send message to: listserv@vm1.lcc.ufmg.br

General mailing list about all types of African information. Includes a lot of discussion about the culture, music and social issues that are part of the music.

Music From Africa and the African Diaspora

http://www.matisse.net/~jal/africanmx.htm

The Music from Africa and the African Diaspora is a large collection of music links that is compiled and listed by African country. The site features African countries as well as the Caribbean region and links to artists from each area.

French Music

majordomo@wimsey.com
   Message body: Subscribe chanter-liste

Discussion about all French language groups and singers. This is a multilingual mailing list, in other words, use any language you are comfortable with. Groups and singers like RudeLuck, Celine Dion and hundreds more are discussed on this list.

Irish Traditional Music

listserv@irlearn.ucd.ie
   Message body: Subscribe IRTRAD-L "your name"

Irtrad-l is a mailing list that focuses on all aspects of Irish traditional music both old and new.

Celtic Music Calendars

Send message to: majordomo@celtic.stanford.edu
Message body: info lists

A set of lists, one for each US state and Canadian province. Each has a single posting each month, listing upcoming Celtic music events in each state/province.

Hawaiian

alt.Music.hawaiian

Discussion about traditional and current Hawaiian music and artists.

Indian

rec.music.indian.classical

This group attracts a lot of interest. There are 70-80 new messages posted everyday. One heated thread focused on the morality versus music dilemma that is often discussed with other genres like rap or metal.

Middle Eastern Music

middle-eastern-music-request@nic.gunet.fi

This is a digested list meaning that it only comes out in one mail packet once a week. It has discussions in English on Middle Eastern music including countries from Morocco to Afghanistan.

New Zealand Music

Kiwimusic
Send message to: kiwimusic-request@athena.mit.edu

Discussion of New Zealand pop bands and specifically those on the Flying Nun, Failsafe and Xpressway labels.

• *Latin/Spanish Music*

alt.music.mexican

Posts here are often in Spanish or English or a combination of both. Alt.music.mexican covers all the Mexican musical styles and the artists who make the music. The newsgroup is open for discussing Tejano, Ranchero, Banda, Norteno and Mariachi. The group also focuses on singers and musicians from Mexican pop, rock and hip-hop categories. In addition, other Latin American music might be discussed here from time to time.

Latin Music Mailing List

Latammus
    Send mail to: listserv@asuvm.inre.asu.edu
Discussion of all music and styles of Latin American music.

Andean/Latin Folk Music (Andean Music Mailing List)

Send message: majordomo@lvande.us.net
    Message body: subscribe andino

Dedicated to the discussion of Andean/Latin Folk Music and culture, including technique, announcements, instruments, sources, discographies and related discussion.

• *Reggae/Ska Music*

Reggae
Dub Mailer

Send message to: majordomo@priscilla.ultima.orgMessage body:
    Subscribe "your E-mail address"

Dub is a high volume mailing list discussing anything remotely related to both reggae and ska styles.

rec.music.reggae

This is a heavy traffic group discussing all aspects of reggae music and life-styles. The best and worst recordings are discussed as well as classic Jamaican music. The group also attracts discussion about ska and Caribbean dancehall music.

Jammin Reggae Archives

http://orpheus.ucsd.edu/jammin/

The Jammin Reggae Archive is a collection of FAQ's for the rec.music.reggae newsgroup and links to almost everything reggae related on the Net. As you can see on the following page, the site is visually pleasing and offers a good introduction to reggae. There is a connection to a Reggae dictionary, tour information, a catalog of essential recordings, a directory of US clubs, sound samples and a lot of other reggae resources.

JAMMIN REGGAE ARCHIVES

Welcome to the Archives!

A collection of information about and Web Links to Reggae Music.

Quicklink

[Archives |.WAV Sounds |.AU Sounds |Reggae |Bob Marley |Radio |Bands |Other |Records |Biz]

alt.music.ska

Ska came out of Jamaica in the early 1960s, moving to the UK and the world. Reggae grew out of this style in the late 1960s. The basic sound is a heavy beat with lots of horns and organ. The group has about 20 posts per day discussing this sound. A FAQ can be found at:

http://www.cis.ohio-state.edu/hypertext/faq/usenet/music/ska-faq/top.html

Country Music

Country music has escaped the regional confines of the south and has emerged in the past ten years as an important national style of popular music. It runs the gambit from traditional styles like bluegrass and swing, to sounds that are almost indistinguishable from the mellow top 40 sound. As the Internet attracts more people this musical sub-topic is taking off with fan pages and general sites. All the record companies are getting in the act by featuring their own country artists in a single place.

• *General Country Starting Points*

History of Country Music

http://orathost.cfa.ilstu.edu/public/oratClasses/ORAT389.88Seminar/Exhibits/
JohnWalker/0home.html

Country Western music has been part of the popular music scene in the United States since the turn of the century. The history of Country music is featured in a site called, History of Country Music, which is housed in an exhibit site at Illinois State University. The opening screen is shown on the following page.

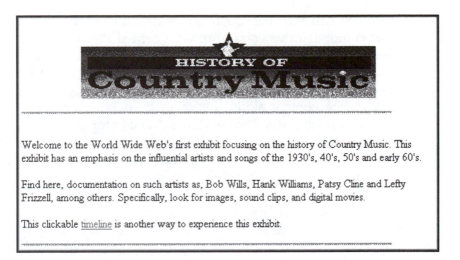

Welcome to the World Wide Web's first exhibit focusing on the history of Country Music. This exhibit has an emphasis on the influential artists and songs of the 1930's, 40's, 50's and early 60's.

Find here, documentation on such artists as, Bob Wills, Hank Williams, Patsy Cline and Lefty Frizzell, among others. Specifically, look for images, sound clips, and digital movies.

This clickable timeline is another way to experience this exhibit.

The project divides the music by periods from the beginnings in the early 20s and 30s to the Nashville sound of the 50s. Each one of the five periods has sound samples and pictures of the important artist of each period.

Country Connection

http://digiserve.com/country

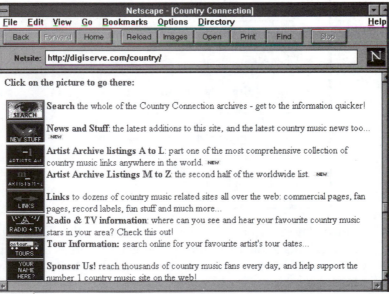

As you can see, the Country Connection bills itself as the Web's most comprehensive country music oriented site. It may well be with over 125 artist profiles and 700 different country music references, this site is a key bookmark for anyone with any interest in country music.

While the content alone is enough to make this site essential, the biggest surprise is that the developer and curator of the Country Connection is British. Michael Blanche started the site in 1994 when he was 17, to fill a need for country music on the Net. Michael says he is also committed to getting the word out about country music around the world.

"The majority of Britons think that if you like country music, you spend your spare time dressing up as a cowboy and running around the country-side firing off blanks, slapping your thighs and whooping 'yee-hah.' Happily this situation is changing, and country music artists are getting more exposure over here."

The artist section includes text, image, and sound links for each of the 125 plus artists. As you can see in the graphic below, in the index, there are icons for each artist indicating what type of information is online for each artist.

- Alabama - text - web -
- Deborah Allen - text -
- John Anderson - text -
- Archer/Park - text - image - sound - web -
- Chet Atkins - text -
- Hoyt Axton - text
- Bellamy Brothers - text -
- Matracea Berg
- Clint Black - text
- Suzy Bogguss - text - image - sound - web -
- Lisa Brokop - text - image - web -
- Garth Brooks - text - image - web -
- Brooks And Dunn - text -
- Jimmy Buffett - text -

In addition to all the artist information, the Country Connection includes links to all the different country resources available on the Net. Commercial sites, fan pages, lyric and chord sites are referenced on Mike's pages.

Nashville Scene

http://www.nashscene.com/

Nashville Scene is a weekly newspaper that features schedules, upcoming events, and news about town. If you're interested in trying your hand in the business in Nashville, checking out this site is well advised.

• Country Music Mailing Lists

Bluegrass

bgrass-l@ukcc.uky.edu
    Send message to: listserv@ukcc.uky.edu

This is the discussion list for the International Bluegrass Music Association (IBMA). All bluegrass music topics are discussed here including bands, performers, publications, recordings, reviews of live shows, history and what not. Old-time bluegrass and country music is also discussed on this fairly active list.

Country Music

Country-l

Send message to: maiser@rmgate.pop.indiana.edu
    Message body: Subscribe Country-L

List for all types of discussion about country music. It covers everyone from the pioneers, to the Nashville glory days, to the current state of the style.

ROCK MUSIC

As you tune across the radio dial you are hit with several different styles of rock music. Some of it may be called classic, pop, metal, grunge or alternative. All of these styles have a home and fans on the Net. Because of the popularity of rock oriented music, there are more resources for this type of music than for any other style of music.

In this section we'll look at some general resources for rock oriented music and some specific resources for different genres of rock music.

Rock Music Resources

• *The Rock and Roll Hall of Fame*

http://www.rockhall.com

This is another good starting point for exploring the roots of rock music and learning what artists might be in the roots category in 25 years. The Rock and Roll Hall of Fame in Cleveland has put together a site that can keep the curious fan or music buff entertained for a long time to come.

As the site unfolds in your web browser, you are greeted with a opening page that has a, "Today in Rock," section that features birthdays and other events from the history of Rock music. You are also presented with a graphical menu that, along with features about the museum and facts about Cleveland, you find the real heart of the Hall of Fame—the artists and the music.

The Museum

I.M. Pei., architect of countless buildings and museums—including the Grand Louvre in Paris, the John F. Kennedy Hospital in Boston and the Morton H. Myerson concert hall in Dallas—has designed a stunning masterpiece dedicated to popular music. The web site has some excellent pictures of the Rock and Roll Hall of Fame. It also has a summary of each of the exhibits that are featured at the museum. On the web, you can take a virtual tour of the museum or dig down deep and find out some history of the music.

The People

Hank Ballard

In the Inductee section, you will see all the current performers, producers and business people that have been inducted into the Rock and Roll Hall of Fame. They are listed by the year they were inducted. By clicking on an inductee like Hank Ballard, you get a brief written bio that talks a little about the artist and his contribution to rock music. The treatment of Ballard includes the bare minimum, that he led a band called the Midnighters that scored some R&B hits with three songs in the mid 50s that all had the name Annie in the title. The site also mentions that he wrote, "The Twist," yep, the one that made Chubby Checker big. The neat part of the bio is that audio files are available in all formats. You can listen to a bit of the music with what appears to be the real narration from the museum, just like if you rented the headsets and were strolling around.

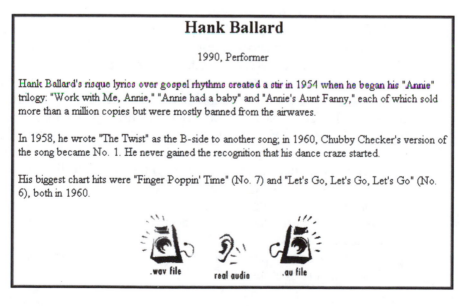

Hank Ballard

1990, Performer

Hank Ballard's risque lyrics over gospel rhythms created a stir in 1954 when he began his "Annie" trilogy: "Work with Me, Annie," "Annie had a baby" and "Annie's Aunt Fanny," each of which sold more than a million copies but were mostly banned from the airwaves.

In 1958, he wrote "The Twist" as the B-side to another song; in 1960, Chubby Checker's version of the song became No. 1. He never gained the recognition that his dance craze started.

His biggest chart hits were "Finger Poppin' Time" (No. 7) and "Let's Go, Let's Go, Let's Go" (No. 6), both in 1960.

.wav file   real audio   .au file

The Music

What do T.Rex, Pinetop Perkins, Deep Purple and Kurtis Blow have in common? Well, according to the Rock and Roll Hall of Fame, they all recorded a song that made it on the list, "The 500 Songs that Shaped Rock." This list can be found at the WWW site, and if you're so inclined and find yourself in Cleveland, Ohio, with a little time on your hands, you can see the actual list in its own exhibit. The list was put together by the museum's chief curator, Jime Henke, who got input from critics and rock writers. We weren't consulted and neither were millions of other fans. This list has caused such a stir that a separate forum is set up on the site for fans to make comments and suggestions. In fact, even The *New York Times* and *USA Today* have gotten in the act with articles quoting fans who lament about why, "We are the Champions" by Queen and any tune by Emerson, Lake, and Palmer weren't included.

As you have seen in this book, music does cause a certain passion in people; the Rock and Roll Hall of Fame web site was smart to recognize it and give everyone a forum.

• The History of Rock and Roll

http://www.hollywood.com/rocknroll/index.html

"The History of Rock and Roll," was a 10 part mini-series presented on U.S. television in 1995. The special chronicled the Elvis years, the British invasion, Woodstock, new wave, punk, MTV, rap and hip-hop. The website is an excellent introduction to rock music and is divided into five multimedia sections.

"Show Buzz" has information about all the episodes with a brief overview of each. This is a good place to start if you want to get a feel for different eras of Rock and Roll music. For example, the Elvis section discusses the development of electric guitar, black music influences on Rock music, and the general reaction by society to the music.

The "Quotables" section features transcripts of the interviews that were in the mini-series with artists like: Bono, Springsteen, Pete Townsend, the Van Halen group, and David Gilmour. George Martin of Beatles fame discusses the final days of the Beatles. Quincy Jones give the business and production prospective of the history of popular music in a detailed discussion.

In the "Soundbite" section you can hear actual quotes from the artists. All the sound samples contain some fun comments. Gene Simmons of KISS talks about blowing fire and catching his hair on fire. Billie Joe from Green Day tries to define alternative music.

"Video Vault," has several audio and video movies online, which are fairly short to minimize bandwidth, but just enough to give someone an intro to an artist. Again, the producers of the web space, Warner, picked some good clips including: Iggy Pop talking about the punk days of the seventies and James Hetfield from Metallica talking about music and life.

The "Sights," include pictures of several of the musicians that were featured in the mini-series.

Rock and Roll

http://www.pbs.org/rocknroll.rr.html

This is the PBS story of rock and roll. Like the "History of Rock and Roll" series above, this covers the basics. However, here you are more likely to find a much greater wealth of quotes, sound samples, and stories about your favorite artists.

Rock Web Interactive

http://www.rockweb.com/

Rock Web is an interesting combination of online band information and feature articles. The goal of Rock Web is to provide a meeting place for bands and their fans. According to the introduction, it is a place where the fans can congregate and dig into the vibe of the band, read about them, listen to music, and participate in discussions.

Rock Web Interactive works with each band to find out what the band wants to say to their fans by using the new medium of the Net.

• Online Electronic Magazines

Addicted to Noise

http://www.addict.com/ATN

Addicted to Noise is an extensive monthly electronic online magazine devoted to music and music culture. It features music news, music reviews, and full length articles. The editor is Michael Goldberg, who was named "Music Journalist of the Year - 1995" by the judges for the

Music Journalism Awards for his work with *Addicted to Noise* after only five months of online publication. The magazine changes almost daily and features some of the best known music writers and critics whose credentials include *Cream*, *Rolling Stone* and *Spin*.

According to the editor, *Addicted to Noise* was started because Michael Goldberg felt there was a void in the world of music writing. The publication focuses its efforts on strong writing about music. With a staff featuring: Dave Marsh, Jaan Uhelszki, Lenny Kaye, Greil Marcus and others, Goldberg has accomplished his task. We keep coming back to this site to read the articles. While the writing keeps you coming back for more, as you can see, the graphics are outstanding.

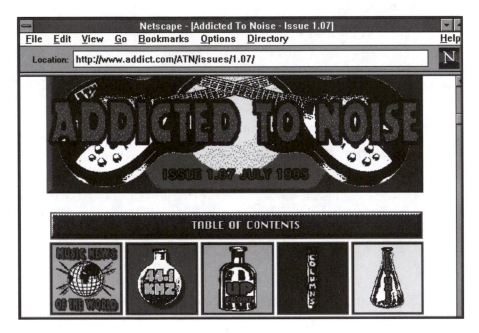

Here is a summary to just a few of the things you will find on Addicted to Noise.

Addicted to Noise: Music News of the World

This section is updated everyday. It is edited by Jann Uhelszki. It includes music label news of the day, updates on tours, upcoming concerts, and a notice for an important rock and roll birthday. As you can see, when you go to this area you are greeted with the news summary

Today's News

Sunday, December 3

<u>Secret Offspring Gig At "Punk" Club</u>
<u>Addicted To Noise One Year Anniversary, Part 2</u>
<u>Stop The Presses!! Springsteen Didn't Perform With Joe Ely</u>
<u>Rage Against Machine Rages Again</u>
<u>The Amazing ATN CD Sampler</u>

for the day in the form of a clickable menu. Archives of previous days news are also available so you can catch up.

Addicted to Noise: Columns

Columns are short form pieces written by Greil Marcus, David Was, Bill Wyman, Dave Marsh and other notable music writers. These differ from the normal columns you will see in a traditional magazine. In a recent issue, Greil Marcus had a piece about Marianne Faithful that was injected with sound samples in three popular formats and original photos by the ATN staff.

Addicted to Noise: Cover Story

These are long form articles that focus on a specific topic. In a recent issue, Dave Marsh tackles Kurt Cobain's suicide in a seven page article, by really getting to the heart of the note that was left by Cobain and taking a look at what might have been in his mind. Joey Ramone from the Ramones gets on the road and does a well written article about Offspring. In another issue, Michael Goldberg takes on Neil Young in a long form interview complete with a quicktime movie clip of a music video from "Mirror Ball." As you can see on the next page, Addicted to Noise creates an electronic cover for each issue. All of the articles are peppered with relevant sound clips and photographs.

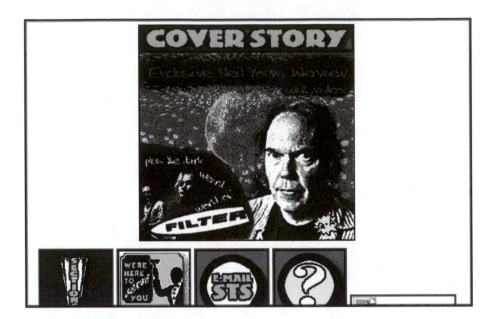

Consumables Online

Send message to gajarsky@pilot.njin.net
http://www.westnet.com/consumable/Consumable.html

Consumables Online is an electronic magazine that contains reviews, interviews, commentaries and other reading selections. The reviews primarily focus on alternative styles, but pop and rock are also covered from time to time. It's updated every 10 to 14 days.

Earfood

http://www.tumyeto.com/tydu/music/earfood.htm

This is really part of a site that is called "tum yeto Digiverse," a web space oriented to skate culture. Site owner Tod Swank wanted to expand the site by adding music features to the web space. So, the Earfood section was started, headed up by music feature editor Clea Hantman, a free-lancer for *Warp*, *Options* and *Details*. Some of the recent music features include the history of the band Kiss, a discussion about silly band names and an introduction to Acid Jazz music. In addition to features, it includes a large collection of interviews and music reviews. You can see the opening screen on the next page.

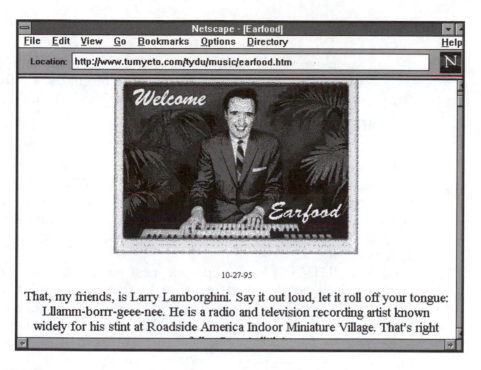

Netscape - [Earfood]

File   Edit   View   Go   Bookmarks   Options   Directory   Help

Location: http://www.tumyeto.com/tydu/music/earfood.htm

Welcome

Earfood

10-27-95

That, my friends, is Larry Lamborghini. Say it out loud, let it roll off your tongue: Lllamm-borrr-geee-nee. He is a radio and television recording artist known widely for his stint at Roadside America Indoor Miniature Village. That's right

Epulse from Tower Records

Send message to: listserv@netcom.com
Message body: Subscribe epulse-l

Epulse is the electronic version of *Pulse*, Tower Records' free music electronic magazine sent weekly. *Epulse* contains excerpts from the hard copy magazine, readers "desert island discs," music reviews and music news. There is always a weekly music trivia contest with a give-away. Lots of product is recommended, but for some reason, it never comes across as a blatant promotion for Tower Records—kudos. The big surprise is what is going to be in each week's issue. The electronic magazine doesn't follow a certain format; it is almost like a collection of notes that end up on the editor's desk, are thrown up in the air, and placed where they fall.

Strobe

http://www.iuma.com/strobe

Strobe is a bi-monthly magazine based in LA covering new music and alternative culture.

Seconds

http://www.iuma.com/Seconds/

Features in-depth interviews and articles about groups and musicians just a little bit out of the main stream. A recent issue featured: The Cramps, Orbital, The Jesus and Mary Chain, and a lot more.

MTV Online

on America Online (keyword: MTV)

This is a very dense little site on AOL with lots of fun tuff to do. In the beginning all MTV had was their chat room, MTV Yacks. It was and remains a miserable experience for most users. "Kurt lives," someone shouts. "Reznor rules," someone else says. Yacks is mostly about 14 year old kids getting a chance to hang out in cyberspace. Our advice. Stay away.

However, MTV has loaded up their most recent site with tons of great downloadable files, both images and sounds. (If you must have a photo of VJ Kennedy, you have plenty to choose from here.) Just like the channel itself, the site has its own MTV News area where actual scripts read by Kurt Loder appear as they do on his teleprompter. You can also access things like MTV's current "heavy rotation" list, those videos that are currently inundating your TV.

MTV Arena, a spawn from the awful MTV Yacks, is sometimes quite good. In it, MTV brings stars online and allows us to shout various questions. In a section called The Goods, you can order cool MTV gear like t-shirts and hats, but their most recent addition to The Goods is their Blockbuster Music shopping experience. Much like the Tower Records site—also on AOL—you can search for artists and purchase right online.

However, Blockbuster looks a little cheaper on average, and it has the added bonus of WAV files (clips or artist's songs) online as well. Before we bought the Deep Blue Something CD, we previewed three of the tracks. Bravo for MTV, but expect to see Blockbuster break away into their own site soon (perhaps by the time you read this.)

• *Rock Music Mailing Lists*

AOR MUSIC

Striktly for Konnissuers
   Send message to: the company@aol.com

The list covers Album Oriented Rock music from primarily the 70s and the 80s. Artists like Journey, Survivor, Bon Jovi and Queen are discussed on the list.

BREAKBEAT MUSIC (Breaks)

Send message to: majordomo@xmission.com
   Message body: subscribe breaks

Breaks is the Internet mailing list dedicated to discussions, chat, news and information on breakbeat music. This encompasses the whole group of different breakbeat style s from old-skool, happy hardcore to jungle, hardstep and darkside.

HARD ROCK LIST

Send message to: listproc@lists.colorado.edu
   Message body: Subscribe hardrock "your name"

This is a digested list that is mailed every couple of days; it covers anything about hardrock music. If the topic concerns hardrock, it is welcome on the list from commercial to alternative to progressive, know and unknown, big and small; all band discussion is all right with the exception of speed and thrash styles.

HARD ROCK/HEAVY METAL, WOMEN OF (ladykillerz)

Send message to: ladykillerz-request@arastar.com
   Subject: asdf
   Message body: subscribe ladykillerz "Your Name"

Some of the bands discussed here include: Ann Boleyn (Hellion), Doro Pesch (Warlock), Heart, Lisa Dal Bello, Lita Ford, Mother's Finest, Pat Benatar, The Runaways and other bands featuring female artists.

INDEPENDENT MUSIC

Indie List
　Send message to grumpy@access.digex.net

A weekly or bi-weekly mailer focusing on independent bands. Each mailer contains reviews of live shows and recordings.

INTELLIGENT DANCE MUSIC

Send message to: idm-request@hyperreal.com
　Message body: subscribe

Covers the new breed of dance music as exhibited by bands like Future Sound of London, the Aphex Twin, and labels like Warp and Astralwerks.

METAL

Send message to: majordomo@inet.it
　Message body: Subscribe metal

All aspects of metal from thrash, grind, death, old and new are discussed on this list.

NEW RELEASES

Send message to new-releases-request@cs.uwp.edu

This is a great way to keep up. This list is usually sent once a week and features a summary of the CDs, singles, and vinyl that will be released over the next few weeks.

NEW MUSIC LIST

Send message to: majordomo@xmission.com

Cutting edge and experimental music is the focus of discussion on this mailing list.

PROGRESSIVE ROCK, OBSCURE (Gibraltar)

Send message to: gib@mailhost.tcs.tulane.edu
　Message body: indicate you want to subscribe

The topic is obscure progressive rock and related music, such as fusion and neo-psychedelia. Subscription is manual. Just drop a note and ask to subscribe or unsubscribe. Gibraltar is a weekly digest of progressive rock and related music. Well-known acts, such as Yes and Genesis, are not covered because they have their own lists. Bands such as National Health, Anglagard, Ozric Tentacles and Gong are more typical. Each issue contains news, discussion and many reviews.

PSYCHEDELIC MUSIC LIST

Send message to: listserv@ucsd.edu

Message body: Subscribe "your E-mail address"

General discussion list for psychedelic music and styles of music similar to psychedelic.

PUNK/HARDCORE MUSIC

Send message to: punk-list-request@cpac.washington.edu

Focuses on punk rock music and hardcore music. Discussion centers on bands, concerts, politics and reviews of the original 70s punk and punk styles today.

SYNTH-POP

Send message to: perfect-beat-request@acca.nmsu.edu

Mailing list for the discussion of groups from the synth-pop era of the early 80s like ABBA and others.

URBAN (Electronic Urban Report)

Send message to: EURmailroom@afrinet.net

Message body: Subscribe EUR

This list chronicles the Urban/Black entertainment industry including celebs like Janet and Michael Jackson, Prince, Whitney Houston, Anita Baker, Snoop Doggy-Dog, Notorious B-I-G, 2Pac, Denzel, Whoopi, Shaq and many many more.

> **PLUG IN For More Info!**
> Browse to the website at
> http://www.prenhall.com/~plugin

Artist Homepages

As the Net grew, record companies and bands realized that a crucial link from them to their fan base was created. Naturally as the World Wide Web (see chapter 1) grew exponentially, homepages began springing up. These homepages (usually devoted to a single artist with everything from bios to lyrics to samples of their music) run the gamut

```
┌─────────────────────────────────────────────────────────────────────┐
│ ▬              Netscape - [the ultimate band list: m]          ▼ ≑ │
├─────────────────────────────────────────────────────────────────────┤
│ File   Edit   View   Go   Bookmarks   Options   Directory      Help │
├─────────────────────────────────────────────────────────────────────┤
│ │ Back │ Forward │ Home │  │ Reload │ Images │ Open │ Print │ Find │ Stop │ │
├─────────────────────────────────────────────────────────────────────┤
│ Location: http://american.recordings.com/WWWoM/ubl/M.shtml      N  │
├─────────────────────────────────────────────────────────────────────┤
│ ▨ Madonna                                                           │
│    NEWS - FAQ - AUDIO 1 - AUDIO 2 - LYRICS 1 - LYRICS 2 - TAB        │
│    Mailing List: madonna-request@umich.edu - madonna-digest-request@umich.edu │
│    WWW: Madonna - Bedtime Stories - Madonna Mailing List Digest - The Madonna │
│    Homepage                                                          │
│    Other: Songlist - Madonna filmography from Movie Database         │
│ ───────────────────────────────────────────────────────────────    │
│ ▨ Madredeus                                                         │
│    AUDIO - LYRICS                                                    │
│    WWW: Madredeus - EMI / Madredeus                                  │
│ ───────────────────────────────────────────────────────────────    │
│ ▨ Magic Bag                                                         │
│    WWW: Magic Bag Home Page                                          │
│ ───────────────────────────────────────────────────────────────    │
│ ▨ The Magic Christian Music Band                                    │
│    WWW: The Magic Christian Music Band                              │
└─────────────────────────────────────────────────────────────────────┘
```

from complex and exciting experiences to dull and lifeless promotional tools.

We must take a moment here to talk about the Ultimate Band List. (http://american.recordings.com/wwwofmusic/ubl/ubl.shtml). It is without a doubt the single most important fan link in existence. From it you can access virtually any artist in music. UBL is maintained by Aurelius Prochazka and overseen by the good people at American Recordings. Let's say you're still not tired of reading about Madonna. Well, by calling up the Ms you'll find her name. Click on her name and you'll see separate sites that cover all sorts of information: audio clips, the FAQ (frequently asked questions—all answered), lyrics to her songs; and even tablature (for guitar and piano) so you can play her songs. Let's whisk you away to the server that holds the Madonna homepage.

Once you're there you've got a terrific amount of options or links. Here's a page from the real Madonna homepage. All those words underlined are links. By clicking on them you can zip off to somewhere else and get the complete list of Madonna records, or see what David

Letterman had to say about her, or get a copy of the lyrics to "Take a Bow."

- Transcript of Madonna's Interview on the Late Show March 31, 1994.
- Top 10 Signs that David Letterman is Obsessed with Madonna.
- Madonna's Top 10 List from that infamous episode.
- Madonna's tribute to MTV at 10. Transcribed by Mark Muirhead.
- The Madonna FAQ, Version 2.0.1 Last Update: November 7, 1995
- Discography, maintained by Tero Isoniemi.
- A recent Madonna interview. (7/7/95)
- Madonna Songlist maintained by David Hanna.
- Top Positions of Madonna songs. We argue about this all the time. Finally, someone has put together a list.
- Chris Coombs has started transcribing an html version of the script of *Truth or Dare* aka *In Bed With Madonna*.
- Do you dream of Madonna?

Now that we've got some of the basics, let's turn our attention to some of the stars of the web. These homepages are well worth the visit, even for the casual fan. The very best of the homepages are absolutely stunning, with excellent visuals (photos, graphics, etc.) and even digitized sounds (songs, selections, and pieces of interviews.) You can research the history of Eric Clapton, or track down the chord changes for "Lay Down Sally," download the lyrics to your computer or your printer, or jump over to one of the online CD stores and order the Slowhand CD. It takes seconds.

For a typical recent month, here's a list of the 10 most accessed homepages. (Note we talk about artist and style homepages elsewhere in this section, most notably in the Finding Music Styles chapter.) We'll take you around them briefly, giving you the highlights of some of the pages. Anything going on in artists' homepages will be found on these examples.

Now, don't panic about the long and complicated http addresses. If you read Chapter One, you'll know all about hypertext. And, once you start accessing our site, you'll discover we've got these links already in place for you. You'll be able to click and GO!

Pearl Jam

http://www-personal.engin.umich.edu/~galvin/pearljam.html

The best homepages are pretty much the same: pictures of the band, a list of frequently asked questions (FAQ) and answers, tour dates, links to sites where you can get all the lyrics and chord changes to all the songs, a newsgroup link, and audio clips (portions of songs; sometimes even whole digitized songs themselves.) For example, on this Pearl Jam page—and you can link or jump to other Pearl Jam pages from this one—you can access an FTP site in Sweden that has digitized versions of "Daughter", "Evenflow", "Alive" and "Jeremy". With the right software and speakers, you can jam away to your favorite PJ tune while checking to see if their tour is coming through your town.

Nirvana

http://www2.ecst.csuchico.edu/~jedi/nirvana.html

My favorite section of this page, also known as the Verse-Chorus-Verse page, is the FAQ section devoted to Cobain's equipment. Everything you want to know about his guitars, amps, effects, etc. is all right here. Also, the link to newsgroups has been moderated. This means that instead of seeing the vast amount of posts—the good and the bad—this link shows you posts considered worthy by the homepage keeper. This is a real online time saver.

Pink Floyd

http://humper.student.princeton.edu/floyd/

The first feature you find here may be the best. The most recent person to access the page has his/her address displayed. (As I clicked on to review the page, someone from Czechoslovakia had been there just seconds before me.) This is a great feature when you're looking to expand your E-mail address book. Another Floyd Fan! Also, the page has all the cover art from the band in easy to use, view, and print GIF format. If you're into MPEG viewing (movies) there are some clips from "The Wall," as well.

Aerosmith

http://coos.dartmouth.edu/ljoeh/

Maybe the best band page on the Net. It's a cool looking page—black background! Lots of pictures, and a wav file welcome that is changed monthly. In addition to the usual stuff, you also can access a list of Aerosmith pen pals complete with E-mail addresses. Want to get a ticket for an upcoming show? Someone on here may have an extra one to sell. Check out the link for "extra tickets." (Did anyone say scalp?) Since the band has also made appearances on the main commercial servers, there is an actual E-mail address should you want to tell Steven something about yourself and that great song you'd like to sell him. All in all a very satisfying page and one that is sure to be copied by other artists and fans.

R.E.M.

http://www.halcyon.com/rem/index.html

A low key page, perhaps, but very clean and easy to use. All the requisite stuff is here, including a special set of FAQs that focus on individual group members. Excellent links to other relevant R.E.M. locations, including a link to their record company.

Tori Amos

http://olympe.polytechnique.fr/Tori

http://www.netsurf.org/Tori/

Don't be thrown off by the address in France (.fr). This links you up with all the vital Tori information worldwide. It is a beautiful homepage, carefully put together. It may take a little longer to load than your normal page, because of the complexity of the graphics package, but it is well worth the wait. My favorite section here is the Parodies link. This proves that Ms. Amos' fans—very reverent usually—also have terrific senses of humor. The following post is the description of a new Tori CD, a parody of her Under the Pink.

Under The Sink

I've got a sinking feeling...

Tori Amos follows her sparse 1991 debut, Little Birthrates with the much cleaner, more accessible follow-up, Under the Sink. This extraordinary second effort is awash in emotion. A much more personal outing than the more geo-politically oriented Little Birthrates, the new album plumbs the depths of Tori's soul, leaving the listener drained. It's difficult to pick highlights from this fabulous release; here's a rundown of the new songs:

* Pretty Good Ear

The tragic tale of Tori's expulsion from the Peabody Conservatory at age 11, for her refusal to read music.

* Dog

A lament on the failure of canine society, including the all-too- familiar line Dog, sometimes you just chew right through; Now I've gotta buy another pair of shoes.

* Bills for Her

Tori watches helplessly as a close friend accepts the banks' twisted version of the American Dream, accepting every credit card offer she receives and quickly descending into bankruptcy.

* Pass the Dijon

It was, 'Pass the Dijon' just came one day. We were eating dinner, and it was really quiet. And we were at the table, we were so far apart, and the mustard was way over on the other side, it was almost as if it was, you know, it was as if it might as well be in New York.

* Breaker, Breaker

You know, people always talk about that tension between truckers and police... remember Smokey and the Bandit? What a trip! I could really relate to those guys!... and anyway, it's really, it's much more subtle and covert between the truckers themselves, it's like they're telling you about some road hazard ahead, and all the time they just want you to get lost in some obscure little suburb of Chicago.

* The Long Hand

This is a poignant remembrance of the challenge of learning to tell time. According to Tori, At first I thought it was called 'The Wrong Hand', and it was about growing up left-handed, but then I just realized that it wasn't right for me, that I hadn't acknowledged that, that sinister side of myself.

(cont.)

* The Address

In this sequel to Breaker, Breaker, Tori tries desperately to find her way back to the truckstop, after getting hopelessly lost in Chicago. I have got to pee, bitch!, she angrily intones.

* Ketchup Girl

It was when 'Pass the Dijon' came, she was telling me about this friend of hers, and that's where 'Ketchup Girl' came from. It's about... it's kind of like, really, there are two kinds of women: there are the ketchup girls and then there are the mustard girls. The ketchup girls are those, you know, those wholesome, innocent, vanilla girls and the, the mustard girls are, they're more earthy or worldly. It's like 'This is not really Grey Poupon... you bet your life it is!' you know? It's just you can't really, you can't, I used to think I was a ketchup girl, because that was the right thing to be, it was nice, and I didn't really, I didn't want to be a mustard girl. I thought that was dirty or... But now I understand that, it's ok, and I'm really more comfortable with that now. It's like, when you have a hamburger, and you've got the ketchup and the mustard right there, all mixed up together, on the same burger, and it tastes really good.

* Bicycle

A hair-raising story of a child's first nightmarish experience without training wheels: Bicycle, bicycle, where are you going?

* Crowd on my Tongue

This track will not appear on the US release of Under the Sink.

* Spaced Hog

Wilbur (or was it Tori?) gets into the catnip.

* Yes, Anesthesia

Tori's response to the dentist's first question at her wisdom tooth extraction.

The cover art shows a Cindy Palmano photograph of Tori cramped in a small kitchen cabinet, an apt metaphor for the confinement theme which runs through such songs as Pretty Good Ear and Pass the Dijon.

A back cover photo of a number of phallic mushrooms will be replaced by several bottles of Heinz ketchup on the US release, which will not contain the controversial Crowd on my Tongue.

Steve Clark
clark@cme.nist.gov

Nine Inch Nails

http://www.fsl.orst.edu/rogues/rosero/nin/ninlist.htm

Well I hate to bring you the bad news, but NiN pages go in and out of service very quickly. At various times we've seen terrific pages for the band, but the webmasters never seem to keep anything online for more than a few months at a time. So instead, let us offer you a pretty stable page that compiles the most current list we've seen of NiN online resources. In addition to finding the current homepages, this address will also get you to lyric sites, etc.

The Beatles

http://www.eecis.udel.edu/~markowsk/beatles/beatlesWWW.html
http://www.eecis.udel.edu/~markowsk/beatles/

The first address isn't a traditional homepage, but it is the best place to start for Beatles' fans. It keeps a very up to date list of all homepages that have major Beatles sections (thirty of them as of this moment). It's broken down into pages made by fans, pages about specific band members or records or events, and pages sponsored by commercial entities. Mark Markowski, who maintains this site, also has a terrific Beatles homepage of his own. It's the second address listed above.

10,000 Maniacs

http://www.indirect.com/www/mecheves/misc/10000.html

An exquisite page, filled with nicely chosen and archived photos. There are some nice paintings of singer Natalie Merchant done by artist Gregg C. Wagener. This site also seems to serve as a homepage for Natalie since the group's breakup. Marc Echeveste, a law school student at Stanford in Palo Alto, is the webmaster.

Jimi Hendrix

http://www.lionsgate.com/music/hendrix/

Homepages are a chance oftentimes for fans to pay respects to the music and the musicians that mean so much to them. At times it's possible to forget that as you bounce from homepage to homepage filled with corporate links and online CD stores. There's nothing wrong with commerce by itself, but every once in a while you stumble across a homepage that has a different feel. This page is just flat out different and it's special. We're not even particularly big Hendrix fans, but this page is put together so reverentially that it's impossible not to take notice. Hendrix's story is told here in a series of biographical links, covering his early bands up to his death and beyond to his historical importance. Steve Pesant, the homepage keeper, has really done his homework, unearthing the most significant material about Hendrix.

U2

http://www-users.informatik.rwth-aachen.de/~kaldow/u2.html

Unfortunately this is sort of a workmanlike page out of Germany. It has all the necessary links and so forth. There are solid pointers to lyrics, other pages, bios, FAQ, etc., but overall the experience is a little sterile. Odd actually, for a band that engenders such a fervent following. Might be a place for a better page, if you're so inclined.

"Beyond" Mainstream Homepages

Now, don't get worried if you didn't see some of your favorite artists in that top ten group. The Net world of music is definitely skewed toward mainstream, mass appeal folks. Luckily the World Wide Web is a very catholic place, where all kinds of music co-exist. Like we've already mentioned, you'll be able to take some of our links at the website to find just what you need. In this little section we're just giving you the flavor of the vast palette of artist homepages.

Ludwig van Beethoven

http://www.ida.his.se/ida/~a94johal/beet.chtml

As you discovered in our music styles section, classical music has a fair number of fans on the Net, and pages like the Beethoven one will give you a great opportunity to begin sharing information on topics that too many times seem incompatible with modern life. Johan Alkerstedt's page is a good one and in addition to standard info about the composer's life, you also can access details about principal compositions, etc.

Beethoven, 1823

During his first visit to Vienna in 1787 Beethoven impressed Mozart with his improvisations at the keyboard. Before any formal tuition could take place, however, news that Beethoven's mother was dying took him back to Bonn. By the time he returned to Vienna in 1792, Mozart too was dead. He went instead to Haydn for composition lessons, but the two men were temperamental opposites, and the instruction he recieved from Johann Albrechtsberger

Philip Glass

http://moolah.fml.tuwien.ac.at/~ameno/glass/biography.html

Sticking with composers, here's the great American contemporary composer Philip Glass. In addition to covering biography, the page also carefully chronicles Glass' extra-musical forays into film production.

The Biography

Born in Baltimore on January 31, 1937, Philip Glass discovered music in his father's radio repair shop. In addition to servicing radios, Ben Glass carried a line of records and, when certain ones sold poorly, he would take them home and play them for his three children, trying to discover why they didn't appeal to customers. These happened to be recordings of the great chamber works, and the future composer rapidly became familiar with Beethoven quartets, Schubert sonatas, Shostakovich symphonies and other music then considered "off-beat". It was not until he was in his upper teens that Glass began to encounter more "standard" classics.

Glass began the violin at six and became serious about music when he took up the flute at eight. But by the time he was 15, he had become frustrated with the limited flute repertory as well as with the musical life in post-war Baltimore. During his second year in high school, he applied for admission to the University of Chicago, was accepted, and, with his parent's encouragement, moved to Chicago

I love music because it makes me feel so good. I was in a dark mood one day, for instance, and I popped in a climactic part of Philip Glass' Itaipu, and it picked me up right away. There was also an instance where I was in an OK mood, and started listening to Mary Chapin-Carpenter's song "Only a dream" which is so sad that I had to choke back tears.

What I love about the Net is the fact that it is so easy to find likeminded people. You can meet someone at a bar, convention, or class, and it's pot luck for the most part whether they share your interests. But instead YOU pick the area of interest and once there find kindred souls.

Aaron Woodin
DeltaV@ix.netcom.com

Moby

http://www.cudenver.edu/~dcerman/moby.html

Moby is the most influential person in all of techno. This page is very interactive and fun to play with. (A surprising flaw with many mediocre pages is the simple lack of links—those little underlined sections of text where you can click and jump to somewhere else.) In addition to simple news blurbs, you can access tour info, buy CDs online, and learn more about Moby's own Internet presence.

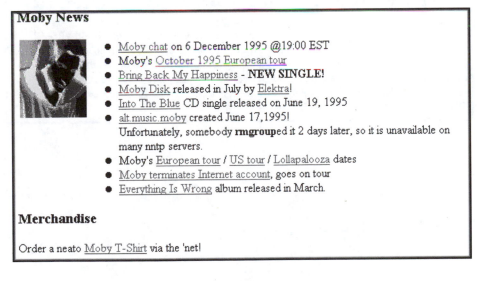

Moby News

- Moby chat on 6 December 1995 @19:00 EST
- Moby's October 1995 European tour
- Bring Back My Happiness - **NEW SINGLE!**
- Moby Disk released in July by Elektra!
- Into The Blue CD single released on June 19, 1995
- alt.music.moby created June 17,1995!
  Unfortunately, somebody **rmgroup**ed it 2 days later, so it is unavailable on many nntp servers.
- Moby's European tour / US tour / Lollapalooza dates
- Moby terminates Internet account, goes on tour
- Everything Is Wrong album released in March.

Merchandise

Order a neato Moby T-Shirt via the 'net!

New Zealand Symphony Orchestra

http://www.actrix.gen.nz/users/dgold/nzso.html

It's not every day you meet the principal double bassist from any symphony, let alone a world famous one like the New Zealand Symphony, but we did find Dale Gold in our travels. He maintains the homepage for the NZSO and it's an excellent example of a page of its type. There are individual links to key members of the orchestra, and on Dale's page for example (go ahead and check it out; it's under the link called "Who Are We,") you can actually hear him play a "few bars from Bottesini." The page also includes information about upcoming dates, where and how to obtain CDs, biographies for the players, and even a notice that they're currently looking to fill a trumpet opening. It's a fascinating and well designed page.

The New Zealand Symphony Orchestra

We've been so busy that we almost forgot to notice our first anniversary on the World Wide Web. It seems like only yesterday that we gleefully announced ourselves as the first symphony orchestra in the world on the World Wide Web, and we are delighted to see that at least 40 other orchestras have joined us online since then. If the 40-fold increase in orchestral presences on the Web each year continues along with the remarkable growth of the Internet, we can confidently predict 409,600,000 orchestras on the WWW by the year 2000!

Bob Marley

http://gene.fwi.uva.nl/~ketel/Broer/music/bmarley.html

Marley, the absolute, reigning, past, present, and future king of reggae music has a number of homepages devoted to his life, music, good deeds and love of ganja. This is the best of the lot.

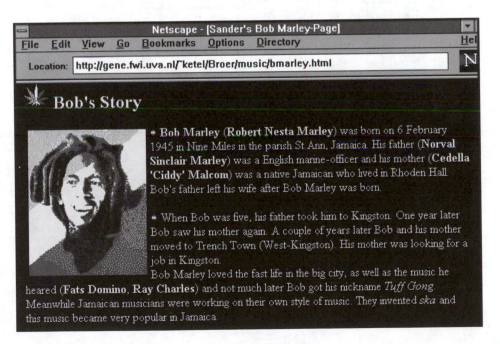

Van Morrison

http://www.harbour.sfu.ca/~hayward/van/van.html

A giant along the same sort of stature as Bob Dylan, Van's presence on the Net is quiet. But like many cult-ish figures, he has devotees like Michael Hayward who runs this very excellent page. There is lots to choose from here and it's a great example of how valuable a single fan site can be. There's an excellent discography here and a great selection of bootlegs that are available as well.

The bootleg section has now been broken into three parts, organized alphabetically by album title. This is so that you don't have to download the entire bootleg discography when viewing a single entry. I'm focussing on CDs, rather than tapes or vinyl, on the theory that CDs should be more "standard" as a point of comparison.

- ## Bootleg Albums: A - K

  The preceding link takes you to the top of the page, or go directly to
    - ☐ Van Morrison & Dr. John: Amsterdam's Tapes
    - ☐ Bluesology 1963 - '73
    - ☐ Can You Feel the Silence... (see Live in Essen, 1982)
    - ☐ The Church of our Lady St. Mary
    - ☐ Copycats Ripped Off My Soul
    - ☐ Dark Knight Of The Soul (Van Morrison with The Chieftains)
    - ☐ Desert Land
    - ☐ Gets His Chance To Wail

      This is a multi-CD set. The preceding link contains overall comparative information on the chronology of the set and a review. More detailed information on the individual titles in the set can be accessed through that page, or the following direct links:

Yanni

http://www.teleport.com/~celinec/yanni.shtml

```
┌─────────────────────────────────────────────────────────┐
│ ─         Netscape - [Unofficial Yanni Web Page]    ▼ ▲ │
│ File  Edit  View  Go  Bookmarks  Options  Directory  Help│
│ ┌────┐ ┌────┐ ┌────┐ ┌────┐ ┌────┐ ┌────┐ ┌────┐ ┌────┐ ┌────┐│
│ │Back│ │Forwd│ │Home│ │Reload│ │Images│ │Open│ │Print│ │Find│ │Stop││
│ └────┘ └────┘ └────┘ └────┘ └────┘ └────┘ └────┘ └────┘ └────┘│
│ Location: │http://www.teleport.com/~celinec/yanni.shtml│  [N]│
│                                                          │
│   1. Yanni Fans List - Email addresses, etc. of Yanni Fans - share the experience with each other.│
│      (Additions temporarily suspended)                   │
│   2. Yanni Picture Gallery - By popular demand, I put some Yanni pictures online. Let's hope it│
│      doesn't overload my server. =)                      │
│   3. LOYOL - Info about the new Yanni fan club at America Online.│
│   4. Biographical Information                             │
│   5. Yanni Quotes                                        │
│   6. Band Members                                        │
│   7. List of Albums                                      │
│   8. Song list from his albums & some soundtracks        │
│   9. 1995 Tour Dates (no concerts scheduled right now)   │
│  10. Review of June 24, 1995 concert in Great Woods.     │
│  11. Review of July 18, 1995 concert in Tampa, FL.       │
│  12. MIDI files of Yanni Songs                           │
│  13. Other "new age" music resources                     │
└─────────────────────────────────────────────────────────┘
```

Celine Chamberlain is another of our favorite souls on the Net. Her Yanni page is a sweet paean to one of her favorite artists, the nearly unexplainable new age-ist, Yanni.

Table of Contents

1. NEW! Yanni press release - answers many questions about current and future Yanni plans.
2. The Yanni Fans Mailing List - An automated mailing list (majordomo) so we can discuss Yanni and related topics. As of 11/5/95 there were around 90 people and it's growing everyday. If you want to talk about Yanni, this is the place
3. Yanni Picture Gallery - Some Yanni pictures
4. Song lists and info from Yanni's albums, soundtracks, and other projects
5. MIDI files of Yanni songs - download some MIDI arrangements of Yanni's songs (contributions are welcome)
6. Yanni Quotes - Yanni's profound thoughts
7. Concert Reviews - Reviews of two 1995 Yanni concerts written by fans
8. Tour Dates - Not a complete list. Only two dates in North America are listed.
9. (Old) Yanni Fans List - Email addresses, etc. of Yanni Fans. (Additions to this list are no longer accepted, but the list is still available for viewing)
10. Biographical Information - What little I've been able to track down about Yanni

John Cage

http://www.emf.net/~mal/cage.html

Cage is a perfect candidate for Net presence. His fans are urbane and erudite (we like using those words) and his stature as a composer and player have much to do with the sociological impact of his music. This page in fact spends as much time talking about his cultural importance as his music. It's a good looking page, and will provide you with lots to think about.

Netscape - [A John Cage Page: Cage on the internet]

File   Edit   View   Go   Bookmarks   Options   Directory   Help

Location: http://www.emf.net/~mal/cage.html

Postmodern Culture references

Seems that a number of articles in the **_Postmodern Culture_** archives make casual or in depth references to John Cage. Here's the ones that keyword searches indicate have some Cage content. While some of these make only casual refence to Cage I've included them, partly to help "screen" these so others looking through Web search engines for Cage info will have some ideas of the utitlty of the documents.

The Ideology of Postmodern Music and Left Politics by John Beverly, from _Postmodern Culture_ v.1 n.1 (September, 1990).
includes a number of Cage references throughout.

Impossible Music by Susan Schultz, from _Postmodern Culture_ v.2 n.2 (January, 1992).
opens with a Cage quote on Schoenberg; no other Cage references.

Beyond the Orality/Literacy Dichotomy: James Joyce and the Pre-History of Cyberspace by Donald F. Theall, from _Postmodern Culture_ v.2 n.3 (May, 1992)
makes only casual reference to Cage.

Rocket From the Crypt

http://www.underground.net/sdrocks/rocket/

Let's finish this section with something a little unusual. One of the truly interesting activities on the Net is searching and finding new things. We stumbled across lots of things in our research for this book, but few things intrigued us as much as unsigned, unknown bands. We love music so much, that it is always a little bit of a challenge to be the first guy with a new CD. If we can whip out some music that no one around us has heard yet, then we're a step ahead. (I was the 11th person in the United States to actually own the debut Frankie Goes to Hollywood album. I know this for a fact, and for a solid year it made for much cocktail party talk.)

So, finding unknown bands, hearing samples of their music (often just off of demo tapes), is a real kick. Here's one of several bands that are getting their first chance at Netwide attention through homepages.

A Warning to Music Fans

Be careful when you promote your page that you've set up to honor one of your favorite artists or groups. One of our favorite bands is the Neville Brothers, but look what happened to another fan.

George Gerhold, a Neville Brothers fan in Washington, D.C., created an extensive Nevilles tribute web page. The page was so well done that Yatcom, a New Orleans Web site and provider gave Mr. Gerhold the space to post the "Unofficial Neville Brothers Page," which contained a history of the band written by Gerhold, an extensive discography he compiled, and a graphic he designed.

Offbeat, the New Orleans music magazine (http://www.netcom/offbeat/), reported that in August of 1995, Gerhold met Charles Neville and told him about his web project. He asked if the band would like to see anything particular on the page or add anything to it. Not long after the meeting, Gerhold received word that, "the Nevilles were really angry after seeing my stuff. I was in shock--I could not understand how something I had created as a tribute to the Nevilles was creating such a problem." Gerhold says he received a letter from Charles Neville as President of Neville Productions that informed that "nobody [is] authorized to distribute an electronic or printed newsletter" for the band, and that if Gerhold wanted to pursue a joint project he should talk to the Neville's business manager, Shannon Chabaud. Chabaud told Gerhold that the situation was being looked at by the band's attorney.

Mr. Gerhold told *Offbeat*, "I am extremely bitter over what happened."

The business manager says she and the Nevilles are concerned about what they feel are historical inaccuracies in Gerhold's bio of the brothers. Craig Hayes, the Neville's attorney, says that while Gerhold's intentions may be "somewhat honorable," he should have asked permission of the Neville Brothers before making the Unofficial Neville Brothers Home Page public. Hayes says he and the band feel strongly about keeping the fan club, newsletter and Web page in the family, and that anything public "needs to be done at [zip code] 70115. We need to get these mid-50s geniuses to sit down and do it on their own," says Hayes. He has not ruled out the possibility of working with Gerhold in the future, but so far has been unable to coordinate any such collaboration.

After the page went down for a while, George Gerhold's page went back up with some suggested disclaimers. It can be found at...

(http://www.yatcom.com/neworl/entertai/music/nevilles/neville.htm)

Concerts & Venues

Pollstar

http://pollstar.com

We're big fans of this site. If you're looking for your favorite band and wondering when they're scheduled to come to or near your city, we'd recommend starting here. The pages are good looking and easy to navigate. In addition to giving flawless (we've found) info about dates and venues, they also include a variety of other music related tidbits we think you'll like. Here's the main page.

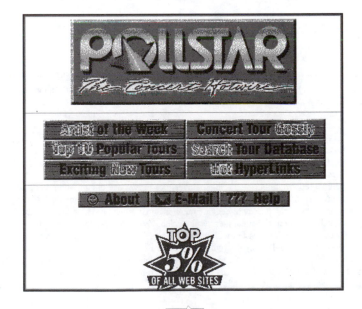

We started with the Tour Database to check one of our favorite singers, Joan Osborne. This screen came up and identified the range of dates we asked for. Clicking on the city or venue gives you more specific information about the dates.

P☉LLSTAR
The Concert Hotwire

Artist of the Week
Concert Tour Gossip
Top 50 Popular Tours
Exciting New Tours
Search Tour Database
Hot HyperLinks

Concert Information for

Joan Osborne

Date	City	State	Venue
12/2/95	East Lansing	MI	Michigan St. University
12/3/95	Detroit	MI	State Theatre
12/4/95	Columbus	OH	Veterans Memorial Aud.

One of the little bonuses with Pollstar is the variety of gossipy things that most music fans love to be in on. We just checked (at the time of this writing) their gossip page. It's cool to be in the know, right?

Concert Tour Gossip
Week of November 27, 1995

Tickets for the **BRUCE SPRINGSTEEN** solo acoustic tour went on sale November 18th, along with two benefit performances that had not been included with the initial announcement of tour dates. The original tour schedule had a starting date of November 26th at the Wiltern Theatre in Los Angeles, but the Boss decided to open the tour in his home state of New Jersey with shows at the State Theatre in New Brunswick and Count Basie Theatre in Red Bank. In Los Angeles, the 4600 tickets sold out, via just 25 Ticketmaster outlets plus phone orders, in 19 minutes. Promoter Brian Murphy of Avalon told *POLLSTAR* that there were about 250 people at every single outlet. Avalon used wristbands in conjunction with a lottery method of selling tickets. After people were issued numbered wristbands, a starting number was drawn at random. Whoever had that starting number became the first person allowed to buy tickets, and whoever had the next number after the number drawn, became number two, and so on. However, Avalon added another element of randomness to the sales. "We didn't sell the building front to back," said Murphy. "We started with the left side sections front to back, then went to the center sections and finally the right side front to back... so the tickets came out more randomly. We were trying to give everyone an equal chance." Springsteen will reportedly stop by the Monday afternoon taping of "The Tonight Show" to chat with Jay Leno before he heads out for that night's gig at the Wiltern.

Ticketmaster

http://www.ticketmaster.com/

Despite their past and ongoing problems regarding their alleged monopoly status, this is the easiest and best way to purchase tickets to most major venues for most major and minor concerts. Their website is good and fairly easy to navigate.

The information they provide ranges from their ticket outlet locations to actual seating charts of nearly all venues. (This is a very handy thing to have along as you go to purchase tickets. Knowing as much as you can about the place will help you find the best seats for you.) In addition, Ticketmaster is not just selling rock music; we found tickets for some friends who wanted to see the road show of Phantom of the Opera. (You can also access the phone numbers of local offices all across the U.S. to order tickets by phone.)

The good news is, Ticketmaster is working very hard to find a way to conduct online transactions for tickets. This will obviously make this site much more valuable. It's one thing to know the information then have to pick up the phone or drive to an outlet center. It's another thing to view the seating chart on your screen and then hit a button to buy a ticket. As of this writing Ticketmaster is working on the obvious security questions of buying online (like everyone else).We have high hopes that they'll have something in place faster than any other possible competitor.

Wilma

http://wilma.com/

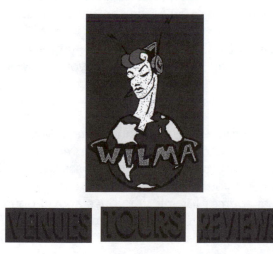

Wilma is a very cool source that is still slowly developing. If you're in search of the more obscure bands and/or venues, this might be helpful. They have a terrific state by state breakdown of venues. We just hit Vancouver Canada, for example, and found this stuff.

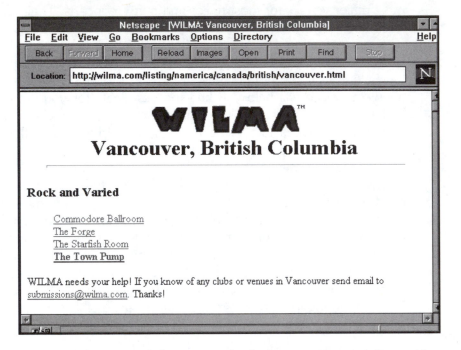

When you click on an individual venue you get their address, phone number, seating capacity, and the name of the person in charge of booking the club. (Obviously a real bonus for bands looking to play!)

In addition to those obvious things, you also can access reviews of ongoing and past concerts to help you make your decisions about future shows.

Yahoo

http://www.yahoo.com/Entertainment/Music/Events/Concerts/

By now you know that Yahoo is a pretty standard "search engine," like Infoseek, Lycos and the others discussed in Chapter One. But to just to remind you, here's a quick and easy way to use it to help you if your usual sources for info (the ones above) don't bring you the help you need. We went to the main menu and picked Amsterdam. We got this very helpful screen with gig and venue information. Even prices.

Netscape - [Amsterdam Concert Guide]

File   Edit   View   Go   Bookmarks   Options   Directory   Help

Back   Forward   Home   Reload   Images   Open   Print   Find   Stop

Location: `http://www.htsa.hva.nl/~jeroensm/concerts`

The Concert Guide

These concerts are mainly in Amsterdam, but if the artist doesn't have a gig in Amsterdam the nearest place is given

mo20nov

DISHWALLA - Melkweg, Amsterdam
BUFFALO TOM/TEENAGE FANCLUB - Paradiso, Amsterdam
THE SANDS - Paradiso Bovenzaal, Amsterdam

tu21nov

THE AMPS - Melkweg Max, Amsterdam

Publications

Now this is an odd little section. As the Internet is spreading and as the World Wide Web increases its coverage, print items like magazines are increasingly showing up online. Naturally this takes some time, but as you see below some major players have gotten involved.

• *Rolling Stone*

on CompuServe (Go RSonline)

Rolling Stone has taken up residence on CompuServe. The interface is decent enough, but it is still developing. The text of current and past issues is available as are a good selection of photos and graphics. Their own voluminous database is mostly online at this time and that makes for great search capabilities. However, loading of complex images takes time and CompuServe is notoriously slow for this anyway. It makes for a rather long (dollars per minute, remember?) visit. Still, with the resources of the print version, it seems destined to be a major online force as well.

• *Spin*

on America Online (Keyword: Spin)

Their online version of the magazine includes current month text and photos in addition to selected past month items. They have a whole raft of cool *Spin* memorabilia to buy as well and the prices are good.

• *Stereo Review*

on America Online (Keyword: Stereo Review)

A well respected high end audio magazine, *Stereo Review* has room for everything from the newest DAT machines available to reviews of an Elvis Costello disk. It's a wide ranging magazine and the online version is fairly slick and easy to use (like most stuff on AOL). An area still under development, but sure to be operating soon, is the buying product area. While it's still too early to tell, we think merchandise from equipment to CDs and tapes will be available in the near future.

Buying Product

While a system called E-cash (electronic cash) has been under development for years now, one of the simplest ways to buy stuff on the Net is the same method used at many mail order places. You give someone (this time by typing) your credit card number and you wait for the stuff to arrive. Some folks are bothered by this and worry about the security. Luckily, encryption programs have been developed and one of the safest is built right into the Netscape browser, so that while your credit card number is in transit from your computer to the vendor of your choice, the numbers are all encoded in such a way that no one (supposedly) could ever figure them out.

Just for reference, some of us long-time Netizens buy stuff on the Net constantly and we can't think of an example of anyone we know ever having their credit card stolen or abused. Still, the encryption is a safeguard and more established vendors will make it easy for you to purchase their wares.

E-cash

The folks at Digicash are at the forefront of the E-cash development curve. Their website can help you great deal with understanding this new concept. Such heavyweights as the Wells Fargo Bank and the US Department of Commerce are associated or involved with Digicash and that should give you a certain amount of piece of mind. Check Digicash out at: http://www.digicash.com/ecash/ecash-home.html

Now, since this is the fan chapter, we're going to focus on the purchasing of CDs, tapes, even vinyl, artist memorabilia, etc. If you want to get a guitar or something, check the next chapter.

(There are over 100 online CD stores. You can get a full listing of them from Yahoo. Next, we'll take a stroll through a few and review the sites we find the easiest to use.)

MasterCard and Visa

If you are still uncomfortable with E-cash and other methods of payment on the Net, wait a while. On the horizon, the big guys have a plan that should be intact by early 1997. Visa International and MasterCard International have developed a technical standard to secure credit card purchases via the Internet. Dubbed Secure Electronic Transactions (SET), the software encrypts credit card information for consumers to ensure that transactions are protected until the they electronically reach the bank. Merchants will be given a code to ensure that the customer is the authorized user. To discourage credit card scams, Visa and MasterCard will verify that merchants are authorized to conduct business. This technology will be integrated in the Netscape browser and any other browser that chooses to license it.

MasterCard developed this software by working with Netscape Communications and IBM while Visa worked with Microsoft. RSA Data Security developed the encryption technology.

Tower Records

on America Online (Keyword: "Tower")

Let's start with one of the major names. Tower is a well established chain nationwide—although centered in the west and in major cities only. Their move off of the Internet to their commercial home on AOL was a little unusual, but AOL's superior ordering interface comes in very handy here. (Like other AOL merchants, you figuratively fill up a little shopping cart as you go.)   Here's their opening screen.

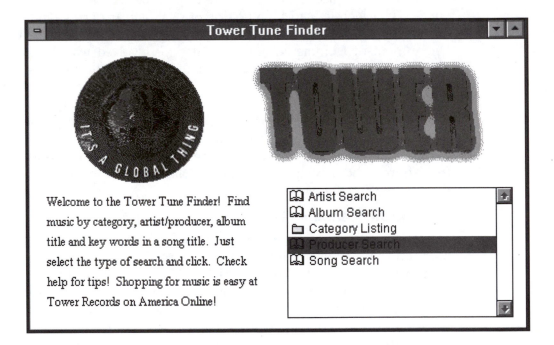

Tower's search function is amazing. When you find a CD or tape you want, like this classic Jim Heath release…

you can get more information about it by clicking on the name. The new screen contains full cover art, song titles, principal players and producers, a price, and even a review or two of the release. Clicking on the "click here to order" button puts the item in your shopping cart. If you've shopped on AOL before they've already got your credit card number and ordering is a breeze.

CD Now

http://www.cdnow.com/

Now here's a place! And if you have any security concerns, CD Now has a completely encrypted method of purchasing. They in fact deal with the sticky concern right on their first page, to allay fears of hesitant Net shoppers. Their search function is extraordinary and quick. (We went in search of one of our favorites, Warren Zevon, notoriously hard to find in anything other than major markets.) In addition to a not-so-brief bio, we had access to all his albums in CD or cassette format.

Warren Zevon

Roots and Influences: <u>The Beatles</u>, <u>Bob Dylan</u>
Similar Artists: <u>Jackson Browne</u>, <u>Greg Copeland</u>

| SORT BY: | <u>ALPHABETICALLY</u> | <u>RELEASE DATE</u> | <u>BEST FIRST</u> |
| VIEW TYPE: | <u>QUICK LIST</u> | FULL | |

Click on the price to put an album in your shopping cart. <u>More help</u>.

Albums:

BAD LUCK STREAK IN DANCING SCH

Tracks   <u>$10.77</u>

Then when we wanted to buy, the procedure was simple. In order to secure your safety, you open an account with them and provide your own password. It may seem a little time-consuming to actually open an account, but if you're a music buyer like we are, you will appreciate the incredible access CD Now! provides; it will be worth the effort. Once an account is opened, your shopping ease increases.

Netscape - [CDnow : account]

File   Edit   View   Go   Bookmarks   Options   Directory   Help

Create New Account [**Create New Account**]

To create your account, we need you to provide us with your first name, last name and a password. The password should be unique but not obvious (like your name). It is good practice to use a new password for your account.

If you will be paying by credit card, your account must be in the name of the cardholder.

1: Login Information

First   Tony
Last   Wozniak
Password   ****   (4 - 10 characters)

2: Shipping info

This is the name and address to which you would like your order shipped.

New Releases?

Sometimes it's hard to know what to look for. Obviously if you have in mind some favorite CD you'd like to buy, all of these services are very user friendly. But what about a new album coming out from David Bowie? You don't know the name; you don't know when it's coming out. The job of finding that information before the CD is available is difficult. Luckily, every week a list called New Releases comes out with complete artist, title, and date information for all known releases for the next year. You can get this list in three different ways:

E-mail:

write to releases@cs.uwp.edu or majordomo@cs.uwp.edu with "subscribe new-releases" in the body of your message.

WWW

http://www.dsi.unimi.it/users/students/barbieri/home.html
http://nabalu.flas.ufl.edu/djemhome
http://www.cloud9.net/new-releases/
http://www.cs.colorado.edu/~miller/new_releases.html

FTP

ftp://ftp.uwp.edu/pub/music/releases
ftp://server.berkeley.edu/pub/music

• *Soundwire*

http://www.soundwire.com/WhatIs.html

Now here we get into some new Net world complexity. The problems we've been talking about as they relate to money are dealt with a number of different ways. Here at Soundwire (and lots of other companies) they are experimenting with two fairly new and still developing systems of money transfer: Netcash and First Virtual. Both of these systems are linked nicely from Soundwire so you find more info there. However, the basic premise is: You send money in a traditional way (check, money order, or credit card over the phone) to a computer "bank," and that "bank" makes E-cash available to you on the Net. (For a small fee, obviously.) The whole theory and system behind electronic cash is complex and beyond the scope of this book. However, the Soundwire folks try to make it easy for you on their page.

Now what about getting CDs and tapes, which is why we're here? Soundwire has a wide selection of alternative, world music, folk and jazz. We'd recommend it as a cool place to go to for locating hard to find or more obscure work. Just for grins we searched for a virtually unknown pre-punk figure, Willie Alexander. We were more than a little stupefied to find him, a cool CD to buy and a relevant bio. Bravo!

Willie Alexander:

Willie Loco Boom Boom Ga Ga (1975-1991)

Seminal garage punk, and former member of The Lost in the mid-'60s (who recorded for Capital), The Velvet Underground in the early '70s (post-Lou Reed), and The Boom Boom Band in the mid-'70s (who recorded for MCA), Willie Alexander has created a musical legacy rich in tradition, outrageous in approach. This disc highlight's Willie's solo career, and includes original versions of the pre-punk classics "Mass. Ave." and "Kerouac," a number of songs available as imports-only, a handful of unreleased material (including the debut of his new band The Persistence of Memory Orchestra), and assorted other nuggets. 22 tracks in all, with a beautiful, 16 page booklet. NR 5502-CD

"Willie's substantial contribution to rock and roll finally gets documented!"—The Boston Phoenix

"A new CD anthology that ranks with the best in Boston rock releases... indispensable."—The Music Paper

---

Music Blvd.

http://www.musicblvd.com/

Holy moley. While it shares many attributes of other CD vendors, Music Blvd. does things just a bit better. Their search function is faster and more comprehensive, and once you're perusing an artist, links are made available to "related" and "influential" artists. For those of us who are music fans, those links are heaven-sent. You can follow a free path down the boulevard or pay a small fee for more information on the paid road.

In the free section, you can look at the music database, purchase CDs, listen to sound samples, read a daily e-zine (electronic magazine) called, "Sound Wire" and scan reviews and charts. A search for the poppy 70s band, Orleans, that scored a top ten hit "Still the One," in 1976 turned up a greatest hits collection issued by WEA, an All Music Guide rating as "best of the genre" and a list of related artists including the Doobie Brothers and John Hall. In addition, you can instantly link to a review of a CD you may be considering buying courtesy the all-powerful All-Music Guide (http://allmusic/AMG). Seven *Billboard*

magazine charts are also made available in the free section every week.

Music Blvd. also features a special level of access if you join the system. Becoming a "backstage pass" holder lets you save money on purchases and have a greater level of access to their estimable database. With your pass, you get online subscriptions and access to back issues to over seven music magazines including *Spin*, *Blues Revue*, *Fanfare*, *Dirty Linen* and more. As a "backstage pass" member you can view all 26 weekly charts from *Billboard*. In addition, the very comprehensive 14 volume encyclopedic reference, *Contemporary Musician* from Gale publications is available for searching. Finally, if all that isn't enough to encourage you to join for less than three dollars a month, you get $.50 cents off every CD you order as a member and there are a lot of contests and giveaways you can enter for free stuff.

RockworldCyberGalleria

http://www.sonnet.com/webworld/homepop2.htm

This cool store is a rather new force on the Net. If you're looking for t-shirts, hard to find posters, and rock memorabilia, this would be the place to start. If they can't find it, they can tell you where to look next. They also feature limited edition and rare instruments, along with signed books, posters and prints.

Now, don't worry. We're not stranding you with only these places to shop. Instead you'll find at the website a complete list of merchants who sell all the music stuff you'll ever want.

> PLUG IN For More Info!
> Browse to the website at
> http://www.prenhall.com/~plugin

The Similarities Engine

http://www.webcom.com/~se

We didn't know where to put this, but since you've just finished finding out how to locate and purchase new CDs, maybe this is as good a place as any. (Also see our blurb about this kind of technology in Chapter 5.) Anyway, Dave Whiteis has got this very interesting tool called the Similarities Engine. In a database function that is a mystery to us (fess up, Dave), he is able to generate a list of albums you'd like based on a list of five current favorite records. Just for fun we entered a collection of stuff we had sitting on top of the CD player and waited about 12 hours for our E-mailed response. The following table shows our input:

Artist	Recording
Dylan, Bob	Slow Train Coming
Zevon, Warren	Mutineer
Springsteen, Bruce	Tunnel of Love
Morrison, Van	Wavelength
Jones, Rickie Lee	Pirates

We got back this list

No.	Artist	Recording	Weight
1	Holly, Buddy	Collection	41
2	Lewis, Huey & the News	Four Chords...	41
3	Mellencamp, John	Lonesome Jubilee	26
4	Bach, J.S.	Cantatas	16
5	Bardens, Pete	Big Sky	16
6	Brandon String Trio	Bustin Out...	16
7	Ellington, Duke	Blanton-Webster...	16
8	Everly Brothers	Heartaches &...	16
9	Kottke, Leo	My Fathers Face	16
10	Marley, Bob	Reggae Legend	16

Key to Weights: The Wt. (Weight) column indicates how likely it is that you would enjoy that particular recording. Use this chart as a guide:

* 100 or more: Highly likely to be a CD that you would enjoy.
* 30-99:   You would probably enjoy most of these CDs.
* 17-29:   You would probably enjoy about 2/3 of these CDs.
*1-16:   You would probably enjoy about 1/2 of these CDs.

The engine showed us a total of 73 suggested CDs and we were a little astonished at how many records we actually owned of that list. If you're a frequent buyer of CDs and are always looking for some new stuff (and who isn't?), we think this engine will prove to be a very valuable resource.

Charts All Over the World

http://www.lanet.lv/misc/charts/

We grew up listening to Casey's Top 40 and all the other top hit shows on the local radio stations, while looking forward to seeing if our favorites had made it to the number one position. Top hit shows are still on the radio, but there is now one for every style of music from classic country, top pop hits, heavy metal, college radio, dance—you name it and it is charted.

Billboard and *Cashbox* have also gotten more sophisticated with the charts, with both radio play and store sales being charted.

The Net has the latest music charts posted every week from all over the world. One of the best starting points is to visit Afis Kluss's site in Latvia (he is the webmaster at the Latvian Academic Network); it is an impressive set of links to hit charts located all over the world. Not only does Afis point us to the hit charts, he also links radio playlists, college hitlists, DJ charts, Internet online music charts and more. The following chart is a sampling of the number one pop hits from around the world gathered from his site during one week in September, 1995.

Charts All Over The World

Australia	"Kiss From a Rose"	Seal
Austria	"Wish You Were Here"	Rednex
Belgium	"Scatman's World"	Scatman John
Canada	"You Oughta Know"	Alanis Morisette
Denmark	"Dub I Dub"	Me & My
Finland	"Shy Guy"	Diana King
France	"Yeha-Noha"	Sacred Spirit
Germany	"Scatman's World"	Scatman John
Great Britain	"Country House"	Blur
Hungry	"Scatman's World"	Scatman John
Israel	"Paninaro'95"	Pet Shop Boys
Japan	"Scatman"	Scatman John
Latvia	"HM,TM,KM,KM"	U2
Netherlands	"Het Is Een Nacht"	Guus Meeuwis & Vagant
Poland	"Trzy Noce Z Deszczem"	Robert Gawlinksi
Spain	"Never Forget"	Take That
Sweden	"Det Vackraste"	Cecilia Vennersten
Switzerland	"Wish You Were Here"	Rednex
U.S.	"You Are Not Alone"	Michael Jackson

As you will find, there is a lot of music an entire country thinks is good, though we may never hear it in our own region.

Fan Newsgroups B

Here is our current list of fan newsgroups. Believe it or not, for several months now we've been reading these groups, taking part in ongoing discussions. Be forewarned, unlike the newsgroups we discussed in the chapter itself, some of these are sporadic and small. But, it you're a big fan of one of these artists, you can be sure that you'll find someone else out there who will want to talk, share information, discuss tapes, etc. Good luck. It's a big list, but you're up to it!

alt.fan.allman-brothers	alt.fan.barbra.streisand
alt.fan.barry-manilow	alt.fan.blues-brothers
alt.fan.capt-beefheart	alt.fan.courtney-love
alt.fan.david-bowie	alt.fan.debbie.gibson
alt.fan.depeche-mode	alt.fan.devo

alt.fan.elton-john	alt.fan.elvis-costello
alt.fan.elvis-presley	alt.fan.enya
alt.fan.frank-zappa	alt.fan.gg-allin
alt.fan.harry-connick-jr	alt.fan.henry-rollins
alt.fan.jello-biafra	alt.fan.jimi-hendrix
alt.fan.jimmy-buffett	alt.fan.laurie.anderson
alt.fan.leningrad.cowboys	alt.fan.liz-phair
alt.fan.madonna	alt.fan.maria-callas
alt.fan.michael-bolton	alt.fan.oingo-boingo
alt.fan.peter.hammill	alt.fan.rickie-lee.jones
alt.fan.run-dmc	alt.fan.samantha-fox
alt.fan.shostakovich	alt.fan.spinal-tap
alt.fan.trisha.yearwood	alt.fan.u2
alt.fan.weird-al	alt.fan.yanni
alt.fan.zoogz-rift	alt.music.+live+
alt.music.abba	alt.music.alanis
alt.music.alanis.morissette	alt.music.aliceinchains
alt.music.america	alt.music.amy-grant
alt.music.army-of-lovers	alt.music.bad-religion
alt.music.banana-truffle	alt.music.barenaked-ladies
alt.music.beach-boys	alt.music.beastie-boys
alt.music.beck	alt.music.bee-gees
alt.music.bela-fleck	alt.music.billy-joel
alt.music.bjork	alt.music.black-sabbath

alt.music.blueoystercult	alt.music.blues-traveler
alt.music.blur	alt.music.bon-jovi
alt.music.boyz-2-men	alt.music.brian-eno
alt.music.bruce-springsteen	alt.music.butholesurfers
alt.music.byrds	alt.music.celine-dion
alt.music.cheap-trick	alt.music.chicago
alt.music.clannad	alt.music.clash
alt.music.counting-crows	alt.music.cranberries
alt.music.ct-dummies	alt.music.danzig
alt.music.dave-matthews	alt.music.dead-kennedys
alt.music.deep-purple	alt.music.def-leppard
alt.music.depeche-mode	alt.music.detox
alt.music.dio	alt.music.dream-theater
alt.music.eagles	alt.music.ebm
alt.music.ecto	alt.music.elastica
alt.music.elo	alt.music.enigma-dcd-etc
alt.music.enya	alt.music.erasure
alt.music.faith-no-more	alt.music.fates-warning
alt.music.fegmania	alt.music.fleetwood-mac
alt.music.foo-fighters	alt.music.genesis
alt.music.green-day	alt.music.green-day.sucks
alt.music.guthrie	alt.music.gwar
alt.music.harry-chapin	alt.music.iggy-pop
alt.music.independent	alt.music.indigo-girls

alt.music.info-society	alt.music.inxs
alt.music.j-s-bach	alt.music.james-taylor
alt.music.janes-addictn	alt.music.jesus-lizard
alt.music.jethro-tull	alt.music.jimi.hendrix
alt.music.jon-spencer	alt.music.joydivision
alt.music.julie-masse	alt.music.kylie-minogue
alt.music.led-zeppelin	alt.music.leonard-cohen
alt.music.lightfoot	alt.music.live.the.band
alt.music.lloyd-webber	alt.music.lor-mckennitt
alt.music.lou-reed	alt.music.luis-miguel
alt.music.mariah.carey	alt.music.marillion
alt.music.marilyn-manson	alt.music.mazzy-star
alt.music.michael-english	alt.music.michael-jackson
alt.music.ministry	alt.music.moby
alt.music.modern-rock	alt.music.monkees
alt.music.moody-blues	alt.music.morrissey
alt.music.moxy-fruvous	alt.music.naked-barbies
alt.music.new-order	alt.music.nils-lofgren
alt.music.nin	alt.music.nin.creative
alt.music.nin.d	alt.music.nirvana
alt.music.oasis	alt.music.offspring
alt.music.orb	alt.music.ozzy
alt.music.pantera	alt.music.pat-mccurdy
alt.music.pat-metheny	alt.music.pat-metheny.moderated

alt.music.paul-simon	alt.music.paul-westerberg
alt.music.pearl-jam	alt.music.pet-shop-boys
alt.music.peter-gabriel	alt.music.pink-floyd
alt.music.planet-gong	alt.music.pogues
alt.music.pop-eat-itself	alt.music.pop.will.eat.itself
alt.music.prick	alt.music.primus
alt.music.primus.sausage	alt.music.prince
alt.music.queen	alt.music.ramones
alt.music.replacements	alt.music.roger-waters
alt.music.rupaul	alt.music.rush
alt.music.s-mclachlan	alt.music.seal
alt.music.seikima-ii	alt.music.shamen
alt.music.shamen	alt.music.shonen-knife
alt.music.sinaed	alt.music.smash-pumpkins
alt.music.smiths	alt.music.sondheim
alt.music.sonic-youth	alt.music.sophie-hawkins
alt.music.soundgarden	alt.music.squeeze
alt.music.stone-roses	alt.music.stone-temple
alt.music.suede	alt.music.supergrass
alt.music.sylvian	alt.music.the-band
alt.music.the-doors	alt.music.the.police
alt.music.thecure	alt.music.tlc
alt.music.tmbg	alt.music.todd-rundgren
alt.music.tom-waits	alt.music.tool

alt.music.tragically-hip	alt.music.type-o-negative
alt.music.u2	alt.music.utah-saints
alt.music.van-halen	alt.music.van-halen.sammy-sucks
alt.music.w-carlos	alt.music.ween
alt.music.weird-al	alt.music.who
alt.music.yanni.aural-enema	alt.music.yes
alt.music.yngwie	alt.music.yngwie-malmsteen
alt.music.zevon	alt.rock-n-roll.acdc
alt.rock-n-roll.aerosmith	alt.rock-n-roll.metal.gnr
alt.rock-n-roll.metal.ironmaiden	alt.rock-n-roll.metal.megadeth
alt.rock-n-roll.metal.metallica	alt.rock-n-roll.metal.motley-crue
alt.rock-n-roll.oldies	alt.rock-n-roll.stones
rec.music.artists.beach-boys	rec.music.artists.bruce-hornsby
rec.music.artists.danny-elfman	rec.music.artists.debbie-gibson
rec.music.artists.queensryche	rec.music.artists.mariah-carey
rec.music.beatles	rec.music.dylan
rec.music.gaffa	rec.music.gdead
rec.music.phish	ec.music.rem
rec.music.tori-amos	

Fan Mailing Lists C

These are fan mailing lists.

#'s

10CC

capnbizr@interaccess.com

Send message: Subscribe Minestrone "your E-mail address" "your name"

Covers old and new information about the band 10cc and all related bands like Godley & Creme and the related solo projects.

10,000 Maniacs

Send message to: majordomo@egr.uri.edu

Message body: Subscribe 10k_maniacs "Your E-mail address"

10,000 Maniacs and Natalie Merchant discussion.

2 UNLIMITED

delaney@acy.digex.net

Send message that you would like to subscribe.

A manually run mailing list for this dance band. Weekly newsletter and news flashes.

A

ABDUL, PAULA

Send message to: majordomo@csn.net

Message body: Subscribe Pabdul-L

AEROSMITH

Send message to: aerosmith-fans-request@dartmouth.edu

Message body: Subscribe aerosmith-fans

A-HA

Send message to: majordomo@lists.best.com

Message body: Subscribe a-ha

ALICE IN CHAINS

Send message to: angrychr@halcyon.com

Message: In subject field type subscribe

ALLMAN BROTHERS BAND

Send message to: listserv@netspace.org

Message body: Subscribe Allman

Discussions of Allman Brothers Band and all the related solo efforts.

ALPHAVILLE

Send message to: listproc@tribble.uvsc.edu

Message body: Subscribe Utopia "your name"

Discussion of Alphaville music and Martin Gold's solo projects.

AMOS, TORI

Really Deep Thoughts List

Send message to:
really-deep-thoughts-request@gradient.cis.upenn.edu

Message body: Subscribe

Discussion and dissemination of information about Tori Amos, her music and anything else related to Tori.

B

BASIA

Send message to: basia-request@jane.tiac.net

Message body: Subscribe

List focuses on music of Basia and early Matt Bianco.

BEACH BOYS

Send message to: Smile-approval@smile.sbi.com

Individual projects, group projects and general music discussion takes place on the Beach Boys list.

BECK

Send message to: agwebb@watserv1.uwaterloo.ca

Message body: Subscribe beck

BEE GEES

Send message to: listproc@cc.umanitoba.ca

Message body: Subscribe Bee-Gees "your name"

Forum for the exchange of information and discussion about the music of the Bee Gees.

BENATAR, PAT

Send message to: majordomo@southwind.net

Message body: subscribe Benatar-L

List server of the Pat Benatar Online Fan Club for discussion of Pat Benatar and the band.

BIANCO, MATT see Basia

BIG COUNTRY

Send Message to: bc-request@specklec.mpifr-bonn.mpg.de
Message body: Subscribe

BJORK

Blues Eyed Pop List
Send message to: listserv@morgan.ucs.mun.ca
Message body: Subscribe blue-eyed pop "your name"

List dedicated to Icelandic popular music artists.

BLACK SABBATH

Send message to: sabbath-request@fa.disney.com
Message body: Send name and Your E-mail address.

A digested list that covers Black Sabbath and former members music careers.

BLUES TRAVELER

Send Message to: blues-traveler-request@cs.umd.edu

BLUR

Send Message to: listserv@netcom.com
Message body: Subscribe ADVERT-L

BOBS

Send message to: majordomo@lists.best.com
Message body: Subscribe netfobs

If you don't know this accapela band that gives popular tunes a bizarre twist, check it out.

BOLTON, MICHAEL

bwoolf@pro-woolf.clark.net
Send message to above address: sub bolton

All aspects of Michael Bolton's music is discussed on this list. Music, concert information, and fan information are all part of this list or try this one:

ai411@yfn.ysu.edu

BON JOVI

Send message to: bjlistsub@aol.com

There are two lists for New Jersey's second favorite son. The AOL based list is a digest that is sent daily, or try this one:

Send message to: ktrappe@silver.ucs.indiana.edu.

Message: In the subject line type in "Bon Jovi request"

BOOK OF LOVE

Lullaby List

Send Message to: majordomo@tcp.com

Message Body: Subscribe lullaby

BUSH, KATE

Love Hounds Mailing List

Send message to: love-hounds-request@uunet.uu.net

A mailing list that mirrors the Usenet group rec.music.gaffa.

BYRDS

Send message to: richruss@gate.net

Message body: In subject line type Subscribe.

A weekly digested list featuring Byrds discussion.

C

CAGE, JOHN

Send message to: majordomo@bga.com

Message body: Subscribe silence "your E-mail address"

Discussion of the music, philosophy, writings, and art of John Cage. The list attracts novice listeners and experts all discussing the composer and classical contemporary artist John Cage.

CAMPER VAN BEETHOVEN

Send message to: majordomo@list.stanford.edu

Message body: Subscribe campervan-etc

Music discussion group concerning everything about Camper Van Beethoven, including related bands such as Cracker and Monks of Doom.

CAREY, MARIAH

Vision List

Send message: vision-request@biographer.wustl.edu

Message body: Include word "subscribe"

CARPENTER, MARY CHAPIN

Send message to: ua700@ciao.trail.bc.ca

Message body: Subscribe MCCIFC "your E-mail address"

A bi-monthly newsletter focusing on Mary Chapin Carpenter.

CARPENTERS

Send message to: schmidt_r@swosu.edu

Subject line: Subscribe

Message body: Subscribe Newville Ave

CATHERINE WHEEL

Strange Fruit

Send mail to: Fruit-request@gdb.org

Mailing list for the fans of Catherine Wheel.

CAVE, NICK

Send message to: goodson-request@geog.leeds.ac.uk

CHAPMAN, TRACY

Send message: tracy-chapman-request@julie.pond.com

Message body: Subscribe tracy-chapman "your E-mail address"

Official mailing list of the Tracy Chapman Internet Fan Club.

CHICAGO

Send message to: chicago-request@acca.nmsu.edu

Message subject: Subscribe

Discussion about the band Chicago and all related solo projects.

CHURCH

Send message to: seance-info@thechurch.Ebay.Sun.com

CLAPTON, ERIC

Send message to: Slowhand-request@daacdev1.stx.com

COCKBURN, BRUCE

Send message to: majordomo@fish.com
Message body: Subscribe humans

CONCRETE BLONDE

Little conversations list
Send message to: little-conversations-request@dover.cerf.net
Send message: Subscribe in Subject line

COOPER, ALICE

Alicefan List
Send Message to: listserv@wkux1.bitnet

Anything related to Alice Cooper goes on this list from collectables to music and tours.

COSTELLO, ELVIS

Send message to: Costello-Request@gnu.ai.mit.edu
or
Send message to: majordomo@rain.org
Message body: Subscribe costello-l

Two separate lists focusing on Elvis Costello.

COUNTING CROWS

Send message to: county-crows-request@ariel.com

CRANBERRIES

Send message to: majordomo@ocf.berkeley.edu
Message body: Subscribe cranberry-saw-us "your E-mail address"

CROSBY, STILLS, and NASH

Send message to: majordomo@blender.digital.com.au
Message body: Subscribe lee-shore

CROWDED HOUSE

Send message to: listproc@listproc.wsu.edu

Message body: Subscribe ch-digest "your name"

CULTURE CLUB

Kissing to be Clever List

Send message to: Kissing-to-be-clever-request@umich.edu

Message body: Subscribe in the Subject line.

This list covers all topics related to Boy George and his solo years.

CURE

Babble List

Send message to: babble-request@anthrax.exst.csuchico.edu

D

DEEE-LITE

Send message to: majordomo@world.std.com

Message body: Subscribe deee-lite

DEF LEPPARD

LepNet List

Send message to: lepnet-request@cs.niu.edu

Low volume list focusing on Def Leppard.

DENVER, JOHN

Rocky Mountain High List

Send message to: emily@sky.net

DEPECHE MODE

Bong Mailing List

Send message to: bong-request@fletch.earthlink.net

Message body: Subscribe bong

Discussion about Depeche Mode and related bands like Recoil.

ANI DIFRANCO

Send Message to: majordomo@word.std.com
Message body: Subscribe ani-difranco

DOKKEN

Breaking the Chains List
Send message to: kirsten@mik.uky.edu

Mailing list about the musicians that were formally in the bands Dokken and Lynch Mob.

DURAN DURAN

Tiger List
Send Message to: tiger-request@acca.nmsu.edu

High traffic list devoted to Duran Duran.

DYLAN, BOB

Hwy 61 List
Send message to: Listserv@ubvm.cc.buffalo.edu

Heavy traffic list that is replicated on the rec.music.dylan Usenet group. Focuses on all aspects of Dylan's words and music.

E

ECHO & the BUNNYMEN

Send message to: Seven-seas-request@dfw.net
Message body: Subscribe seven-seas

ELASTICA

Stutter List
Send message to: stutter-request@webcom.com
Message body: Subscribe

ELECTRIC LIGHT ORCHESTRA

Send Message to: Elo-request@andrew.cmu.edu
List that is oriented to ELO and related solo projects.

EMERSON, LAKE & PALMER

Send Message to: arnold@iii.net

This list devoted to EL&P comes out every couple of weeks or when list traffic warrants.

ENIGMA

Send message to: listserv@yoyo.cc.monash.edu

Message body: Subscribe "your name"

ENO, BRIAN

Send message to: Eno-L-Request@udlapvms.pue.udlap.mx

Issues and music about Brian Eno are discussed on this list. Everything about Eno, avant-garde music, his video's and museum exhibits are fair game here.

ENYA

Send message to: majordomo@cs.colorado.edu

Message body: Subscribe Enya

ERASURE

Send message to:majordomo@tcp.com

Message body: Subscribe vincent-clarke

Erasure and Yaz discussion.

ESTEFAN, GLORIA see Miami Sound Machine

ETHERIDGE, MELISSA

Send message to: Etheridge-request@cnd.mcgill.ca

F

FAITH NO MORE

Send message to majodomo@tower.techwood.org

Message body: Subscribe cv

FERRY, BRYAN see Roxy Music

FIXX, THE

Send message to: theFixx-request@pesto.eng.sun.com

Discussion about the music of the Fixx, its members, and producer Rupert Hine.

FOGELBERG, DAN

Send message to: ai411@yfn.ysu.edu

FRIPP, ROBERT

Elephant Talk List

Send message to: elephant-talk-request@arastar.com

G

GABRIEL, PETER

Send message to: majordomo@ccsdec1.ufsia.ac.be

Message body: Subscribe gabriel "your E-mail address"

GENESIS

Paperlate List

Send message to: paperlate-request@atom.ansto.fov.au

GIBSON, DEBBIE

Between the Lines List

Send message to: BtL@egbt.org

GO-GO's

Send message to: go-gos-request@steffi.dircon.co.uk

GRANT, AMY

Send message to: art-request@ipc.uni-tuebingen.de

Subject: SUBSCRIBE

GRATEFUL DEAD

Dead-Flames

Send message to: dead-flames-request@berkeley.edu

Digested list from the rec.music.gdead Usenet group. The digest is sent out at least once per day.

Dead-Heads

Send message to: dead-heads-request@berkeley.edu

Mailing list that eliminates most of the discussion on dead-flames and focuses on upcoming shows with existing band members, tickets, ride-sharing to shows, and Dead related merchandise.

GREEN DAY

Send message to: greenchs@indirect.com

Subject: SUBSCRIBE GREENDAY

Green Day fans gush about Billie Joe Armstrong and the boys' latest concerts and realeases.

GRIFFITH, NANCI

Send message to: majordomo@world.std.com

Message body: Subscribe nanci "your E-mail address"

GUNS N' ROSES

Send Message to: majordomo@teleport.com

Message body: Subscribe gnr

H

HARDING, JOHN WESLEY

Send message to: rkhw@ukc.ac.uk

Message body: Indicate that you want to subscribe to the John
Wesley Harding mailing list.

HARRY, DEBORAH

Send mail to: lab@indirect.com

List with discussion of Debbie Harry, Blondie and Chris Stein.

HARVEY, PJ

Send message to: majordomo@langmuir.eecs.berkeley.edu

Message body: Subscribe pjharvey

HATFIELD, JULIANA

Send Mail to: listproc@mcfeeley.cc.utexas.edu
Message body: Subscribe juliana "your name"

HEDGES, MICHAEL

Taproot List
Send mail to: mailserv@desire.wright.edu
Message body: Subscribe taproot

HENDRIX, JIMI

Hey Joe List
Send message to: hey-joe-request@ms.uky.edu

HIATT, JOHN

Send message to: shot-of-rhythm-request@chinacat.unicom.com

HIGHWAYMEN

Send message to: listserv@indycms.iuui.edu
Message body: Subscribe Hiwaymen "your name"

Discussion about the power group featuring: Willie Nelson, Waylon Jennings, Johnny Cash and Kris Kristofferson.

HITCHCOCK, ROBYN

Send message to: fegmaniax-request@nsmx.rutgers.edu

HOTHOUSE FLOWERS

Send message to: yaboss@cc.bellcore.com
Message body: Subscribe "your E-mail address"

I

INDIGO GIRLS

Send message to: Indigo-girls-request@cgrg.ohio.state.edu

Discussion of Indigo Girls music, tours, concert reviews and related artists.

INFORMATION SOCIETY

Send message to: automailer@magellan.creighton.edu

INXS

Send message to: inxs-list-request@iastate.edu

J

JACKSON, JANET

Send message to: list@xs4all.nl
Message body: Subscribe Janet "your E-mail address"

JACKSON, JOE

Send message to: majordomo@primenet.com
Message body: Insert "subscribe" in subject field.

JACKSON, MICHAEL

Michael Jackson Net Fan Club

Send message to: mjj@fred.net
Message body: Insert "subscribe" in subject field.

JANE'S ADDICTION

Send message to: janes-addiction-request@ms.uky.edu

Anything related to Jane's Addiction and all other related projects like: Porno for Pyros, Deconstruction and Red Hot Chili Peppers.

JEFFERSON AIRPLANE

Send message to: listserv@netspace.org
Message body: Insert "subscribe 2400fulton" in the subject field.

List related to Jefferson Airplane and the spin-offs: Jefferson Starship and Hot Tuna.

JESUS JONES

Send message to: magazine@cs.rmit.edu.au

JESUS & MARY CHAIN
Send message to: majordomo@macel.st.hmc.edu
Message body: Subscribe jamc

JETHRO TULL
The St. Cleve Chronicle List
Send message to: jtull-request@remus.rutgers.edu

JOEL, BILLY
Send message to: Joel-request@chaos.bsu.edu
Message body: Subscribe "your E-mail address"

JOHN, ELTON
Send message to: the-22nd-row-request@uiuc.edu
Message subject: Subscribe

JOURNEY
Journey-L
Send message to: journey-l-request@wkuvx1.wku.edu

K

KANSAS
The People of the Wind list
Send message to: Kansas-request@world.std.com
Mailer discusses the state of the band Kansas.

KENTON, STAN
Send message to: server@acc.rwu.edu
Message body: Subscribe kenton.list "your name"
Discussion of the band leader Stan Kenton and his alumni.

KINKS
Send message to: otten@quark.umd.edu
Message body: Subscribe
Everything about the Davies brothers band, the Kinks.

KISS

Kissarmy

Send message to: mxserver@wkuvx1.wwku.edu

Kissarmy is a discussion list for all fans of KISS. Any topic from collectables to music to recordings and tours about KISS and the members.

KLF

Send message to: majordomo@xmission.com

Message body: Subscribe klf

The KLF is one of many bands put together by Jimmy Cauty and Bill Drummond. This list covers all of them from the K Foundation, the JAMS, the Timelords and of course, KLF.

KRAFTWERK

Send message to: Kraftwerk-request@cs.uwp.edu

L

L7

Send message to: L7s@aol.com

Message body: Subscribe

LANG, K.D.

Send message to: majordomo@world.std.com

Message body: Subscribe k-d-lang

LAUPER, CYNDI

Send message to: shebop-request@lae.emory.edu

LED ZEPPELIN

Send message to: listserv@cornell.edu

Message body: Subscribe zeppelin-l "your name"

LEMONHEADS

Hate Your Friends List

Send message to: hyf-request@acca.nmsu.edu

Message body: Subscribe "your E-mail address"

LETTERS TO CLEO

Send message to: cleo@world.std.com

Message body: Ask to be added to the list

You couldn't get away from this band in 1996 and you can't miss a beat with the moderated list. This list is moderated and is distributed in a digest format.

LEVEL 42

Send message to: level42-request@enterprise.bih.harvard.edu

Message body: Subscribe

LITTLE FEAT

Send message to: hoyhoy@ultranet.com

Subject: subscribe hoyhoy "your name"

An unmoderated mailing list about the band Little Feat and their music.

LIVE

Official List

Send message to: live-request@mediafive.yyz.com

Live too, the unofficial list

Send message to: listserv@core-dump.async.vt.edu

Message body: Subscribe live

LYNCH MOB see Dokken

M

MADONNA

Send message to: madonna-request@umich.edu

Heavy list volume mailer devoted to Madonna.

MASSE, JULIE

Send message to: majordomo@wimsey.com

List dedicated to French pop star Julie Masse.

McLACHLAN, SARAH

Send message to: listserv@yoyo.cc.monash.edu.au

MELLENCAMP, JOHN

Human Wheels List
Send message to: da2c+request@andrew.cmu.edu

MEN WITHOUT HATS

Send message to: hats-request@cs.uwp.edu

METALLICA

Send message to: metallica-request@thinkage.on.ca

MIAMI SOUND MACHINE

Conga List
Send message to: conga-request@hustle.rahul.net

List devoted to Miami Sound Machine and the music of Gloria Estefan. A FAQ for the list is archived at rtm.mit.edu in directory: pub/usenet-by-group/news.answers/music/gloria-estefan.

MIDNIGHT OIL

Send message to: majordomo@cs.colorado.edu
Message body: Subscribe powderworks

MINOGUE, KYLIE

Send message to: poulet@shell.portal.com

MONKEES

Send message to: majordomo@primenet.com
Message body: Subscribe monkees

MOODY BLUES

Lost Chords List
Send message to: lost-chords-request@mit.edu

Handles 20-30 messages per day.

MORISSETTE, ALANIS (Nails)

Send message to: nails-request@tamos.gmu.edu
Subject: Subscribe

She's angry and she's popular.

MORRISON, VAN

Send message to: majordomo@fish.com
Message body: Subscribe van

MOTT THE HOOPLE

Send message to: hunter-mott-request@dfw.net
Discussion of Mott the Hoople and Ian Hunter.

N

NEW ORDER

Send message to: ceremony-request@niagara.edu

New Order, Electronic, Joy Division, and all the offshoots are discussed on this list.

NEWTON-JOHN, OLIVIA

Send message to: onj-request@anima.demon.co.uk

NIRVANA (The Heart-Shaped Mail Box)

Send message to: Lily@Digital.net
Message body: Ask to be subscribed

Discussion ranges from bootlegs to the FooFighters and Courtney Love. Anything goes.

NITZER EBB

Send message to: nitzer-ebb-request@iastate.edu
Message body: subscribe (e-mail address)

Discussion of this heavy industrial dance band take place on this list.

NUMAN, GARY

Send message to: Numan-request@cs.uwp.edu

A weekly digest about Gary Numan, the creator of "Cars."

O

O'CONNOR, SINEAD
Jump in the River List
Send message to: JITR-request@presto.com
Discussion of music and lyrics of Sinead O'Conner.

OLDFIELD, MIKE
Send message to: majordomo@damp.apana.org.au
Digested list for fans of Mike Oldfield.

ONO, YOKO
Send message to: listserv@vm1.spcs.umn.edu
Message body: Subscribe ono-net "your name"
For those who want to discuss Yoko's life, art, music, and writings.

THE ORB
Send message to: majordomo@xmission.com
Message body: Subscribe orb/orb-digest

ORCHESTRAL MANEUVERS IN THE DARK (OMD)
Send message to: omd-request@cs.uwp.edu
A daily digested list for OMD and related projects.

P

PARKER, GRAHAM
Graham-Parker List
Send message to: majordomo@primenet.com

PAVEMENT
Send message to: mailserv@d31rz0.stanford.edu
Message body: Subscribe

PEARL JAM

Oceans List

Send message to majordomo@tamos.gmu.edu

Message body: Subscribe oceans "your E-mail address"

A high traffic list oriented to the music, gossip, recordings and live shows of Pearl Jam.

PET SHOP BOYS

Introspective Mailing List

Send message to majordomo@tcp.com

Message body: Subscribe introspective

PHAIR, LIZ

Send message to: listproc@phantom.com

PHILLIPS, SAM

Send message to: p9490086@qub.ac.uk

Message body: Subscribe SAM

List centering on the recordings and music of female vocalist Sam Phillips and her husband T-Bone Burnett.

PHISH

Send message to phish-info-request@phish.net

Message body: Subscribe

PINK FLOYD

The Echoes List

Send message to: echoes-request@fawnya.tcs.com

All types of Pink Floyd discussions including recordings, concerts, live recordings and discussion about the band.

POI DOG PONDERING

Poi Ponders List

Send message to: poi-ponders-request@presto.ig.com

POLICE

Send message to: majordomo@xmission.com

Message body: Subscribe police-digest

POP WILL EAT ITSELF

Send message to: majordomo@concorde.com

Message body: Subscribe pweination

PRESLEY, ELVIS

Send message to: pelvis@phoenix.princeton.edu

The scoop on the King's activities plus a daily King quote!

PRINCE

Send message to prince-request@icpsr.umich.edu

All kinds of information about Prince or the artist formally known as Prince.

Q

QUEEN

Send message to: majordomo@stat.lsa.umich.edu

Message body: Subscribe qms

QUEENSRYCHE

Send message to: qryche@ios.com

R

REPLACEMENTS

Send message to: lists@phoenix.creighton.edu

Message body: Subscribe skyway-l

A monthly digest.

ROLLING STONES

Undercover

Send message to: undercover-request@tempest.cis.upguelph

Discussion list for the Stones, their music, tours, history, gossip, and whatever. The list is distributed in a daily digest format.

ROXETTE

Send message to: owner-roxette@eiunix.tuwien.ac.at

ROXY MUSIC

Send message to: avalon-request@webcom.com
Message body: Subscribe avalon

RUNDGREN, TODD

Send message to: awizard-request@planning.ebay.sun.com

RUSH

Send message to: rush-request@syrinx.umd.edu

S

SAMPLES

The Underwater list
Send message to: samples-request@nyx.cs.du.edu

SCORPIONS (The Zoo)

Send message to: listproc@u.washington.edu
Message body: subscribe thezoo "your name"
Discussion of the German rock group and related projects.

SEVERED HEADS

Adolph-a-Carrot@andrew.cmu.edu
Send Message to: Adolph-a-carrot-request@andrew.cmu.edu

This list is centered on the recordings of Severed Heads and the Ralph records label. This Australian based artist has been a part of the Ralph record label group since the mid 1980s.

SIMPLE MINDS

Send message to: new-gold-dream-request@dfw
Subject: Subscribe

SIOUXSIE & THE BANSHEES (SATB-L)

Send message to: Listserv@brownvm.brown.edu

Message Body: SUB SATB-L "your name"

SATB-L is the mailing list dedicated to the discussion of the band, Siouxsie & the Banshees and their members and side projects, such as The Creatures and The Glove.

SLADE

Send message to: slade-request@gnu.ai.mit.edu

Message body: Subscribe slade

SINATRA, FRANK

Send Message to: listserv@vm.temple.edu

The Sinatra list covers recordings, arrangements, lyrics, and anything involving the career of Sinatra.

SOUTHSIDE JOHNNY & THE ASBURY JUKES

Send message to: southside-request@ici.net

Subject: Subscribe

SPIN DOCTORS

Send message to: spins-request@world.std.com

SPRINGSTEEN, BRUCE

Lucky Town Digest

Send message to: Luckytown-request@netcom.com

Message body: Subscribe luckytown

A digested discussion list for fans of Bruce Springsteen. Topics vary from news, lyrics, bootleg reviews, concert tapes, etc.

STEELY DAN

Send message to: steely-dan-request@uluc.edu

Subject: Subscribe

STEWART, AL

Send message to: majordomo@fish.com

Message body: Subscribe al-stewart

STEWART, ROD

Storyteller List

Send message to: rodfans@kbourbeau.kenmoto1.sai.com

STONE ROSES

Send message to: majordomo@best.com

Message body: Subscribe roses-list

STYX

Send message to majordomo@world.std.com

Message body: Subscribe styx

SUGAR/BOB MOULD/HUSKER DU

Send message to: majordomo@csua.berkeley.edu

Message body: subscribe sugar "your e-mail address"

Discussion of Bob Mould and his various groups

SUGARCUBES see Bjork

SUNDAYS

Send message to: arithmetic-request@uclink.berkeley.edu

Subject: Subscribe

T

TALKING HEADS

Send message to: listproc@ukanaix.cc.ukans.edu

Message body: Subscribe talking-heads "your name"

TANGERINE DREAM

Send message to: tadream-request@cs.uwp.edu

TEARS FOR FEARS

Send message to: tears4-fears-request@ms.uky.edu

THEY MIGHT BE GIANTS

Send message to: they-might-be@super.org

Message body: Subscribe they-might-be "your E-mail address"

THOMPSON, RICHARD

Send message to listserver@listserver.njit.edu
Message body: Subscribe r-thompson

THOMPSON TWINS

Send messge to: blackwst@uvsc.edu
Message body: Subscribe Thompson Twins

TIFFANY

Send message to: tiffany-request@acca.nmsu.edu

TLC

Send message to: MaldenTV@world.std.com
Message body: Tell them you want to subscribe

Discussion of this unexplainably very popular band.

TOAD THE WET SPROCKET

Send message to: listproc@sprocket.silverplatter.com
Message body: Subscribe Toad "your name"

TOWER OF POWER

Send message to: majordomo@cv.ruu.nl
Message body: Subscribe top "your E-mail address"

TRAGICALLY HIP

Send message to: listmanager@hookup.net

Message body: Subscribe tragically-hip "your name"

u

U2

Wire List
Send message to: U2-list-request@ms.uky.edu

Electronic magazine devoted to U2 and related topics.

URGE OVERKILL

Send message to: listserv@psyche.dircon.co.uk
Message body: Subscribe mood-control

V

VANGELIS

Direct list

Send message to: direct-request@caltech.com

VEGA, SUZANNE

Send message to: undertow-request@law.emory.edu

W

WAITS, TOM

Send message to: listserv@ucsd.edu

WEEZER

Send message to: weezer-rules-request@ms.uky.edu

Message body: subscribe

This list is for discussing Weezer and any solo projects in which the members are involved.

WELLER, PAUL

Kosmos List

Send message to: kosmos-request@mit.edu

WHO

Send message to: majordomo.@cisco.com

Message body: Subscribe thewho

X

XTC

chalkhills@presto.ig.com

Send message to: Chalkhills-request@presto.ig.com

Mailing lists discusses music and records of XTC.

173

Y

YELLO

Send message to: major domo@cs.uwp.edu
Message body: Subscribe yello

YO LA TENGO

Send message to: tim@vestek.com

YOUNG, NEIL

Send message to: majordomo@fish.com
Message body: Subscribe rust

A very active list for Young fans. It is rumored that in 1994, Mr. Young temporarily sacked a band member who was suspected of passing unreleased demos to a Rustoid (a Young fan) for distribution on this list.

Z

ZZ TOP

Send message to: zztop-request@cabana.ncsa.uiuc.edu
Message body: Subscribe

This mailing list is for the fans of the rock band from Texas, ZZ Top. Topics of discussion include concert information, rumors, press releases, reviews and more.

Newsgroups About Music Styles D

Here are some newsgroups that will help you find information concerning music styles.

alt.music.a-cappella	alt.music.african
alt.music.alternative	alt.music.alternative.female
alt.music.big-band	alt.music.black-metal
alt.music.filk	alt.music.france
alt.music.hardcore	alt.music.hawaiian
alt.music.jewish	alt.music.mexican
alt.music.mods	alt.music.polkas

alt.music.progressive	alt.music.psychedelic
alt.music.pulp	alt.music.rockabilly
alt.music.ska	alt.music.soul
alt.music.swedish-pop	alt.music.techno
alt.music.world	alt.rock-n-roll
alt.rock-n-roll.classic	alt.rock-n-roll.hard
alt.rock-n-roll.metal	alt.rock-n-roll.metal.black
alt.rock-n-roll.metal.death	alt.rock-n-roll.metal.heavy
alt.rock-n-roll.metal.progressive	austin.music
bit.listserv.allmusic	bit.listserv.bgrass-l
bit.listserv.blues-l	bit.listserv.edusig-l
bit.listserv.emusic-l	clari.living.music
comp.music	rec.music.a-cappella
rec.music.afro-latin	rec.music.ambient
rec.music.arabic	rec.music.bluenote
rec.music.bluenote.blues	rec.music.cd
rec.music.celtic	rec.music.christian
rec.music.classical	rec.music.classical.performing
rec.music.classical.recordings	rec.music.compose
rec.music.country.old-time	rec.music.country.western
rec.music.dementia	rec.music.early

rec.music.filipino	rec.music.folk
rec.music.funky	rec.music.hip-hop
rec.music.indian.classical	rec.music.indian.misc
rec.music.industrial	rec.music.info
rec.music.newage	rec.music.opera
rec.music.ragtime	rec.music.reggae

Mailing Lists
for Music Styles

These are mailing lists for music styles.

A

ACID-JAZZ

Send message to listserv@ucsd.edu
Message body: Subscribe acid-jazz "your name"

ACOUSTIC

Acoustic Junction
Send message to: aj-request@cs.cmu.edu
Message body: Insert "subscribe" in the subject field.

AMBIENT MUSIC

Send message to: ambient-request@hyperreal.com

Message body: Subscribe

List covers artists like Eno, Orb and other ambient style musicians.

B

BARBERSHOP

Send message to: bbshop-request@cray.com

Discussion of barbershop singing and the various activities of organizations devoted to this style.

BASQUE MUSIC

Basque-l

Send message to: listserv@cunyvm.cuny.edu

This is a general discussion list for anything about Basque culture. Music, news, literature and politics are all acceptable here.

E

EXOTICA see Strange

F

FILM MUSIC

Film Music List

Send message to: Filmus-L@iubvm.ucs.indiana.edu

Film and television music is discussed on this list. Reviews of film scores and dramatic music for television music are included here. Both classic and new films and television shows are open topics.

Music and Moving Pictures List

Send message to: mailbase@mailbase.ac.uk

UK based mailing list for the discussion of the techniques and practices used in making music for moving pictures including: film, TV, computer graphics and games. This list attracts practitioners, theorists, musicians and anyone who is just interested.

FINISH MUSIC

Finlandia

Send message to: majordomo@phoenix.oulu.fi

Finnish classical and modern composers, their life and works, performing artists and orchestras, Finnish discussions, recordings and music in general are discussed here.

FOLKTALK

Send message to: folktalk@wmvm1.cc.wm.edu

Discussion list for U.S. traditional and contemporary folk music. In addition, topics on this lists include English, Celtic and other varieties of folk music.

FOLK MUSIC

folk_music list

Send message to: listserv@nysernet.org

This list deals with tours, reviews, and release information on artists like David Wilcox, Nanci Griffith, Maura O'Connell and others.

FUNK MUSIC

Funky Music List

Send message to: funky-music-request@mit.edu

Discussion of funk, rap, hip-hop, rhythm and blues, and related beat based music are all welcome on the list.

G

GOSPEL

Send message to: maiser@rmgate.pop.indiana.edu
Message body: Subscribe gospel-l

Discussion of gospel with an emphasis on southern gospel styles.

GRUNGE

Grunge-L
Send message to: Listserv@ubvm.cc.buffalo.edu

List with fairly heavy traffic focusing on everything related to grunge rock. Tour dates, reviews, gossip, interviews and articles.

J

JAZZ
Send message to: Listserv@brownvm.brown.edu
Message body: Subscribe JAZZ-L
This is a list for jazz buffs to keep up with favorite groups.

M

MUSICALS

Send message to majordomo@world.std.com
Message body: Subscribe musicals

General discussion of musical theater.

S

STRANGE

Exotica List

Send message to: majordomo@xmission.com

This is the list that focuses on that music from the '50s and '60s that never really made the transition from LPs to CDs. This would include Hawaiian, novelty, electronic, surf, party and other strange type tunes.

SPACE MUSIC

Send message to: space-music-request@cs.uwp.edu

Discussion of artists who use electronic instruments, are not commercial and create sound spaces or music defined as "cosmic" or "floating." Artists like Eno or Tangerine Dream are not discussed on this list.

Mailing Lists
for Record Labels

There are several mailing lists that discuss the music on a specific label.

4AD

4AD List

Send message to: listserv@jhuvm.hcf.jhu.edu

Message body: Subscribe 4AD "your name"

Covers the bands signed currently or in the past to the 4AD label like: Cocteau Twins, Dead Can Dance, Belly, Throwing Muses, Pixies, Breeders and anyone else halfway related.

BOMP RECORDS

Send message to: listserv@netcom.com

Message body: Subscribe to bomp-l "your name"

21 year old independent label. List covers any surf, garage, or punk style bands from the '50s through today.

METAL BLADE RECORDS

Send message to: metalblade-request@arastar.com

Message body: Subscribe metalblade "your name"

A list to discuss Metal Blade artists and receive announcements.

NETTWERK RECORDS

Send message to: nettlist-request@nettwerk.wimsey.com

Message body: Subscribe

Nettwerk artist from the past and present like Sara McLachlan and MC900 Ft. Jesus are discussed on this list.

ON U SOUND

Send message to: on-u-request@connect.com.au

Discussion of groups on this label like: Tackhead and Dub Syndicate.

RALPH RECORDS

Adolph-a-Carrot@andrew.emu.edu

Send message to: Adolph-a-carrot-request@andrew.emu.edu

List dedicated to the records and groups that are part of the Ralph record family. Ralph has released the records of the Residents, Yello, Tuxedomoon, Snakefinger, Fred Frith, MX 80 Sound and others.

TRANSMISSION COMMUNICATIONS

Send message to: com11@transcom.brisnet.org.au

Australian based label.

ZZT RECORDS

Send message to: majordomo@xmission.com

Message body: Subscribe zzt

Devoted to bands on the ZZT label like Art of Noise, Frankie Goes to Hollywood, Seal and 808 State.

186

MIDI 3

In a way we hesitated about including this chapter in the book. At first glance it might appear that MIDI programming and sequencing (very cool activities) don't necessarily fit in a book about the Internet. However, this is a music book and one of the foremost sets of resources we've found Netwide has to do with MIDI. In the end it seemed we couldn't avoid MIDI. In addition, Internet functions like FTP and E-mail are natural carriers of music files. So, that's how this chapter came about. In it we'll discuss:

- the history and description of MIDI
- basic MIDI setups for your computer
- software and online companies
- MIDI resources on the Net
- actual MIDI applications
- a wide-ranging MIDI glossary put together by Eugene Confrey (Appendix G)

Art can be created for many senses; chefs create art for the taste and smell senses, painters for the visual, sculptors for the visual and touch senses, and music artists create something for the auditory sense. The point of art, whether it's a dessert, a poem, or a song, of any kind is to evoke an emotional reaction or climate. Music is such an amazingly illustrative sense that artists can actually create an entire "space" through their craft and involve you in the feel of the melody, the beat, and touch your life through the lyrics.

Peter DiFalco
pdifalco@ecst.csuchico.edu

It was inevitable that with the proliferation of MIDI (Musical Instrument Digital Interface) that the computer would become another instrument in music making. Players who are conversant with computers have an almost limitless access to sounds, songs, software, recording help, professional associations, other musicians, record companies and publishers.

This chapter is going to introduce you to some of the basic features of MIDI and how it, along with your access to the Internet, will expand your musical world.

MIDI BASICS

MIDI is a way for musical instruments (keyboards, drum machines, computers, keyboard controllers, sound modules, etc.) to talk to one another. Since the early 80s, MIDI has swept through the music world, making it possible for single musicians to compose vast orchestral pieces (or just a slamming dance track) all by themselves. MIDI makes it possible for you to have at your disposal every sound, every instrument and every textured tone. It also allows you to be able to shape, edit, change, those sounds—moving a single note if you wish—fix a mistake. It's all happening on the computer so you have the same kind of editing functions (more or less) as you do with word processing.

MIDI has had its biggest impact on songwriters and musicians. With the technology (a computer, some software, and just one keyboard)

you can write, perform, record and create entire songs (symphonies) on your own.

You don't like that part of the song you just played? Erase it and play it again. You think the tempo's too fast? Click a button and slow it down. Did you play that part unevenly? Let the quantize function fix your mistakes. Countless musicians of every type have embraced MIDI sequencing. You can't dial down the radio and NOT hear some song that has been sequenced or MIDIed in some way.

MIDI HARDWARE

What you really need is a computer (and we know you've got one up and running if you're this far in the book, right?), a MIDI interface card, a couple of cables, some software and a keyboard. That's the bare bones system. Even with that you can begin working in MIDI, and getting ready to let the Internet help expand your musical ambitions.

Let's start throwing some brand names around now, so you can get a more realistic idea of some stuff to use if you don't already have some. Even if you've got a keyboard and a computer you'll want to stick around because we'll be talking about optimum configuration of that stuff. (By the way, we don't endorse any kind of equipment. We're just running through some manufacturers and companies that are way into MIDI and who you might want to check out. None of this brand name stuff is an endorsement. You should get into a good store and play the stuff; decide for yourself what you want to work with.)

KEYBOARDS, DRUM MACHINES, TONE MODULES

Well, MIDI compatibility is the first step. Believe it or not there are still keyboards out there being made that aren't fully compatible. Watch out especially for keyboards that only have MIDI In and MIDI Out (these are weird looking holes in the back somewhere.) You will definitely benefit from having a keyboard with MIDI Thru as well. Most major keyboard manufacturers are making terrific boards, but be sure you get a board with multi-timbrality (the ability to play more than one sound at a time), which will aid you tremendously as you compose or write. This means that with just one keyboard you can get yourself a symphony worth of sounds. Some fine makers include Yamaha, Roland, Kawai, Kurzweil, Alesis, Peavey and Akai. Your first stop should be the Harmony Central website, specifically their Keyboard section. Here's the URL for the site, but we do a more thorough job talking about it later on in the MIDI Resources section: http://harmony-central.mit.edu/Synth/.

Once you have one keyboard, you have access, of course, to all the sounds it has "on board." However, because of the limited ability most keyboards have to make sounds (usually only a few at a time), you might be looking for another way to make noise. Well, it used to be that you'd have to get a whole other keyboard. But not anymore. Now many home studio musicians have sound or tone generators hooked up in their MIDI setups along with their main keyboard. You get the benefit of the extra sounds, but don't have the hassle of having more big keyboards around. (How many hands have you got, right?) The Proteus line of sound modules is a terrific example, as is the line of Roland SoundCanvas. (The SoundCanvas, in fact, has its own user group on the Internet.) The group is so well run and so full of information, it's almost reason enough to think of getting into a Sound Canvas yourself. You can't buy help as good as the help you can get on the Net from actual users who care enough to post their ideas and problem solving in a public way.) See the next page for more.

Follow the same strategy for finding info on drum machines, everything from the current champ Alesis to old favorites like the Roland 707, 808 and even Roger Linn's seminal Linn Drum.

Kat Percussion
http://www.mw3.com/kat/

While we're talking drums, we have to take note of Kat Percussion, makers of the terrific drumpad MIDI controllers. Their site offers decent product info and support.

190

Alesis

http://www.mw3.com/alesis/

Alesis makes cool stuff. They're responsible, of course, for the formidable ADAT digital recorder. But their Quadra Synth is an industry standard, and their line of reverb units is terrific. (I've got two hooked up to my keyboards right now!) Also at this site is their ever-evolving "Dream Studio," a sort of virtual recording studio that Alesis is crystal balling.

Peavey World

America Online (Keyword: Peavey)

Peavey is well-established on AOL, and their information in AOL's MusicSpace is well presented. They also are brave enough to include a wide open forum section where Peavey users share problems and solutions. Their pages include a healthy dose of "Look at our new stuff," but for Peavey users, some of the technical help here surpasses most visits to a music store. There's also a good selection of sounds for the Peavey DPM series of keyboards.

Roland SoundCanvas Users Group

http://www.spacestar.com/users/gevans/scug/scgroup.html

As noted previously, this group focuses on help for the popular SoundCanvas family of sound modules. Since Roland itself doesn't have their own website, the so culled SCUGs work very hard to keep fellow users up to date on trouble-shooting, updates, etc. The users also make their own MIDI compositions available on the site for downloading.

MIDI SOFTWARE (SEQUENCING)

In many ways the software you use to compose is far more important than the hardware. Just like any really good word processing or database software, you'll have to find one that you understand, that talks in your language, and that you can live with. It's not easy and there are seemingly countless programs out there.

Many major programs have their own support right online. So let's look at a handful of those:

Twelve Tone Systems

http://mozart.mw3.com:80/12tone/12thome.htm

Twelve Tone—still run by founder Greg Hendershott—makes the very popular Cakewalk Professional, now in version 3.01. We feature this software in our MIDI examples below. It's an okay page with links to other Twelve Tone software.

Passport Audio

http://www.mw3.com/passport/passprod.htm
(their new product page...updated regularly)

http://www.mw3.com/passport/passport.htm
(their homepage)

Passport was founded in 1981 by David Kusek, and its current top of the line software—Master Tracks 6.0—is terrific. Their products are available cross-platform (for both Mac and Windows) and this page introduces you to the special features for each software. The page has an E-mail address that will enable you to reach Passport (passport@aol.com), but limited information on pricing and availability (not uncommon).

Big Noise Software

http://www.icba.com/bignoise/

Headed up by Richard Johnson, Big Noise is a rather new player in the MIDI software game. (Their main software is the SeqMax, also available coupled with a package of their other products, MIDI mixer, etc.). But their website leaves the others far behind with its E-mail order form and easy to follow ordering instructions. Big Noise knew what they were doing when they got online and we predict their fine (and still developing) software will get a much wider audience because of their excellent online presence.

Opcode

http://www.opcode.com/products.html

Opcode—featured prominently on our CD ROM—is a maker of terrific MIDI sequencing software. (We feature their Macintosh products, but they manufacture cross platform.) They also make fine notation and audio recording software. Opcode stands at the forefront of the field.

I do think that the Net will (eventually) bring musicians from all over the world closer together, and thus creating a "virtual studio", which may result in some really interesting pieces of music. Music brings people together, and the Net will only encourage that.

Martijn Berlage
Berlage@stack.urc.tue.nl

Kraft Music & Computers
http://www.execpc.com/~kraftmus/kraftmus.html

Kraft stocks both Mac and Windows sequencing software, MIDI interfaces, multimedia soundcards, keyboards, drum machines, and samplers. To get all the way in to a MIDI setup, you'd be hard pressed to find another online location with so much. And the website is attractive and complete. Discounted prices aren't shown on the screen, but we can assure you from experience that they will indeed cut you a good deal.

Dan's Sound and Music
http://www.cyserv.com/dans/about.html

A long time retail location in Texas, it now has a website featuring a complete list of their very fine, very large consignment list (with prices). Dan's makes sure the equipment is in good shape and you can contact them via E-mail for more details. All MIDI stuff, of course, but also pro audio gear: recording, mixing, etc.

MIDI RESOURCES

Because of the natural connection of computers and music, it's not surprising that the Internet is full of terrific sources of information about making music with machines. In this chapter we will focus on a number of the best and most usable sites. You'll find everything here from MIDI primers to sources of MIDI songs to play on your own equipment, to users groups of popular MIDI products. (We'll also hook you right up with the folks at major companies so you can get the goods from people in the know.)

> *PLUG IN For More Info!*
> *Browse to the website at*
> *http://www.prenhall.com/~plugin*

MIDI Homepage

http://www.eeb.ele.tue.nl/midi/

We met Heini Withagen pretty early on in our search of the Net and his MIDI homepage is terrific and fun. Heini lives in the Netherlands and his page not only features excellent links to MIDI primers and MIDI song files, but also includes info about him and his terrific helicopter pilot girlfriend Anne-Marie.

One of the things that you'll find that matters the most on the Net is the personality behind the pages. There are some pages that never change. Pages that are lifeless and dull. It's obvious to us after months and months of hyperlinking around the Net that the difference between a good and a bad page is enormous. Good pages are lively, have modest changes month to month. The links are updated regularly so you never hit dead ends. It's part of the sociological interest we have in the Net that's made this page (and the ones that follow) such a pleasure to view and use.

Let's look at Heini's first page.

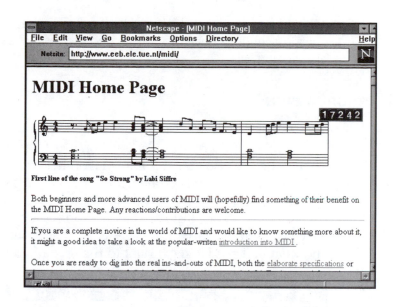

Like we've been saying, MIDI primers abound on the Net and Heini puts a really good one right up front in his page. And, below you'll see another important feature of any decent page—the links. Heini has linked his site to a wide variety of other MIDI links. By clicking on any of the ones below you will be taken somewhere else on the Net where you'll be able to find what you need.

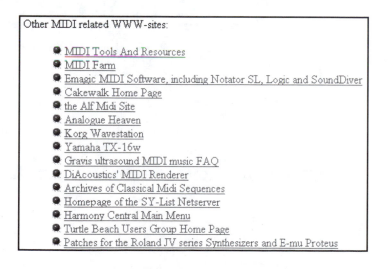

You'll notice that one of Heini's links is to Harmony Central. We've already been introduced to this terrific site, but let's look at some more of it now!

Harmony Central

http://harmony-central.mit.edu

The folks at Harmony Central don't just feature MIDI resources. Their large site also contains information helpful in finding equipment, selling equipment, and getting your band heard! It's a wide ranging set of pages that is laid out nicely and run by Scott Lehman at MIT. Here's his table of contents. Instead of a long torturous search through links—which is often the case on pages—Scott lays it out very early. It's easy find what you need and get right to the area of your interest.

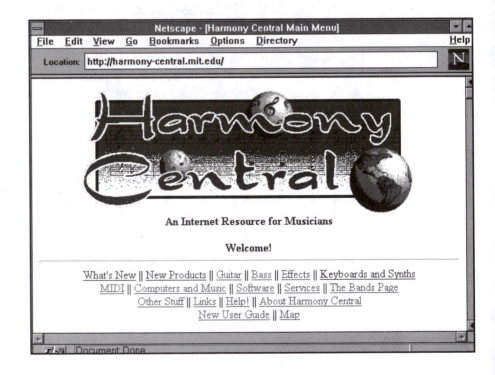

For example, under the MIDI link we can access information about software, hardware, etc. Products are introduced here as well, and if you've ever been in a music store you know how horrifying that experience can be. But not here at Harmony Central. Instead of dealing with commission-driven salespeople and wandering around tons of equipment you'll never be able to understand in the space of a single visit, Scott does the legwork for us. Let's see how he handles new products. (One of his table of contents links).

Clicking on it takes us to a list of products that are available for the MIDlist. Here's a sample first page of Scott's summary and review of a cool piece of Yamaha equipment.

Netscape - [Yamaha MU5 General MIDI Tone Generator]

File   Edit   View   Go   Bookmarks   Options   Directory   Help

Yamaha MU5 General MIDI Tone Generator

The MU5 has a built-in host computer interface and MIDI terminals eliminating the need for a separate MIDI interface. The MU5 can also act as a stand-alone MIDI interface.

The MU5 is battery powered. It provides full General MIDI level 1 compatibility with 128 General MIDI voices and eight drum kits. It also boasts 28-voice polyphony and it is 16-part multitimbral.

The MU5 comes with built-in two-octave (ten-octave range) keyboard. It can also be used to play notes on the MU5 or on a connected external tone generator, to enter notes into sequencer or computer, or to send program changes.

It features an LCD display and has controls for selecting any of the 16 Parts, and Muting or Soloing parts. The LCD display also allows monitoring of those Parts with a bar graph display. A set of editing functions give freedom to customize operation to suit specific applications.

$299

For more information contact:
Yamaha Corporation of America
Audio, Guitar and Synthesizer Division
P.O. Box 6600, Buena Park, CA 90622-6600

And yes, after this I think I'd like to have one of these. When I walk into my local music store this coming month, I will go in with more information than ever before. Harmony Central has done the work for me and now I won't be completely at the mercy of the store.

Synth Zone

http://www.rain.org/~nigelsp/midilink.htm

Nigel Spencer's series of pages is rather impressive. And he just seems to be getting warmed up. Check out his main page and it will lead you to other great midi pages, plus most of the available pages for manufacturers (a shifting category), and voluminous caches of keyboard reviews, MIDI files, etc.

MIDILINK

http://ally.ios.com/~midilink

Here's another major MIDI site. It's a virtual clearing house of MIDI information. It's constantly updated and well-linked to other places. In fact it's one of the first places you should go. Also, because they have strong support affiliation, they are very current and their links are updated more often than most one person homepages. Their links, however, do often lead to places where you'll have to spend money to get the info you want. Unlike the homepages that precede this one in this section, it has a more commercial feel, which of course is both bad and good.

- IBM MIDI Programs/Utils-168K, 2201+ files
- Atari MIDI Programs/Utils-31K, 883+ files
- Macintosh MIDI Programs/Utils-64K,1180+ files (5000 reg Mac files not listed here)
- Amiga MIDI Programs/Utils-20K, 512+ files
- ENSONIQ (EPS/ASR/TS & others including SampleVision .smp, Giebler and other formats)-44K, 2287+ files
- YAMAHA TX16W Samples in Giebler format-6K, 273+ files
- ENSONIQ Mirage Samples-12K, 242+ files
- Roland Corp Samples (S-50/S-550/700 Series)-19K, 1200+ samples on 240 diskettes
- MIDI Song Files A-M-110K, 3383+ files
- MIDI Song Files N-Z-57K, 1692+ files
- KORG Users Group -14K, 292+ files
- Synth Sounds & Patches-41K, 2238+ files
- IBM DEMO Programs-45K, 575+ files
- Sound Card Files-72K, 2828+ files
- WAV Files-162K, 10,663+ files

Like you can see in the previous page, you can actually access and download new sounds for your keyboards and new songs to play and manipulate with your sequencing software. And just because these manufacturers are mixing some commerce with music doesn't mean they've forgotten about the most basic needs of a beginning MIDIst. In fact at this same site (free of charge) you can access plenty of terrific MIDI help.

MIDI Composers Exchange

http://www.mindspring.com/~s-allen/homeboy.html

Talk about a resource for players! Here's a place to upload your latest MIDI created composition and to listen to songs and compositions by other players from around the world. The site is maintained beautifully by Steve Allen and is updated frequently. On one of our visits we downloaded a gorgeous piano piece from a composer in Denmark, and a very funky piece from a songwriter in Pennsylvania. Files download in *.MID format, which you'll be able to play easily on most sequencing software (like Cakewalk).

Classical Music MIDI Archives

http://www.prs.net/midi.html

If you're looking for some classical pieces to play and/or examine in their MIDI form, there is no better place to start. Whether you're looking for big names like Beethoven or more obscure composers like Gustav Holst, you'll find a terrific sampling of pieces here. They download in *.MID format as well.

MIDIWEB

http://www.digiface.nl/midiweb/index.html

This page comes out of the same country as Heini's earlier page. It's run by Raymond Zwarts and like Heini's it's an excellent page and getting better every day. The special feature of this page is that, for the most part, Raymond is updating it with our help. It's designed to be a user supported site. Obviously this has some terrific advantages. If you want to be involved in a MIDI homepage, but don't have the time, energy, or resources to do your own, Raymond has in place a page where you really can make a difference. (And we know, because we've sent stuff to him that he's incorporated.)

Like we observed earlier, the finding and acquisition of MIDI equipment will be on your mind as your abilities and facilities increase. Raymond's page features an open market, The MIDI Goodies Market. It's a terrific idea and one we haven't seen done this well before.

People send in their advertisements—equipment they have and want to sell; equipment they're looking to buy. It's a big classified ads page that is updated virtually non-stop.

FINDING SONG FILES

One of the first and easiest things you may want to do with your newfound MIDI ability, is to download some of your favorite songs and play them on your own MIDI setup. Imagine if you were given the chance to orchestrate the new Janet Jackson single. Wouldn't you want to pick a slightly funkier bass sound or maybe swap out that little tinny snare drum and put a big wallop of a sound in there? How about if you want to put your own piano part in there where Janet probably should have anyway? Well, that's more or less how MIDI files work. By searching some of the MIDI databases on the Internet or even on the commercial servers like AOL, Prodigy and CompuServe; you can find current and past songs by almost all artists, download them, import them into your MIDI software, and play away. However, these files currently fall in a legal grey area. Some MIDI websites in fact no longer even post these files for downloading because of their fear of lawsuit. How this will all play out is a mystery. The fact of the matter is, lots of sites have song files available, as do Bulletin Board Systems (discussed below). Until this issue gets completely resolved, files will simply be available. Here are some places:

FTP

Now remember we talked about FTP in chapter one. Well here's a really good opportunity for us to use our FTP function in order to get some songs to play on our Cakewalk. (Remember, you've got a free Cakewalk demo right on the CD ROM, so you can actually listen to and modify these songs as we go along. The only thing you can't do is save songs...you have to buy the full software for that.)

But anyway, FTP to the following and get some songs already formatted in Cakewalk and, therefore, are very easy to use.

```
ftp://ftp.cs.ruu.nl/pub/MIDI/SONGS/cakewalk/
```

Or, just remove the "cakewalk" from your FTP address (ftp://ftp.cs.ruu.nl/pub/MIDI/SONGS) and get their total listing of MIDI files.

While we're at it, here are three more sites: one in Japan, one in San Diego, and one in Finland. The one in San Diego has a decidedly more "classical" fare. Pick up some of your favorite fugues right there.

```
ftp://ftp.pu-toyama.ac.jp/pub/
ftp://ftp.ucsd.edu/midi/scores/cakewalk/
ftp://ftp.funet.fi/pub/msdos/sound/cakewalk/
```

In Chapter One we talked a little about BBSs, and indeed we'll find a good amount of MIDI files there. So, let's start with them.

BBSs

As the world computing network has exploded, BBSs have fallen out of favor. It doesn't mean, however, that they should not be consulted or used. BBSs—at least the ones that remain up and running and current—are a more serious labor of love than any website. (And we do mean labor.) Many BBSs are run out of private homes where the operator must not only take care of the site, but must run and maintain several phone lines, computers, modems, software, etc. It's a terrific amount of work and when operators are willing to give so much time to their BBS, you can almost always count on the fact that you will be able to find something worthwhile.

Thankfully, for us, all the BBSs sort of hang together, and once you get on a good one, it's easy to find a local BBS that will serve your needs. We're not going to give you a list of all the BBSs in the country because it would take up literally scores of pages. Instead we'll show you a handful of the best. From any of these you'll be able to access a local BBS near you.

Just some quick reminders about BBSing. First, you'll need to call them up and log on as a new user. This means sometimes filling out a registration online. Do it. It's the only way to get access. BBS operators want to know you before they open their hearts (and their hard drives) to you. Next, it's smart to leave a message or an E-mail for the Sysop (system operator). That way you can let the Sysop know what it is you need, and he or she will be able to direct you where to go on the BBS (or maybe another BBS) to get the information you need.

The first time you're on a BBS you may not have much access, but usually Sysops are online several times a day and you'll be able to get a little free time access to look around and determine if the board is worthwhile for you and your time. (One additional note: BBSs often have subscriber or registration fees. These are often small and/or nominal—$20 a year—and you will certainly get your money's worth in free software and shareware even if you just download a couple of things.) Keep in mind that BBSs are run by people and somebody has to maintain the system. You'll find quickly that a couple of good BBSs may be all you need. That's not too much to assure yourself of good access to information. Plus, the BBS system is quite friendly—compared to the Internet, say—as it is run by a small group of folks who in some cases have been doing this for ten years or more.

Now, be forewarned that some BBSs tend to go in and out of business pretty quickly. We've done our best to list below only those boards that have done a great job of staying up, in business, current and useful. We're doing something a little unusual here. The first one gets our star treatment. It is definitely worth your time and a long distance call (except for those lucky folks who live in the DC area.) The rest is a list of boards in the MIDILink network (not all of them!), a group of BBSs committed to keeping MIDI information available in the system. Messages on any of these boards get posted nationwide on other boards in the link. Of course this connects you nationwide with folks looking to share info. In addition, the boards all share a group of "conferences" that are very similar to the Internet's Usenet newsgroups. The conferences cover everything in the MIDI world: software and hardware for IBM and Macintosh platforms (including smaller conferences for specific programs like Cakewalk, etc.), multi-track recording, sampling, legal issues in MIDI, and even collaborative songwriting discussions. All in all it's a great deal. If you're fortunate enough to live in a medium to large sized city, you can probably get on a board that carries the MIDILink network.

• *Washington MIDI Users' Group*

(703) 532-7860

This long time group, run by the very likable and knowledgeable Mike Rivers, should be your first stop. Mike's board is well run, professionally managed, and complete. Whether you're tracking down songs (plenty of original compositions, as well, from writers all across the country), looking for equipment to buy or sell, or if you need some specific software support—you can get all of it here.

MIDILink BBS's

Name	City	Phone
Boston Rocks	Boston, Mass.	617-397-8888
Chicago Music City BBS	Chicago, Ill.	708-499-0911
Crescendo	Baltimore, Md.	410-792-7208
Darkside BBS	Westchester Co., NY	914-628-0535
MIDIEX	Dayton, Oh.	513-285-1173
MIDIum BBS	Los Angeles, Calif.	818-764-4538
Music Quest BBS	Plano, Tex.	214-881-7311
Neverland BBS	Seattle, Wash.	206-885-7209
Nightside BBS	Hamilton, Canada	905-572-1065
Omaha MIDI Systems	Omaha, Neb	402-291-0619
Quarter Note BBS	Boulder, Col.	303-939-9923
The MIDI Board	Bayonne, NJ	201-858-8011
Urban Mixing Productions	Reading, Penn.	610-376-0743

On Kate Bush's 1989 album "The Sensual World" she "responded," in an oblique way, to the phenomenon of computer-based communication, in a song called "Deeper Understanding." The song tells the story of a sad, lonely person and his (or her) computer, through which he (or she) finds deep fulfillment in a "virtual" relationship with the incorporeal but beatific "personality" of the machine. The song is remarkable for its evenhanded consideration of both the virtues and dangers of computer-based communications.

Andrew Marvick
IEDSRI@aol.com

THE MIDI INTERFACE

While the following clip (courtesy MIDILink) talks specifically about Mac MIDI interfaces, much of the technical information is identical for PC interfaces. One of the things to check as you look for a PC interface, is to find one that is Roland MPU-401 compatible. That's the benchmark and you'd be hard pressed to find one that didn't have that standard. These cards typically fit into one of the slots in your computer and are then connected to your main controlling keyboard with a pair of MIDI cables. The interface helps whatever software you have talk to the keyboards connected. There is a short learning curve with any interface as you have to find the best settings (IRQ settings, but don't worry about that now) for your machine. Nearly all interfaces come with their own diagnostic software which will tell you how to set up the interface based on your machines' needs.

MACINTOSH MIDI EVENTS AND INTERFACES

INTRODUCTION

All MIDI interfaces, whether for Macintosh, IBM PC, or other computers, are responsible for converting MIDI events (originating in the computer software) into a serial data stream. This data travels on the cables connecting MIDI devices.

The serial MIDI cables that connect to and from the computer's MIDI interface are shielded, twisted-pair cables, that are terminated at each end in a 5-pin DIN plug. Pins 4 and 5 are connected to the twisted-pair, which carry the MIDI signal. The MIDI signals are isolated from one device (e.g., computer) to another (e.g., synthesizer) through the use of "Opto-Isolators", which serve to aid in noise reduction of the MIDI signals and also to provide protection in the event of a shorted or damaged cable or interface. The electrical interface is a 5 milliampere current loop, in which a logic-0 is represented by current ON.

Typically, a MIDI event will consist of two or three 8-bit bytes of data, although certain MIDI events such as "system exclusive" can contain a great number of bytes. A "note-on" event, for example, requires 3 bytes to represent the type of event, the note number, and the attack-velocity values. Other events, such as program changes, channel pressure, and the like only require 2 bytes.

The MIDI specification allows each event to be associated with one of 16 MIDI channels (numbered 0 to 15, but sometimes referred to as 1 to 16 in some MIDI instrument documentation). The channel is transmitted as the lower 4 bits in the first byte of each "channel message" MIDI event. In addition to channel messages, the MIDI data stream can contain system common, system exclusive, and system real-time messages.

MIDI INTERFACES

All Macintosh MIDI interfaces, with rare exceptions (e.g., the MacProteus NuBus card) are external "boxes" that connect to the computer's modem and/or printer ports and provide one or more pairs of MIDI IN and MIDI OUT connectors. The most inexpensive MIDI interfaces connect to either the modem or printer port and provide a single pair of MIDI IN and MIDI OUT connectors. More expensive and elaborate interfaces connect to both the modem and printer ports and provide two or more pairs of MIDI IN and MIDI OUT connectors. For example, the Opcode Studio Plus Two interface connects to both the modem and printer ports, and provides two pairs of MIDI IN and MIDI OUT connectors, for a total of 16 channels per pair, or 32 MIDI

(cont..)

channels in total. Even more expensive and elaborate MIDI interfaces, such as the Mark of the Unicorn's "MIDI Time Piece" interface connect to both the modem and printer ports to provide 8 pairs of MIDI IN and MIDI OUT ports, for a total of 128 MIDI channels. The MIDI Time Piece (MTP) can be chained to another like MTP, and it to another, up to a total of 4 MTP interfaces. Together this maximum configuration offers a total of 512 independent MIDI channels, both input and output. The top-of-the-line MIDI software (e.g., Opcode's Vision and Mark of the Unicorn's Performer) provide the ability to support this large number of channels through a feature known as cabelization, in which you designate to which cable a particular group of channels are assigned.

Even the most inexpensive Macintosh MIDI interface (e.g., priced $60) can accommodate the input and output of events on 16 MIDI channels. However, when an application requires the use of more than 16 channels, a more expensive interface will be needed. Generally speaking, all Macintosh MIDI software recognizes channels on both the modem and printer ports. Therefore, in most cases, channels are labeled M0-M15 and P0-P15 in the MIDI software.

Interface Manufacturer	Ports Used M or P	Total Channels	Price
Passport MIDIInterface	M or P	16	$79.00
MOTU MIDI Time Piece	M and P	28	$375.00
Opcode Professional Plus	M or P	48*	$59.00
Opcode Studio Plus 2	M and P	32	$199.95
Opcode Studio 5	M and P	240	$1295.00

* Some MIDI interfaces offer a different number of IN and OUT ports for connection to the MIDI bus. An example is the Opcode "Professional Plus" interface, which connects to either the modem or printer port, and offers three MIDI OUT ports and one MIDI IN port.

LET'S MIDI

Well, with the help of Cakewalk Pro for Windows our choice of MIDI software lets actually begin doing this stuff. We're going past the simple playing of already available MIDI files; we're going to make some of our own. In this little demonstration below, we'll hit some of the highlights of MIDI sequencing. The CD ROM has a demo version of Cakewalk on it and you might want to take it for a little spin. The stuff we'll be covering in this section though is most easily done with the full version, which is conveniently available from the good folks at Twelve Tone Systems.

Most good software packages will have these same features, although in a slightly different format. Don't worry about it too much. One good day with your computer on, the manual on your lap, a soda at your side, and your phone set to redial the 800 technical support number of your software; and you'll be able to do just about everything you'll ever need.

Okay, here's the opening screen that appears when you start Cakewalk. It looks complicated, but a lot of this is empty space waiting for you to fill it. The software is so good that a lot of that stuff is there to tell you things when you need it.

File	Edit	View	Insert
New...			
Open...			Ctrl+O
Save			Ctrl+S
Save As...			
Merge...			
Extract...			
Info...			
Print Preview...			
Print...			
Print Setup...			
Exit			Alt+F4
1 c:\cpw30\latin.wrk			
2 c:\cpw30\ballad.wrk			
3 c:\wincake\scott2.wrk			
4 c:\cpw30\nomanst.wrk			

The page is very clean and empty, waiting for your music. The top third of the page you'll recognize as a very Windows styled environment. In fact many of the same sorts of functions you have in any word processing program are also here. Under FILE for example, you have commands for opening and saving files. Those print commands come in hand, too, of course, when after you're done with a new song you want to print out the "sheet music." Those bottom four lines are the most recently used files. You can recall them quickly with the push of one key.

Also along the top you'll notice some buttons or keys that make sense. Look at the RECord, REWind, and the arrow (PLAY) functions, which are just like a tape recorder. And that is, of course, the closest comparison for software sequencing. It's like the computer is acting as the world's greatest tape recorder. You play your music and the machine captures it perfectly. As we find out later, though, this tape recorder is very special.

The bottom part of the page is where your "tracks" are. Just like multi-track recording, as you sequence you'll be "recording" one track at a time. This gives you complete control over your song at all times. In this version of Cakewalk Professional (3.01), you have 256 tracks available. We only see 12. (Most of our sequencing uses between 4-12 tracks, so this screen size is usually enough for us. You, of course, may have different needs and can configure the screen any way you want.)

Lets load up an already recorded song so you can see what that bottom section looks like with some music in there.

	Name	√	Loop	Key+	Vel+	Chn	Patch	A 1	B 5	C 9	D 13	E 17	F 21	25
1	Play-thru tra(	√	1	0	0	1	12							
2	Bright piano	√	1	0	0	3	1							
3	Acoustic bas	√	1	0	0	2	32							
4	Horn section	√	1	0	0	4	61							
5	Kick drum	√	1	0	0	10	32							
6	Congas	√	1	0	0	10	---							
7	Rim shot	√	1	0	0	10	---							
8	Tom fills	√	1	0	0	10	---							
9	Bell ride cym	√	1	0	0	10	---							
10	Claves	√	1	0	0	10	---							
11	Cowbell	√	1	0	0	10	---							

Track/Measure

This song (one that comes, by the way, with Cakewalk 3.01) has 11 tracks. From the left, the screen tells us this:

- **Name** of the track or instrument.

- The ✔ (check mark) means the track is on and not muted (a very useful function so that you can preview one track at a time to make sure you've played each part the way you want).

- **Loop** (do you want that part to repeat during the song—a very useful feature when creating long songs that have similar or repetitive parts.)

- **Key** (is the track in the same key as the song—tracks can be modified, for example, to match the desired key of a singer.) We use this function a lot. Just making the music is one thing. When you want to sing with it, or play guitar, for example, you might find the key is too high or low. In a recording studio or just on a tape recorder that means re-recording the whole thing. With sequencing, it means you push a button and you change the key of the music. Easy!

- **Vel**(ocity) helps you determine volume or loudness of the pre-recorded track. You may find as you add more instruments that the cowbell you started with sounds a little puny. Click on velocity and bump it up a bit and you'll have the strong sound you need.

- **Chn** (channel) is easy enough. This is where you make sure each track is being played by one instrument. Depending on the number of sounds your keyboard will let you play (multi-timbrality), how many keyboards you have, or how many tone modules you have; this number can go as high as 256! Now if you're like us, 16 or so is plenty. Look in this column on the sample song. See how the first few tracks all have different numbers. That means, in this example, that the writer of this song has a piano sound ready to go on MIDI channel #3. His keyboard or tone module has a setting for this and he/she's selected it. The software can be told the same info. When channel 3 plays on the software, the MIDI connection sends info (the notes) to channel 3 on the keyboard. But what about all those 10s? Well 10 (and sometimes 16) is a standard drum channel. Most keyboards dedicate either 10 or 16 as the drum channel. Now, since the playing of drums is a multi-faceted and difficult procedure, most computer composers make their drum parts out of several different tracks. Here for example our songwriter has separated such drum parts as the kick (or bass drum) from the cowbell, rimshot (snare), and so forth. Naturally this feature also increases the amount of freedom we have in working with each track since the whole drum kit isn't all together.

■ **Patch.** This is another way your software talks to your keyboards or modules. Look at "Bright Piano" again, in the graphic above. The software and the keyboard have been set up on channel 3. The patch is the exact sound that will be used by that information. In this case, 1, is one of several piano sounds available on most standard keyboards or modules. (The others, in case you want to know, are 0,2,3,4 and 5, the latter two being electric piano sounds.) Why do I tell you this? Just to show you that a lot of sequencing has been standardized. How do I know these numbers? Not a big deal. Turn your keyboard on and you'll see these same numbers on virtually every machine.

Anyway, that's a little taste of things. Remember we're not really trying to teach all of MIDI to you here in this little chapter. We're just hitting some highlights so that you'll be excited about getting up and running. Most sequencing software manuals are well written (despite the jokes about technical writers), and usually there's a technical support number to call when you're really stumped.

Now, how does that music get on that screen? (And by the way, don't worry about those dots. They just denote exactly where in the song a specific sound is playing.) Well let's see if we can configure a little piece real quickly here.

A lot of composers start with some kind of piano part. A piano is a nice full instrument with lots of range and at the very least you can play through the song and then have something to work with. I'm starting with a clean page. (I'm just going to show you a part of the page to keep it simple.)

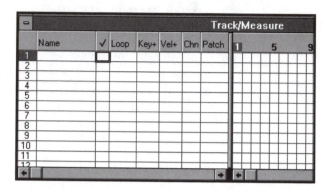

I decide to start with a piano and set it up on channel 1. I choose patch 0, which from my experience is a nice acoustic piano. I type piano in the name slot to remind me and I'm ready to record. Remember those tape recorder-like buttons from before?

Well here's that section of the screen again. On the left you can see 1:1:000. That's my counter which shows me where I am in the song. In this case I'm at the very beginning, first measure, first bar. Then you can see the recorder functions. Then on the far right is the tempo (100.00) That's a nice tempo and remember, if I record this whole song at 100 and then decide I don't like it, I can just click on those arrows and move it up or down!

Okay, so I press RECord and a metronome starts. It clicks 4 beats (or 8 or 12 or 100—whatever I want) and I start playing my piano part.

Suddenly the song is stared. There's the first track. I recorded 9 bars of piano. Let's see how it looks on a musical staff.

Wow. It's really on there. It's too bad you can't hear it right now. (But of course you can. In fact I didn't know it as I played it, but this is the theme music to PLUG IN. Check out the CD ROM. Give it a listen. It's in the SONGS directory.

Enough of the pitch, let's get back to songwriting. Now that I have a piano part, I start adding things to it. I move down to the second track, choose a new channel and a new patch, and put in a bass part. Then a string part. Then some drums. Let's take a look.

	Name	√	Loop	Key+	Vel+	Chn	Patch	1	5	9
1	Piano	√	1	0	0	1	0			
2	Bass	√	1	0	0	2	32			
3	Violin	√	1	0	0	3	40			
4	Kick Drum	√	1	0	0	10	1			
5	Snare Drum	√	1	0	0	10	1			
6	Hi Hats	√	1	0	0	10	---			
7										

Now this is just the beginning, naturally. But I'm on my way. Through editing functions I can take parts of the piano, bass or violin and copy them to use again elsewhere in the song. Much of music sequencing works just like word processing. Look at these commands under EDIT: cut, copy and paste. Those are all things we've been using for years in Windows or in Macintosh. Nothing to it. There are even some more hip commands lower down (Groove Quantize!) But they're just other editing features that really help us make our music. (Quantizing, by the way, is the function that looks at where you've played your notes and puts them right on the beat for you. Very useful for us musicians who are so busy trying to play something good that we're sometimes a little off time.)

Edit	View	Insert	Realtime	Mark
Undo Delete Track			Ctrl+Z	
Redo			Ctrl+A	
History...				
Cut...			Ctrl+X	
Copy...			Ctrl+C	
Paste...			Ctrl+V	
Paste To One Track...			Ctrl+Shift+V	
Quantize...				
Groove Quantize...				
Interpolate...				
Length...				
Slide...				
Retrograde...				
Transpose...				
Velocity Scale...				
Fit				▶
Run CAL Program...			Ctrl+F1	

Well let's get back to our song and look at one more nice feature that nearly all sequencing software has. Since we've been stressing how alike simple tape recording is to this procedure, here's a mode we'd all like to have as we listen to music. This is the "fader" view of our Plug In song.

214

You'll see that there is a fader (volume and pan control, mostly) for each track we've recorded. You can see how easily we can modify the volume of each track (independent from each other!). Look, I've also modified the pan of each track. (This determines from which stereo speaker the sound comes from.) I've moved that snare over to the left, for example, so it sounds more like a real drum set.

Now this is a crude and quick example. For the finished Plug In song, I'll have to do a lot more work. But this is a good start, and I did it all in about 5 minutes. It was fun, easy, and as I'm typing this very sentence of the book, I'm also listening to it come pouring out of my speakers.

More MIDI Help

Gene Confrey is another of our new friends. His name will pop up in your early ventures through the Internet. We found him to be an excellent source of information. A MIDI primer and glossary were things we could have done, but he did both of them first and better and we wanted you to hear it straight from him. The text that follows this paragraph all comes from his articles published on the MIDILink website discussed at length above. Thanks Gene.

GENE CONFREY SAYS

MIDI has been around for about 10 years, since musicians and engineers first discovered how to couple electronic instruments, then, later, how to link the instruments with computers.

The Musical Instrument Digital Interface has had a dramatic history since the 1980s. Synthesizers, sound cards, and sampling techniques have grown remarkably sophisticated in the 1990s. Similarly, software for MIDI-computing has developed apace. Sequencers--for recording, playing, and editing. Notation programs for scoring and printing music. Musical accompaniment software.

A lot of this was created to run in Microsoft's Disk Operating System (DOS).

Then, in the 1990s along came Windows, a graphical environment designed to make personal computing more convenient. Today, more and more music programs are programmed to run as Windows applications.

TERMS USED IN MIDI-COMPUTING

This reference provides a listing of terms important to the activity of MIDI-computing. In its simplest usage, computing involves the use of computers (programmable electronic devices) to process data. For example, storing, editing, and retrieving information.

MIDI-computing is distinguished by the application of a device known as a MIDI, which stands for: Musical Instrument Digital Interface. By means of a MIDI electronic circuit, musical instruments--like keyboard synthesizers--can be connected to computers, or connected to other synthesizers.

The result? Messages can be sent back and forth-messages that produce melodies, harmonies, changes of pitch, and volume.... To illustrate: One musical message, like a piano melody played on a keyboard, can be "recorded," (that is, encoded) on a track in computer memory, then another message can be layered-superimposed--on the melody line. The other message might be, for instance, the sounds of an orchestral string ensemble. Captured by this process are the elements of a digital recording, like that of a compact disc. Gone are the scratches and other noises of the traditional phonograph record. Gone is the wow and flutter often associated with tape recording.

This musical arrangement (melody, harmony, tempo, pitch, etc.) can then be edited on the computer screen. Errors can be corrected, specific notes deleted, chord changes introduced. Then, the ultimate product--a performance, a musical score--can be printed by the computer, using standard musical notation. That's what MIDI can do.

This document is designed to explain and define many of the terms currently used in MIDI-computing. This compilation of terms used in MIDI computing is designed for the novice, who is not sure what MIDI is all about.

A

ACCENT: Stress given to a musical tone.

AFTERTOUCH: The change in pressure on a key after the initial attack. Determines vibrato and other characteristics.

APPLE MACINTOSH: Apple computers were among the earliest computers to offer MIDI-computing capacity. Others now in the field include IBM-compatible PC's, Atari and Amiga.

ASSIGNING PATCHES: When about to play an electronic instrument, such as a keyboard, one first selects a patch (voice, instrument), then plays away. In Midi recording, the sequence is reversed: play first, then assign a patch. If you don't like the sound of the patch (e.g., Rhodes piano), change it (e.g., to a vibraphone).

ATTACK: When the musical note begins. Antonym: Release.

A TRACK AT A TIME: Midi-computing with sequencers is indeed a form of multi-track recording. Nonetheless, one should keep in mind that most of the work (recording, creating song files, editing...) is done one-track-at-a-time. Whether you are running a Song View window, an Event List, a Piano Roll, or a Tempo Map, your orientation is primarily toward a selected track and the Midi events therein.

B

BAR: A synonym for measure--musical time, a grouping of beats.

BEAT: Literally, a single stroke or pulsation. Tempo is expressed in beats per minute. The beat value affects the metronome.

BUFFER: A temporary storage area in memory.

C

CANCEL: An often-misunderstood command. It does not mean delete (e.g., the file) or "send" it to the "moon." It usually means, simply, turn off the display now on the screen.

CHANNEL: In ordinary language, a channel is a path for passing data. In MIDI, channels are used to separate different sections of a song that are going to play together. Each channel is assigned to a single instrument in any particular instant of time. One channel is usually reserved for a percussion voice. To channelize means to move to another channel.

CLOCK: A clock is used to synchronize two devices. In MIDI, the term clock is used to denote a single time source, which everything plays along with. MIDI clocks are actually special messages that are sent 24 times (normally) per beat, and are used to synchronize two sequencers, or a sequencer and a drum machine. Normally, the sequencer's clock is the important one. Other clock sources are rarely used, and, typically, only when doing a final recording.

COMPOSE-ARRANGE: Two activities that can be facilitated by MIDI-computing. The composer creates music. The arranger enhances it--by scoring for other voices or instruments.

CONFIGURATION: Before any Midi-computing can be done (playing, recording, editing, etc.), software and hardware MUST be configured--set up for operation. In Windows, this process takes place in the Control Panel (of the Main Window), involving settings for drivers, Midi Mapper, etc. In Midi applications, look for the phrase "Midi Setup." The most important part of the configuration process is selecting the correct send and receive ports.

CONTROLLER: (1) Most often, it means the instrument: keyboard, guitar, drums... (As in Master Controller.) (2) A second meaning, in sequencing, refers to a setting, a parameter, such as Controller 7 = Volume. In this sense, a controller is a MIDI event.

CONVENTIONAL NOTATION: Sometimes called "Traditional Musical Notation." Sometimes "standard" notation. You know, those old-fashioned things, like notes, rests, slurs, clefs, dynamic marks....Some things that go beyond guitar chords, or piano-roll entries.

COUNT, CLICK: These terms refer to metronome sounds. The former is usually a one-measure count-in before the sequencer starts recording. A "click" is a tone on each beat for the entire song. Obviously, the meter (4/4, 3/4) and tempo (90, 120 BPM) settings will affect these sounds. The sounds will vary according to the settings selected. The sound may come from the PC's speaker or a sound module.

COUNT IN: A command in a sequencer that plays a metronome for several measures until you are ready to record.

CRESCENDO: A gradual increase in volume. Antonym: Decrescendo.

CUT-AND-PASTE: In word-processing, this function means moving text from one place in a document to another. In MIDI, one can copy a section of a musical passage and paste it elsewhere.

D

DEFAULT SETTING: In MIDI, as in general computing, this is a choice made by the program (when the user does not specify an alternative).

DIGITAL: In MIDI, the phrase digital recording is contrasted with analog recording. Long-playing phonograph records are analog recordings. That is, they capture information in a continuously-variable form. A fluctuating waveform. Telephone lines work on the same principle. Digital, in contrast, involves binary numbers--1s and 0s. MIDI-computing represents digital encoding.

DOWNBEAT: The maestro's downward stroke, indicating the first beat of a measure. In contrast, the upbeat is unaccented.

DURATION: The length of time (number of beats) of a note or chord.

E

EDIT: Editing, in MIDI, involves altering, deleting, revising the musical passages that have been captured in a digital recording, and are now displayed on the monitor screen. This display will offer two options: (1) The notes are listed by track and number, by event (like "Note on"), by the specific note G4, the beat, the channel, etc. (2) The second option for editing is to use a musical notation display. Here, the notes are arrayed in clefs, (a) like a piano-roll or (b) in conventional musical notations. Editing options include changes in notes, measures, transpose, volume... (The piano-roll display is sometimes referred to as "graphic notation.")

EDIT MENU: Another drop-down menu of the Menu Bar. As in word-processing programs, it usually includes such commands as Undo, Cut, Copy, Paste... When a command is dimmed, it's unavailable. For instance, you cannot "paste" unless you have "copied" or "cut" part of the loaded song file. The commands listed in this menu vary by program. For the most part, however, Edit menus do what the word implies: alter, adapt, refine... You can undo those musical fluffs. You can cut, copy, paste, clear and delete tracks.

ENABLE-DISABLE: Antonyms, meaning to turn on or turn off. Synthesizers and sequencers have many controls requiring such action (like MIDI THRU).

ENVELOPE: The changes of a tone, e.g., attack, sustain, decay, release.

ERROR MESSAGES: The message says "Something's wrong!" In MIDI, you might be told that "Memory is full." Or you've committed a "Track Error." Or you have made a "Protect Error" (attempted to write to a protected disk).

EVENT: In ordinary language, an occurrence, a happening. In MIDI, the signal that is transmitted-like note on, note off, program change, control change...

EVENT WINDOW: If there is such a display in a sequencing program, it provides an astonishing degree of detail about Midi events. Illustrative data shown in such a listing: For a specific track, when did the event occur (beats and clock ticks)? What type of event (a program change, a note on...)? What channel? What note? What was the length of the note? Given such data, it is possible to edit lines. You can change a time signature or the tempo. Or change a patch or channel, after touch, a marker, a track name, a cue-point. You can delete an entire line, sound a note, change the duration of a note, insert a rest, search for a type of event... All such options are defined by the scope and limits of the specific sequencer. The Event listing itself is a non-graphic display (although some sequencers use icons to differentiate controller events). Moreover, sequencers often provide other graphical displays for editing Midi data, such as Pitch Bend, Channel Pressure, Key Pressure, Modulation or the entire range of controllers.

F

FADERS: Controls for changing effects gradually, like decreasing loudness.

FIELD: Traditional computing defines this as a location in a record. Examples: name, address, zip code, etc. Illustrative fields in MIDI: Song title, Track name, Instrument, Channel...

FILE TYPES: A MIDI File Type 0 is a single (multiple-channel) track. A MIDI File Type 1 contains one or more simultaneous tracks.

G

GANGED: When tracks are "ganged," they will move simultaneously. (Analogy: A variable capacitor in an early radio receiver.)

GENERAL MIDI MODE: A convention specifying how a sequence (a song) should be constructed, so that it will play on a variety of hardware.

GLOBAL EDITING: Affecting an entire file or program. Transpose is illustrative. The contrasting function is local editing, like changing one event.

H

HARDWARE SEQUENCER: Sequencing can be performed by software programs or by hardware. Hardware sequencers also work with synthesizers, controllers, sound modules--creating and editing songs. A hardware sequencer is--as the name implies--hardware, containing a single-purpose program, one designed to provide sequencing.

HUMANIZE: A term that is used in the sense of introducing random irregularities in note-timing and velocities, in order to reduce the mechanical character of a performance.

HUNG NOTES: A "bane" is a source of woe. This is the bane of Midi-computing. Sometimes it seems that a stuck note will haunt you forever. You click on "Stop," yet the note continues to resound. You close the song file. (Still twanging.) You leave the sequencing program. You leave the directory. You climb out of Windows. Occasionally, a "Panic Button" reset will turn off all notes. Failing this, turn off the computer. And do something else.

I

IMPORTING/EXPORTING: That which there is no more important feature of music software programs! Take exporting. Here is a song file you have just created in Master Tracks. As such, it has its .MTS extension--suitable for this sequencer, but unplayable elsewhere. Saved as MYSONG.MTS, it is proudly displayed in the Track Editor. So, in the File Menu, select "Export Midi File." Then choose the format (Type 0 or Type 1). OK. Now, you can save it--reincarnated as MYSONG.MID. Look in Windows File Manager, and there it is as a Midi file, playable, incidentally, by the Media Player, and by any program that plays standard Midi files. Sequencers can also import and play Midi files. Selecting (from the File Menu) the "Import" command will show a list of Midi files in that program directory. Clicking the usual two dots [..] [changing to the parent directory] will show the way to other .MID files. Select, load, and play away.

INITIALIZATION: Initial means the beginning. To initialize is to set a program to a starting position-to prepare the program for use.

INSTRUMENTATION: The selection of instruments in a MIDI arrangement.

INTERPOLATE: This word pops up in some Midi programs. Basically, the word means to alter by insertion. It is designed to search for events and change their parameters.

IRQ: The Interrupt Request line and the Port Address MUST be set correctly when configuring Midi software and hardware. A sequencing program or a sound card will not operate properly if these settings are incorrect. Some interface cards provide a diagnostic utility to help identify problems such as an address conflict--with a video card, for instance.

K

KEYBOARD: Reminder: In MIDI-computing, one has to remember which one is involved in a documentation reference--the computer's or the controller's.

KEY SIGNATURE: Musical notation shows this in terms of sharps and flats after the clef. Software sequencers sometimes show a song key as "F Major/D minor," and indicate the number of sharps or flats. B Flat Major/G Minor has two flats, for example.

L

LOOPING: Used to repeat a section of a recording. In Midi, loop means to go around again. You loop a track, or a song file, or an album, or a drum pattern.

M

MARKER: Something used to record a position. MIDI markers identify, for example, musical cues. They work like tab stops in a word-processor.

MAPPING: The process of identifying patches and keys, so that sound files can be played properly. A key map will translate values for MIDI messages, so that the correct keys will be played. A patch map functions to identify the correct patches (sounds, instruments). For the beginner, mapping is one of the toughest nuts to crack. Let's see if we can identify some fundamentals. For starters, the verb "map" means to delineate, to assign a set of symbols. Maybe "translator" would be descriptive. In Midi, this "mapping" involves (1) patches (voices, instruments), (2) drum sounds. The manufacturers of synthesizers (like the one in your keyboard or the one in your sound card) will have installed factory presets. However, suppose you decide to work in General Midi, a standard that is becoming increasingly popular. OK, maybe you're in luck. The reason: Under the General Midi Specification there is: (1) a General Midi Patch Map, (2) a General Midi Percussion Key Map. (Notice the distinction between "patches" and "keys.") So, where do you find these patch maps and key maps? You can usually find them by poking around the Help files. Try "Search." And there are the patches: Number 1 is acoustical piano, 12 is vibraphone, 16 acoustical guitar, 67 tenor sax, etc. (If you have found this, number 127 is applause; if not, number 128 is gun shot.) Even in General Midi, mapping drum sound keys may require some fussing. Formidable fussing, but not insuperable. Here's the problem: the specific percussion sound is a function of the General Midi Percussion Key Map and some possible idiosyncrasies in your synthesizer. As a consequence, some of the drum sounds will sound neat--but some may sound wrong. So, what do you do? Answer: You map your system. Moral: He who enters the arena of Midi-computing may take on the characteristics of a little ol' mapmaker.

MASTER CONTROLLER: Although pianists may think otherwise, the term "Master Controller" and "keyboard" are not synonymous! The Master Controller can be any Midi instrument that can transmit musical data, like notes, for instance. Thus, piano keyboards do indeed qualify. But so do guitars, violins, wind instruments--even drums.

MELODY: One of the elements of music (the others being harmony and rhythm). Melody is a succession of tones--hopefully pleasing.

MERGE: To combine or blend into one. Example: Merging two tracks.

MESSAGES: The net effect of MIDI-computing is sound: melodies, harmonies, rhythms... But the MIDI message (the MIDI event) itself is not a sound. Transmitted are digital commands--about 1,000 events per second.

METER: The basic pattern of note values, e.g., beats per measure.

METRONOME: A device to mark time by producing a repeated tick. The older type--a triangular box with a vibrating arm--was succeeded by an electrical unit. In MIDI, the ticks are computer-generated.

MIDI: A protocol. The musical instrument digital interface comprises a MIDI card and cables connecting the computer to an electronic instrument, such as a keyboard. The MIDI card (a printed circuit board) is normally mounted in an expandable slot inside the computer. Keyboard synthesizers can also communicate with other synthesizers by means of a MIDI connection.

MIDI PITCH WHEEL SWITCH: Determines whether continuous controller information (e.g., note on, key pressure, control change, program change...) will be recorded.

MIDI SOUND GENERATOR: For authentic reproduction of acoustical instruments. It uses samples--instrument sounds stored as digitized audio. This is actually another term for synthesizer--converting MIDI events into real audio sound.

MIDI THRU: One of three ports (connections): MIDI In, MIDI Out, and MIDI Thru. MIDI In receives information from other equipment. MIDI Out sends information to other equipment. MIDI Thru duplicates the information, and sends it to other equipment. By means of the latter, a synthesizer can echo messages to other synthesizers.

MODULATION: In music, one usually thinks of modulating as passing from one key to another--by means of intermediate chords. In MIDI, modulation usually means applying a vibrato effect to a sound.

MPU-401 COMPATIBLE: The reference is to a standard interface. (It derives from Roland's initial design.) Importance: MS DOS MIDI software often supports this user base, but not always.

MULTI-TIMBRAL: In sequencing, a multi-timbral sound module can play several parts on different channels simultaneously. A multi-timbral device is one that is prepared to sound like more than one instrument at a time.

MULTI-TRACK RECORDING: Normally, one records on a single track ("Normal Mode" recording). Multi-track recording is feasible, however. Example: From a guitar, with each string on a different channel.

MULTI-VOICE MODE: A setting on a multi-timbral tone generator (such as a keyboard) for receiving multiple MIDI channels, each channel having a different voice (instrument).

MUTE: A sequencer command to turn off specified tracks. Reason: So you can listen exclusively to one track.

N

NOISE: That disturbance of a signal that might occur if your MIDI cables are too long--exceeding 15 meters in length, for example.

NORMAL MODE: When a (controller) keyboard has this setting (as contrasted with split, or fingered modes), the sounds are all of one voice--from the lowest note to the highest. In this mode, the resemblance is to an acoustical instrument.

NOTE NUMBERING: Electronic piano keyboards (Master Controllers) vary in their number of keys. Some have 88, like the normal acoustical piano. Many have 61 keys. The sections of a keyboard are identified by octaves. For instance, middle C is C3; the tone above D3, then E3, etc. One octave higher is C4, D4, etc. In a 61-key keyboard, the lowest tone would be C1. Just as some acoustical pianos have more than 88 keys the display keyboards in sequencing programs might show as many as 128 keys (ranging in sound from low "growls" to high "tinkles"). Given this circumstance, the octave-numbering might begin with C-2, and extend to G-8. Another aspect is note numbering for drum sounds--with middle C being designated as number 60, C-sharp number 61, etc.

NOTE ON/NOTE OFF: Given an Event List, why does the display show only "Note on"? The answer is that "note on"

comprises: (1) the note turned on; (2) its duration (measures, beats, clocks); (3) its note-on volume; (4) its note-off volume.

O

OCTAVE NOTATION: MIDI software and electronic keyboards use notations like F4 to represent the specific note (F) located in the 4th octave of an acoustical piano.

ONE TRACK, ONE INSTRUMENT: This is the general rule. Example: the flute on track 4; the guitar on track 7. But there is a prominent exception. Presuppose a melody line on track 3, featuring the acoustical piano. After the first chorus, the piano becomes tedious. Do a program change at the beginning of the second chorus (utilizing the Event Editor), and substitute another patch.

OPEN COMMAND: Loads an existing disk file.

OVERDUB: If you have a track with Midi data in it, and then record over this track, normally the original recording is erased. With this switch toggled on, you can put sound on sound. This is useful for superimposing percussion sounds on a song.

P

PAN: To pan is to move the sound between full left and full right in a stereo sound field. It resembles the "balance" function of a stereo receiver/amplifier.

PANIC: Sudden terror, as when a musical note in a sequence gets stuck. Panic buttons in sequencing programs are largely intended for amusement, not for decisive action. There are exceptions, however. The Panic command usually shuts off notes and resets the sustain pedal.

PARAMETER: A tough word to define. In mathematics, it's a variable or an arbitrary constant. In MIDI, it's a value assigned at the beginning of an operation. Examples: pitch bend, sustain, voice number, volume, reverb...

PATCH: In some early keyboard synthesizers, one selected "instruments" to play (e.g., vibraphone, clarinet...) Later, the term "voice" emerged, in part, because some of the sounds went beyond instruments (police whistles, human voices, etc.). In contemporary MIDI-computing, the word "patch" is prominent--one reason being that a single keyboard setting, like 99, may encompass a large range of percussive sounds. In any event, to a sequencer, the patch setting will determine the nature of the sounds.

PATCH LAYOUT: A potential source of trouble for MIDI users. Manufacturers of synthesizers have not standardized the correspondence between patches and numbers. On a Roland keyboard, the celesta patch number might be 24; on a Yamaha 09. Microsoft's MIDI Mapper is designed to help rectify this.

PIANO ROLL DISPLAY: There are several ways to enter and edit notes in Midi-computing. An Event List is one such way. Here you can type in data: note events, patch changes, velocity, duration of notes, channel numbers, etc. The graphics are traditional music notation. Sequencing programs often use multiple displays.

PIANO ROLL EDITOR: A common notation used for editing by many sequencers. The notes of each track are shown as horizontal bars--the vertical position representing pitch; the horizontal length representing duration of the note (or chord).

PITCH: The property of a musical tone--determined by frequency.

PITCH BEND WHEEL: A wheel on the keyboard that allows notes to be bent up or down. (Example: a sliding trombone sound.) "Pitch bend" is a MIDI message.

PLAY LIST: A list of tunes to be performed in succession. The sequence is pre-programmed.

POLYPHONY: From the Greek, meaning variety of tones. In MIDI, the question is: "How many notes can be played simultaneously?" Maximum polyphony cannot be exceeded.

PORT: It's a location in hardware where data is passed in and out. In setting up MIDI, one must make port assignments, so that channels can be correctly addressed. The musical signals may go 'round and 'round, and they come out where? A port is a location where data pass in and out. You have a port for the printer, and maybe one for your modem. In all probability, your friendly computer will tell you that you have some LPT ports and some COM ports. The printer is likely connected to the former; the mouse to the latter. For our purposes (Midi-computing in Windows), what matters most is the distinction between the INPUT PORT (for recording) and the OUTPUT PORT (for playing song files). If you have configured your system correctly, this selection will be displayed in every musical software program in your possession.

PORT ADDRESS AND INTERRUPT SETTINGS: Addresses are locations within the computer. These addresses are used by devices (such as a MIDI keyboard) to communicate with the software. An interrupt setting signals when the device is ready to send or receive data. Addresses and interrupts must be unique for each device.

PROGRAM CHANGE: This is a channel voice message to a Midi device. The message orders a patch (or program number) change (e.g., from a guitar to a flute). Such changes are reflected in the Event List.

PULSE: The tick of a computer clock is sometimes referred to as a "pulse." Example: One clock pulse might be defined as 1/240th of a quarter-note.

PUNCH IN/PUNCH OUT: Suppose you have recorded three choruses of a 32-bar song, and you are disappointed with your performance of the final 8-bar bridge. Punch-in recording will enable you to re-record these measures at the precise beginning and ending.

PUNCH-RECORDING: A feature that allows automatic on-off recording at specified points.

Q

QUANTIZATION: To quantize is to force all notes played to fall on the nearest beat specified. It shifts events (like note-on) to an exact rhythmic position.

QUANTIZE: A process that a jazz musician--skilled at improvising rhythmically--may never quite understand. Quantization aligns to the nearest fraction of a beat. Quantize to an eighth note, and all eighths fall on that pulse. Result? A tasteful 12-bar blues may sound stiff and mechanical. Commands such as "humanize" or "swing" try to undo this perversion, but can make matters much worse! Quantization is useful where a high degree of precision is needed--a sequence on the way to a notational program for scoring and printing. If one must use quantization (that is, timing correction), it is not necessary to maximize the process. One can choose a percentage between none and full. In a snap-to-grid display, quantized notes line up with the closest grid line.

R

REAL-TIME: In MIDI, there are two types of recording procedures: (1) real-time; (2) step-time. The former resembles traditional recording--as with a tape recorder. Step-time recording is really sequential: note-by-note, chord-by-chord.

RECORD: In the world of sound, to register something reproducible on a disk, like a phonograph record, or on magnetic tape. Traditional recording captures the amplitude (height) and frequency (number) of wave forms. MIDI-computing does not really "record." It encodes messages, digitally--by means of numbers. Because of established usage, however, the words "record" and "recording" often appear in MIDI computing, along with "play," "rewind," "fast forward," etc. In MIDI-computing, these words are really metaphors. A typical sequencer will "record" all of the MIDI events received, along with the time they were received.

RESET: Keyboards, like computers, sometimes "lock up." To restore normal operation, the System Reset is used. There is another meaning in MIDI software: Reset means to return to the first measure.

S

SAMPLING: Emulating the sound of an acoustical instrument by digitizing (converting to digital sound) the waveforms produced by the instrument.

SAVE AS: If no filename has yet been assigned, this is the command to use. If your MIDI file has already been christened, and you have edited it, the appropriate command is Save.

SELECT: Do you want to edit (insert, delete, copy, cut...)? You must first "select," i.e., highlight, block...

SEQUENCER: So called because such a program arranges melodic and harmonic patterns in successive positions. Strictly speaking, one should define a sequencer as something that stores note-on and note-off events in memory, then plays them back.

SEQUENCER MEMORY: It is in RAM (Random Access Memory). It is measured in the number of events that can be accommodated.

SLIDER: An input-device to increase or decrease volume. Also refers to an on-screen image (like a button control) that one can move with a mouse.

SMPTE: Usually indicates a standardized time code developed by the Society of Motion Picture and Television Engineers. The time code is used in the MIDI world as a way of synchronizing MIDI to external events. Where will you encounter this? Beginners probably won't, but the commands and procedures may be lurking around the menus, asking whether you want to "generate the SMPTE Time Code," and when you want to start the SMPTE stripe (hour, minute, second, frame) and how many frames a second you want to run at.

SNAP-TO-GRID: A grid consists of two sets of lines that crisscross. A snap-to-grid feature facilitates step-entry of notes.

SOLO: If you want to listen exclusively to one track, you can mute all other tracks. Alternative: Select a track to "solo" (a feature that some sequencing programs offer).

SONG CLEAR: To erase the contents of all tracks.

SOUND DEVICE: Any device is part of the system's hardware. Examples: a printer, mouse, modem, etc. A sound device might be, for instance, a MIDI synthesizer, a CD-ROM drive, a videodisk player.

SOUND DRIVER: Device drivers are software that control communication between devices (a mouse, printer, modem...) and the computer. A sound-driver controls the sound card or the sound device, such as a MIDI-compatible synthesizer. The sound driver must be correctly configured for your computer.

SOUND MODULE: The component in a device (such as a keyboard) that produces the sound (e.g., a violin melody, a drum rhythm). This is another term for MIDI sound generator.

SOUND RECORDER: Microsoft's Windows accessory that can play, record and edit sound files in the WAVE (non-MIDI) format.

SPEED; PITCH: Perhaps the most important capacity of a sequencer. Tempo can be changed without affecting pitch. Thus, a difficult passage can be recorded slowly, then played at a faster tempo-- with no change in pitch.

SPLIT MODE: Divides a keyboard into two sections, each of which can play a different instrument. Example: From the split-point (like C#3), the left hand can be producing the sounds of an organ, while the right hand plays a flute melody line.

SPLIT-POINT: In a split mode, the location on a keyboard where one voice (instrument) is differentiated from another. G2, for example, might be set to allow one voice (say, choir) in the left hand, another voice (say, violin) in the right hand.

STANDARD MIDI FILE: Identified by its extension (.MID, some-times.MFF or.SMF), this is a file that can store MIDI messages, such as songs. The data in a MIDI file can be played, manipulated, edited...A MIDI file comprises actions performed on an instrument (keys pressed, how hard...) There is a standard MIDI file format. A principal advantage of a MIDI file: It uses comparatively little disk space.

STEP RECORDING: The key is patience, like building a ship in a bottle. Some people, unkindly, describe this as "typing in your music." Gentle reminder: One track at a time. One note at a time. (OK, some-times admittedly one chord at a time.) (OK, admittedly, one can do regional editing!) But the principal focus is STILL: One track/one note! Anyway, which approach to step-recording is best? It largely depends on whether you are more comfortable with numerical input or graphic input. As pointed out elsewhere, there are many ways of entering notes into a sequence. You can play your favorite Midi key-board. You can type them into the Event List (the alphanumeric list of Midi events). You can select them in a notation program, and sprinkle them over the Grand Staff. When the subject is "Step-Entry," however, we are usually emphasizing one of two methodologies: numerical input or graphic input. And the latter (the graphic) subdivides into two categories: Using a pencil-like insertion tool; using a Midi keyboard.

SUSTAIN: To sustain is to hold a note (or a chord). The musical tones fade out gradually.

SYNCHRONIZE: To make synchronous or simultaneous. Example: to synchronize a drum pattern to play with melodies and chords on a synthesizer. MIDI synchronization is a coordinating func-tion--involving a sync signal.

SYNTHESIZER: (Often shortened to synth.) A device driven by a microprocessor, which contains a programmable chip. Examples of instruments that can control synthesizers: guitar, keyboard, wind, string, drum controllers. The keyboard itself does not produce musical sound. A synthesizer circuit, built into the keyboard, accomplishes this function. Originally, a synthesizer was so called because it synthesized acoustic instruments. Nowadays, the term refers to the sound-generating circuitry of any MIDI gear. Another term is sound module.

SYSTEM EXCLUSIVE MESSAGE: A Sysex message involves a specific Midi device, for example, a particular make and model keyboard. One purpose of such messages is to exchange patch information between the device and the computer. Or store drum map names, play-key numbers, reverb depth. Usually a Sysex involves a "bulk dump," i.e., one continuous file.

T

TEMPO: In music, the rate of speed (like allegretto). Electronic keyboards provide controls to set or change tempo. A quarter-note setting may range from 40 to 240 beats per minute. Software sequencers also set and change tempo. Examples of tempo settings: Viennese waltz 190 bpm; disco-rock 104 bpm; swing 166 bpm. Sequencers display the exact beat (e.g., beat number 29) of the music being recorded or played.

TIME BASE: The number of clock ticks per beat. Illustrative range: 120-768.

TIME SIGNATURE: In traditional musical notations, this is expressed as a fractional sign, like 3/4. The denominator indicates the unit for the beat; the numerator shows the number of notes per measure.

TONE GENERATOR: Essentially, a synthesizer without a keyboard.

TOUCH RESPONSE: A feature of some electronic keyboards, enabling one to control loudness according to how hard the keys are pressed.

TIMERS: What are all those spinning numbers in the main windows of sequencing programs? There are two principal indices of the passage of time or the position in a song. The first one shows how much time has elapsed since you started to play or record your sequence. If, upon completion of play or record, it reads something like 0:04:26.688, the length of the song is four minutes, 26 seconds, and 688 frames. (The last number comes into play when one is doing some precise synchronization with a film or video tape--an adventure that the novice is unlikely to take on.) The second array of numbers reveals where you are in a sequence--the play position. If it reads something like 36.2:00, you are currently at measure 36, beat 2. If your sequencer has an automatic rewind option (and you have enabled this switch), when you click "Stop," the play position number will jump back to the starting position. Two displays: Time elapsed. Play position. By the way, timing resolution refers to clock pulses per quarter note.

TRACK: In MIDI, the term "track" designates a location where one records or plays back a musical message---usually a portion of the total arrangement. To illustrate, one might record an oboe melody line on Track Two, then record a bowed bass line on Track Three. When played, the sounds can be simultaneous. Most MIDI software now accommodates 64 tracks of music, enough for a rich orchestral sound. Important: Tracks are purely for convenience; channels are required.

TRACKS: The number of tracks available in sequencing programs varies widely: 16, 64, 128, 256, etc.

TRACK SPLITTING/MERGING: It is possible to merge or split tracks. In the case of the latter, after you select a track, you must decide whether you want to split by channel, or by type of event, or by individual notes. Why in the world would you want to split by note, for instance? Example: You have one percussion track on channel 10. But you want to see what these percussive sounds are, and perhaps edit some of them. So, split the track. Merging allows you to combine data from selected tracks into one track. After this is done, the channel designation will read "multiple," as will the patch-name column.

TRANSPOSE: To perform a musical composition in a different key. In Midi, one may often change the position of an instrument sound. A bass sound, for instance, may have to be lowered one or two octaves.

TRANSCRIPTION: The word has been used extensively in music. Example: arranging for some instrument or voice other than the original. In MIDI, a common usage refers to converting a MIDI file into musical notation for printing. This is accomplished by notation software.

TUNING: 440 Hertz is the normal tuning value. However, the pitch of a synthesizer can be altered-raised or lowered. Changes in the tune value are expressed as plus or minus cents.

u

UNDO: This command could be a life-saver. It reverses your last mistake, such as inadvertently recording or inserting MIDI data. "REDO" undoes an "UNDO." In word-processing, this command (found in the Edit Menu) is a means of reversing actions: removing the text you have just typed; revoking a delete command; reversing a formal decision. Midi programs written for Windows provide a comparable feature. "Undo" applies to a track. Perhaps the most-utilized action is "Undo Record," when your performance is somewhat less than legendary.

v

VELOCITY: Velocity is the MIDI way of determining how hard a note is pressed on the keyboard controller.

W

WAVEFORM: A representation of a wave's amplitude over time.

Z

ZOOM: Just as the zoom lens of a camera magnifies an object while keeping it in focus, this feature of sequencers facilitates the editing of notes, especially in step-recording. Moving, deleting, changing the duration of a note--all this is more easily done when the image has been magnified. When one is scrutinizing not seven beats in a display, but perhaps two. One way to increase magnification is to use the plus (+) sign on the computer keyboard.

Eugene A. Confrey, Ph.D.
70732.301@compuserve.com

The Business of Music 4

Record labels, bands and music professionals are finding that the plugged in world is a place to meet, exchange information, and generally do the stuff business does best, make money. The online world is no longer a sterile environment where business is taboo; real commerce is being conducted on the Net. Record companies aren't just posting sound samples to share music with fans, eventually they hope someone buys the product. Independent musicians are not putting up sites for their own ego, most hope that they might get noticed and signed. Aspiring musicians in addition to learning more about playing their instrument might one day want to get rewarded for their talents.

In this chapter, we will look at some of the resources on the Net designed for music professionals. We'll discuss how to find what's already out there, and then we'll help you get your music related product or service online in the plugged in world of music.

MUSICIAN RESOURCES

Regardless of what instrument you play or what style music you make, you will find a group of people just like you online. There are interest groups, mailing lists, and web sites for all types of musicians on the Net. In the following chapter, we will examine some of the resources specifically available for guitar players, from hard-edge music to classical styles, it is all online. At the end of this chapter you will find a list of all the mailing lists and newsgroup resources for all types of instruments. Or you can check out all of the resources online by using the Plug In homepage.

Sources For the Guitar Player

Most of the resources for guitar players fall into two different categories: the music and the equipment. Most of the music is listener transcribed chords and solos from songs that are placed on the Net in a tablature format. Tablature is a visual way of displaying musical notes or chords by showing the finger position on guitar strings. There are also several software packages on the Net that can help with transcribing music for practice.

• *General Information*

alt.guitar

This group is a general discussion group that focuses on guitar playing, various equipment, effects and anything to do with the instrument.

rec.music.makers.guitar

Another general discussion group that focuses on the musicians and equipment.

rec.music.makers.guitar.acoustic

Discussion of anything dealing with acoustic guitars.

• *The Music*

alt.guitar.tab

In a nutshell, suppose you want to try playing "Tears in Heaven" by Eric Clapton, but you can't afford sheet music since you don't have a gig. Jump on alt.guitar.tab and send a message requesting the tear-jerker and you will likely get a handful of responses. You will either have some musician who will transcribe the song for you or you'll be told that it is at OLGA (see the next page).

Classical Guitar Home Page

http://www.teleport.com/~jdimick/cg.html

If you are remotely interested in classical guitar and the music, you need to see John Philip Dimick's Classical Guitar Home Page. John is a professional musician in the Portland area and has been active in the Oregon classical music scene for over 25 years. He has put a considerable amount of work into this site. It includes beginner information such as, types of guitars, exercises, and suggested approaches to learning classical guitar. John has posted many of the more popular classical songs for guitar in standard notation at his site. In addition to the songs in standard notation, you will also find classical guitar pieces in MIDI format. Here is the opening screen of the site.

Netscape - [The Classical Guitar Home Page]

File   Edit   View   Go   Bookmarks   Options   Directory   Help

Location: http://www.teleport.com/~jdimick/cg.html

The *Classical* Guitar Home Page

John Dimick's Classical Guitar Home Page

OLGA: Online Guitar Archive

ftp://ftp.nevada.edu/pub/guitar

While the legality of posting actual sheet music on the Net is still being debated, there appears to be nothing that anyone can do about fans posting their own chord changes and lyrics for songs by their favorites. This is an invaluable resource for fans and musicians. In some cases songs are available in many formats—lyrics only, lyrics and chord changes, or full tablature—for piano, guitar or bass. And where does one go for this bonanza? Straight to Nevada. Actually: ftp.nevada.edu —also known as OLGA [online guitar archive]. (Check Chapter One again for help on how to FTP.)

The main site is maintained by Jim Carson and Cal Woods. This site is very busy and difficult to log onto. However, there are several mirror sites located around the world that maintain the same information. A primer to OLGA and all of the mirror sites is posted on Thursdays in the alt.guitar.tab newsgroup and in the rec.music.makers.guitar.tabla-ture group.

The Online Guitar Archive is an FTP site that is probably one of the best resources for all levels of guitar players on the Net. It includes several sections ranging from lessons to a huge archive of music.

There are more than 9,000 songs posted on OLGA in tab and chord software formats. A search of the band U2 yielded over 40 different U2 tunes. As one guitar player told us, OLGA is participatory in nature. Anyone can contribute in this worldwide learning experience.

In the lesson section you will find information about practicing scales, learning new techniques, playing power chords and other exercises.

rec.music.makers.tablature

Another tablature discussion group that is very similar to alt.guitar.tab.

• *Guitars and Amps*

Most of the major manufacturers of guitar equipment are accessible in the plugged in world of music. This makes the Net one of the best places to begin when you need good general information about equipment.

The Basics

To get started, go to Webguitar resources:

http://comp.uark.edu/~cbray/html/guitar/html.

You'll find a comprehensive list of all guitar resources on the web.

The Acoustic Guitar FAQ is located at

http://www.io.com:8001/~galvis/rmmga.html,

which is the Acoustic Guitar home page. If you are interested in keeping up with amplifiers subscribe to alt.guitar.amps.

Here are some specific resources from manufacturers.

Abel Axe

http://www.tcd.net/~abel

Abel Axe makes a unique guitar. The body is solid aluminum. The manufacturer claims that it creates more sustain, and better tones and harmonics than a wood top guitar.

Fender Guitars

Fender World

http://www.fender.com/fenderworld.shtml

Fender World opens with a great graphic of Stevie Ray Vaughan and Jimi Hendrix playing the Stratocaster. The amplifier on the opening screen is a clickable menu that lets the guitar player travel to several neat areas of the site. The Welcome section has an area called, "Ask the Pro," which is a collection of frequently asked questions about the company and the products.

Frontline Online is an electronic version of the Fender magazine, *Frontline* with a lot of information for the guitar player. It includes interviews with great artists like Bonnie Raitt—who also happens to endorse Fender gear. The magazine also has a new product section and general guitar news.

The entire product catalog is online in a section called Gear. The section lists every product divided by category. By clicking on the Electric Guitar/Telecaster icon, a graphic of a 1950s style Telecaster pops up on the screen with a listing of every model of the Telecaster that is currently available.

Gibson USA

http://www.gibson.com

From the opening screen, Gibson offers the Net user several jumping points. Gibson in addition to its guitars has several other products and brands like Dobro, Orange Amps, Tobias, Zeta and Oberheim. One of the neatest services that Gibson offers is a search routine. If you have an old Gibson guitar and want to know its age and history, you can search a database by serial number and then check its value with the online version of *Vintage Guitar* magazine. (See the website about *Vintage Guitar* noted below.).

Guitar Oriented Magazines

Guitar Player

http://www.enews.com:80/magazines/guitar_player/

The Electronic Newsstand is the host for *Guitar Player*. It has the table of contents from the current issue, an article or two, and subscription information.

Total Guitar

http://www.futurenet.co.uk/music/totalguitar.html

Total Guitar is a British based guitar magazine. The best of the monthly magazine is available online with equipment reviews, instruction and features.

Vintage Guitar

http://www.vguitar.com/vintageguitar.html

From the *Vintage Guitar* homepage you can view the table of contents of the current issue or order back issues and specialized books oriented to collectors of guitars.

• Equipment Resources

Musician's Web

http://valley.interact.nl/AV/MUSWEB/home.html

Now this is a good idea. The folks at Musician's Web have started a page that compiles information from several companies in a given month. One click and a lot of your search is over. In a recent month, for example, they featured products and links from several terrific companies including: Ovation, Sonor, Takamine, Trace Elliot and others. (Note, not all of these companies have websites.)

MidAtlantic Music

http://pages.prodigy.com/DE/mamusic/mamusic.html

A relatively famous music store, MAM has recently gone online. While they, too, struggle with buying and selling online, they offer E-mail responses to queries about their product lines, which are too numerous to mention. Suffice it to say, they have anything you want in guitars, basses, drums, etc. Once electronic cash becomes secure, companies already online will reap huge benefits from their early visibility.

Lark in the Morning

http://www.mhs.mendocino.k12.ca.us/MenComNet/Business/
Retail/Larknet/larkhp.html

Now here's a website (and quite an address, too). The folks at Lark sell both hard to find and world music instruments. Their website is easy to use, graphically pleasing. Besides the terrific array of stringed, wind, and percussive instruments, they also sell books, cassettes and CDs. Their selection of videos include several instructional tapes for dulcimers, congas, etc. Terrific site!

Sweetwater Sound

http://www.sweetwater.com/

Sweetwater Sound is a mammoth equipment supplier and recording studio in Ft. Wayne, Indiana. Their website has a little something for everyone, and we recommend you check it out fairly soon in your search.

Their site also includes a recording primer written by session cat Roger Nichols. We have done a fair amount of studio work ourselves over the years and we learned a lot by visiting their page and reading through some of their tips.

Tape Machine:

- Machine on input. Monitor through the machine (good idea in case you are overloading the machine input) make sure that whole signal path is working right. (what you see on the meter may not be what you think is going there.
- Listen to output of machine with no music playing. Listen for hums, crackles or buzzes. If the meter is reading something, then there is probably a hum or other noise that you didn't notice.

Now they also sell equipment of all types and their customer service is legendary among us mail-order buyers. So, it was no surprise to find a bunch of great FAQs (Frequently Asked Questions) about nearly every piece of equipment they sell and service.

Q6: I would like to use my K2000 with my sequencer and I would like the K2000 to play more than one sound at a time (to function multitimbrally.) Is this possible?

A6: Yes, and it is very easy to do. First you need to make sure that the K2000 is in MULTI mode. To check this, press the MIDI mode button

Mission Recording

http://webcom.mission.com/

One of Mission's assets is their well-established consumer interface. They are customer ready and their secure credit card service will put your mind at ease. Plenty of catalog pages of their equipment all with current (and very low) prices. Click on items you want, pick the type of delivery you want, and give them your credit card number. Excellent supply of stuff; everything is here from microphones to multi-track recorders.

NEW

Now- Secure credit card server!

We've lowered our Prices!

On

    AZDEN- Wireless mics
    AUDIX- OM5-$179.95 OM3xb-$109.95 mics
    Sound Forge-$334.95
    Our Music Quest prices are the lowest
    Our Symetrix prices are the lowest!

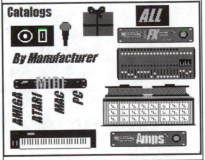

MIDI Equipment Mailing Lists	
Analogue Heaven	analogue-request@magnus.acs.ohio-state.edu
EMU Emax	emax-request@foobar.hpl.hp.com
K2000	k2000-request@jyu.fi
netjam	netjam-request@xcf.berkeley.edu message with Subject: request for info
EPS	eps-request@reed.edu
Roland Samplers	sgroup-request@lotus.UWaterloo.ca
Roland D-70	cyamamot@kilroy.Jpl.Nasa.Gov (Clifford Yamamoto)
Roland U20/U22	phantom@nwu.edu (James Choi)
TX16W	Steve Selick selick@cs.bu.edu
Yamaha SY	sy-request@chorus.fr
SQ-x/KS-32	kjs32-request@cygnus.com
Cubase	CUBASE-R@oldearth.Corp.Sun.COM

LABELS

There are hundreds of major and independent record labels that are accessible on the Net, either on the World Wide Web or by E-mail. Each label uses the Net as a way to promote its artists and releases, as well as keeping in touch with their customers. Most of the labels follow the same format. They offer a quick summary of the philosophy of the label, and a summary of the music and artists, including links to the official homepages of the artists. There is usually a section for downloading samples and a complete listing of the current catalog. All of the labels are reachable on the Plug In homepage. Here are a couple of examples of the way labels are using the Net. We've found the best way to track down labels is through the very fine webpage listed next, maintained by the good folks at KZSU on the campus of Stanford University. Their list is updated constantly and we found their links to be very current.

KZSU—Labels with Websites

http://kzsu.stanford.edu/~music/label-www.html

• *Virgin Records*

http://www.vmg.co.uk

As you can see from the screen below, Virgin Records' UK web site assumes the identity of a raft that is adrift in a sea. The site is actually called, The Raft.

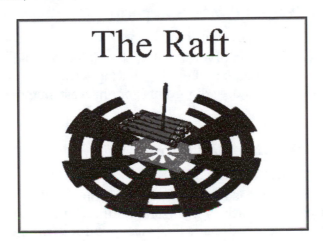

The Raft

From the opening screen, you can jump to the Releases and News section that takes you to a list of the featured artists like: The Future Sound of London, The Verve, and Boy George. Each artists' news and gossip section features things like the current chart performance of a single that may be out, tour information, and random news reports. The Artist section jumps the to a full in-depth look at an specific artist with a glimpse of the music with downloadable sound samples. Audio files containing interviews with band members are also available here. The Raft does a great job of piquing the interest of the browser in exploring new artists and their releases. It is a good example of how to market new music on the Net.

• *Sony Music*

http://www.music.sony.com/Music/FeaturedArtists.html

The largest of all record companies in the free world, Sony has only just begun to unleash their power on the Net. Sony's artist list ranges from Frank Sinatra to Kris Kross and includes enough artists to make this page and its links one of the biggest corporate sites we've seen. They have weekly updated sections for new releases, tours, etc. and a nice section called the Vault where they catalog their entire Sony inventory of CDs and tapes. (Go make a sandwich while this baby loads.)

• *Warner Brothers Records*

http://www.iuma.com/Warner/

Nice selection of artists with audio and video clips. Staff-written bios (we're guessing, based on the glowing terms used) and up to date info about tours and studio events for the vast number of bands on the huge label.

• *Windham Hill Records*

http://www.windham.com

The granddaddy of New Age, Windham Hill takes a more straight forward approach to marketing on the Net by including all of the elements of a good marketing mix: **product**, **place**, **positioning** and **promotion**.

At the opening screen, the viewer is offered the option of choosing a quick tour. This screen **positions** Windham Hill as the premier provider and innovator of New Age music. It discusses the history of the company and the goals for this independent label. The **product** is discussed in a section called, "Our Music." It profiles over 25 artists and nearly 50 of the top releases, containing detailed information on the recording. In another area called, "The Listening Room," music is available for downloading.

The page also **promotes** the label in some additional ways in an area called, "Tune In." Tune In **promotes** the radio stations that play Windham Hill recordings. A chat line offers fans of this music an area to exchange information with other fans about recordings, concerts, or anything else. Finally, there is a place to request that a direct mail piece be E-mailed to a friend of yours who you think might be interested in Windham Hill's web site.

Windham Hill tells the visitor how to get the music in the, "Keeping in Touch" section; the area fulfills the **place** element of the marketing mix. The label lists every way they can be contacted including: E-mail, fax, regular mail, international E-mail, and phone numbers.

Eventually when the Net is a more secure environment, Windham Hill will incorporate online ordering of product.

DJs

There are a lot of club DJs, Mobile DJs, and remix DJs that are using the Net.

Club DJs and remix DJs tend to be oriented to the music, the beat and the equipment. Most of the discussion between these styles of DJs tend to be music oriented. Here are a few newsgroups and sites that might be of interest to all DJs interested in the music, equipment, and the sound.

The Net Mix

http://rampages.onramp.net/~tgurley/tnm.htm

This is a complete reference point, including mailing lists for DJs, rave information, equipment information, and a DJ primer.

• *Newsgroups*

alt.music.makers.dj

A discussion group that has everyone from experienced professional DJs to beginning mobile DJs participating in this ongoing conversation. Discussion focuses on the music, the equipment, and even social aspects of playing music.

alt.music.dance

Dance music is the topic on this group. All styles that would be played at a popular club are part of this group.

alt.music.karaoke

Information for karaoke DJs including equipment, karaoke releases, and contests are discussed here.

alt.rap

This has been the home of the official rap dictionary for several years. It lists a lot of terms found in rap music and lists song references for the words. General discussion of rap music and hip hop is the general thread of this group.

alt.rave

Rave happening, dress, music, and spinning the mix are discussed here.

alt.techno

Heavy beat music with beats starting at 130 beats per minute are debated here.

Mobile DJs are the companies that do school parties, wedding receptions, and company parties. Mobiles are using the Net to conduct their business. If you want to communicate with corporate America, the Net is the place to do it. The DJs are using the medium to send proposals to companies and individuals, transmit contracts, and even to post web sites promoting their business. Here are some sites that might be helpful for mobile DJs running a small business.

alt.wedding or soc.wedding

Weddings are a big part of the of the mobile DJ's business. Both of these newsgroups frequently discuss music and mobile DJs.

Net Music

http://data.tennessee.com/NetMusic/

While we're talking DJs, let's take note of a fairly new member of the Net. Net Music has recently taken up space on the web with their online discount music store. The website is easy to use and they have products and prices neatly displayed. They have everything from microphones to full PAs, speakers, lights, and lighting rigs. The place is looking to expand into musical equipment, too. Check out their used gear section for the best prices.

PLUG IN For More Info!
Browse to the website at
http://www.prenhall.com/~plugin

GETTING YOUR BAND or MUSIC BUSINESS on the NET

With the labels, manufacturers and other professionals getting online, don't you think that your band or music business should be there too? In this section, we will show you how to get promotions on the Net for your band or business. We'll refer to bands here, but this could easily apply to a CD store, Mobile DJ company, production studio, or anything else music related.

Establish your Presence

The first step is to get an account that provides an Internet E-mail address. In the first chapter we discussed how to get a direct account on the Internet with a PPP or SLIP dial-up account. Every area now has Internet providers that will get you access to the Net. The main thing to look for is good service and a provider that will give you server space with your account for setting up a web page.

Look Around

Step two, look at what other bands or businesses like yours are doing on the Net. You may decide that you just want to send an E-mail promotion to all the people in your area that might like the music that your band plays; or you might like to put your band on the World Wide Web for anyone to take a peek at. Explore the web; you can use some of the links to independent bands on the Plug In homepage. Visit the pages of different bands. Jot down what you like and dislike about each of the different sites you visit and what you want to use in your own space.

Create a Web Site

The third step is to create your web space; this can be simple or elaborate. In the following section, you will see some basic information on working with HTML—the language used to place documents on the World Wide Web. However, the basics of your web site should consist of: the name of the band, contact and booking information, a brief summary of the style of music, and some sort of mission statement. (You know. "We want to save the world from evil, by playing our guitars really, really loud!") Below, you will see the homepage for one of our bands, True Story.

True Story

http://web2.airmail.net/bhate/band.htm

True Story

24 hour info & booking line: (214) 941-0722

CD Release Date: January 19, 1996...Stay tuned for release party gigs!

One dark night these boys from the Church were driving and listening to Mission tapes, when a deep howling blues tune took over the AM dial. It was like nothing they had ever heard before. Thumpa thumpa thumpa (and a stained voice sings): "...my bucket's gotta hole in it" thumpa thumpa.

• *Writing HTML Documents*

If you can use a simple word processor and follow a few instructions, you can post your own homepage in minutes.

The code is simple to learn. HTML describes the basic document structure. In other words, it is a set of styles that defines a document. The mark-up coding defines what certain elements look like.

Below, you will see some of the code we used to write True Story's homepage (http://web2.airmail.net/bhate/band.htm).

Each command in brackets <> is a tag that tells the web browser how to display the document.

```
<HTML>
<HEAD>
<TITLE>True Story: the band </TITLE>
</HEAD>

<a> <img src=story1.jpg> </a>


<BODY>
<H1>True Story</H1>
<P><hr><H4>One dark night these boys from the Church were
driving and listening to Mission tapes, when a deep howling blues
tune took over the AM dial. It was nothing like they had ever heard
before. <P>

<P>thumpa thumpa thumpa (and a strained voice sings) "...my
bucket's gotta hole in it" thumpa thumpa.<P>
</BODY>
</HTML>
```

<HTML> is the first and last tag of every document; it indicates that the document is in the HTML language.

The <HEAD> tag specifies that the lines within it are the prologue to the text.

Each document needs a <TITLE> tag. The text inside shows up at the top of the document screen.

HTML links to other documents with an anchor tag <a>. In the one above, we anchor our graphic of the band which is titled story1.jpg.

The main part of the document is written between the <BODY> tags. Header size is noted with the codes <H1> through <H6>, <H1>

being the largest. Paragraphs are noted with the <P> tag. Horizontal rules or lines (to create space between different sections of text) are inserted with the <HR> tag.

Those are some basic tags, but when you start writing HTML on your own, you'll need a good guide. We'd suggest you try out *HTML for Fun and Profit*, published by Prentice Hall.

Here is the homepage for our Mobile DJ business:

Sound Associates

http://rampages.onramp.net/~tgurley/sound.htm

Netscape - [Sound Associates: Mobile DJ's]

File   Edit   View   Go   Bookmarks   Options   Directory   Help

Location: http://rampages.onramp.net/~tgurley/sound.htm

Sound Associates - Mobile DJ's

PO Box 595593

Dallas, TX 75239

1-800-395-2398

Who Are We

The Sound Associates is a mobile DJ company based in Dallas, TX. We do about 125 parties a year in the Texas area. The company is owned by Ted & Jeff Gurley (Gurley Entertainment Corporation).

We've been doing parties since the mid-70's and have accumulated over 5,000 CD's, LP's and yes 45's in our library. Primarily we do weddings, company parties, reunions and school dances. We have three sound systems and a light show. We're members of the ADJA (American DJ Association) and operate as a business not a hobby. We tend to price on the high end ($450-700) because we feel there is a value to our experience, professionalism, and service.

• *Shameless Promotion*

Once you have set up your page you need to get it out to the masses, let people know about your group, show them a picture, let them hear what you do. There are several sites which feature independent bands and music, that you might want to post your information with.

• Sites That Feature Independent Bands

Internet Underground Music Archive (IUMA)

http://www.iuma.com

IUMA was started in late 1993. It was the first site to offer free downloadable music on the Net. As the site developed, it grew to contain over 500 bands (signed and unsigned) and their music—available to listen to or purchase. It has expanded to include live concerts, music magazines, record labels and more. This is IUMA's opening screen.

M.et.al Archives

http://www.webjammers.com/projects/bands.html

This site features bands that are just starting out and not signed with a record label. The bands have all created their own homepages and E-mailed ben@webjammers.com the URL (the address) of the homepage. B.K. DeLong created the site because he felt there needed to be a place on the Net for new bands, unsigned bands, and unheard of bands to get some attention. If you want to get your band noticed send him a link to your site or just check it out to find out about some future stars.

Rock Web Interactive

http://www.rockweb.com/

Rock Web is an interesting combination of online band information and feature articles. The goal of Rock Web is to provide a meeting place for bands and their fans. According to the introduction, it is a place where the fans can congregate and dig into the vibe of the band, read about them, listen to music, and participate in discussions.

Rock Web Interactive works with each band to find out what the band wants to say to their fans through using the medium of the Net.

Virtual Music Spotlight

http://www4.ncsu.edu/unity/users/d/decox/WWW/TVMS.html

This is another site that will link your band's page or even create one for you if you like. The good folks at Virtual Music are also willing to help you put your demo on the Net. If you are interested, send a message to decox@unity.ncsu.edu or to pxixxo@unity.ncsu.edu.

Virtual Radio

http://www.microserve.net/vradio

Virtual Radio is another site that features the music of several bands with new music in DAT quality audio, available to be downloaded to your computer. Once you locate a band you are interested in, with the help of a search tool you are presented a screen with a picture of the band, a brief bio, and the opportunity to download either a sample of music or a complete song. Video of the bands and the real-time audio format are also available.

Complete Songs!

Welcome to **Virtual Radio**(TM) the only non-stop user-definable music broadcast that brings you the latest in new music. Virtual Radio gives you a wide variety of choices -- you can choose which song you'd like to hear and download it to your machine. This isn't a sample, this is a radio-quality broadcast of the **entire cut** many times right off the band's **master DAT**. Each CyberTune(TM) page contains band info, a description of their music, and images of the band. Virtual Radio is the new way to be exposed to today's music -- never miss out on a hit again. Each **CyberTune** is made available with permission of the band and Cyberspace Promotions.

We can be reached via e-mail at **vradio@ugly.microserve.net**

Recently named a Point Survey **Top 5% Site!!!**

One of our favorite regional acts that probably could stand some of the national limelight is the nuclear polka band, Brave Combo. They've got a site and we've got a shot of it here.

Brave Combo

http://www.microserve.net/vradio/bravecombo/bravecom.html

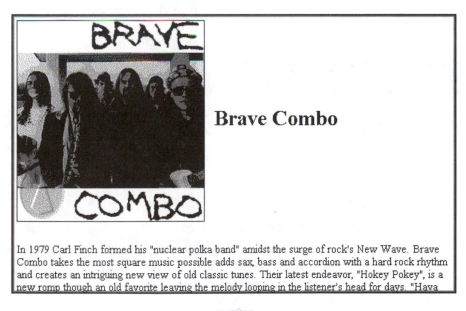

In 1979 Carl Finch formed his "nuclear polka band" amidst the surge of rock's New Wave. Brave Combo takes the most square music possible adds sax, bass and accordion with a hard rock rhythm and creates an intriguing new view of old classic tunes. Their latest endeavor, "Hokey Pokey", is a new romp though an old favorite leaving the melody looping in the listener's head for days. "Hava

You can also put your band into the Virtual Radio mix! It costs only $1 per day to be on Virtual Radio. You can include photos, bios, samples, or complete songs and ordering info.

The site features secured transactions for collecting credit card orders and acting as a distribution point for independent bands.

Worldwide Alternative Jukebox

http://www.nbn.com:80/aaj/

The Worldwide Jukebox provides a site for bands to post samples and information for a small flat fee. Signed and unsigned bands are both represented here. The page about Better Than Ezra, for example, features a discography, bio, reviews, tour schedule, booking information and a few samples.

OTHER RESOURCES

Business of Music Basics

There are two really good primers for bands who not only want to do business on the Net, but also just trying to break into the music business. At the Worldwide Alternative Jukebox listed above, there is an excellent artist reference section that discusses everything from distribution to press kits to getting airplay.

• *Harmony Central*

http://harmony-central.mit.edu/Bands/

Scott Lehman at Harmony Central has put together a good guide that covers several things a starting band might be interested in. He provides links dealing with copyright information and trademarking your band's name.

• *WILMA*

http://www.wilma.com

If you are interested in playing various clubs and venues check out the reference called WILMA, the Worldwide Internet Live Music Archive at. Here, you will find a summary of hundreds of live music clubs around the United States and the world accessed via a searchable database; the information includes contacts, address, seating, and anything else that has been contributed. This site relies heavily on user input.

General Business Guides

• *Commerce Net*

http://www.commerce.net

Information about how to do business on the Net with links to many different business resources.

• *Internet Business Center*

http://tsunami.tig.com/cgi-bin/genobject/ibcindex

A great resource designed for anyone interested in doing business on the Net.

• *U.S. Patent and Trademark Office*

http://www.uspto.gov

The government makes it easy for you to find out basic information about patents and trademarks, and how you can trademark your band name or patent a new instrument.

General Guides to the Music Industry on the Net

• *Music Industry Guide*

http://soundwave.com/mig/migindex.html

Finally, here's a great, comprehensive site about the business of music. The Music Industry Guide has an extensive collection of directories for anything remotely connected to the business of music.

■ There is a handy directory of recording studios around the United States that is organized by state. Each listing gives a thumbnail sketch of the studio and its' equipment. Contact information and phone numbers are listed here.

- There are guides to all of the major record labels and thousands of independent record labels again with contact information, addresses, phone numbers and even some peoples names to send tapes to.

- There is a directory of concert promoters and booking agencies all over the world with contacts and all the important information for getting in touch.

Making money in the music business requires hard work and a lot of self-promotion; the Net can help make this easier than ever before. Good luck!

I use the Net primarily to keep abreast of what's happening in the music business. All the best rumors fly around there, although it takes some effort to separate the fact from the fiction. New releases are almost always talked about by the readers before any other source gets a hold of the release date. Invariably, you run into some one on the Net who knows one of the artists, or the producers, or the sister of the artist, etc. You get some good first hand info on the artist or band that has some reliability. Finally, you can't help but comment extensively on what and why you like the music you do.... and you get to do it to a group of people who will actually listen and agree...

Frank Lafone
hflafone@mailbox.syr.edu

Instrument Oriented Mailing Lists

These are instrument specific mailing lists for musicians and students of music.

A

ACCORDION

Accordion@cs.cmu.edu

Send message to accordion-request@cs.edu

The accordion list is a discussion list about accordions, concertinas and melodeons. This list appeals to players, makers, and repairers of these instruments. List topics include all kinds of information about playing free-reed instruments, contact points for supplies and repair, and reviews of recordings.

ANALOGUE ELECTRONIC INSTRUMENTS

Analogue Heaven

Send message to: Analogue-request@magnus.acs.ohio-state.edu

The Analogue Heaven mailing list is oriented to musicians who are interested in analogue music equipment. Discussion of old and new synthesizers, sequences, drum machines, and effects units are common on the list. The list often has items for sale and repair, and use tips.

B

BAGPIPES

bagpipe@cs.dartmouth.edu

Send message to: bagpipe-request@cs.dartmouth.edu

List for bagpipers. Any topic related to bagpipes is open here. Any Scottish, Irish, English, or Celtic instrument can also be discussed here.

BASS

The Bottom Line Mailing List

Send message to bass-request@uwplatt.edu

Discussion of both the electric and acoustic/upright bass.

BASSOON see Doublereed

BRASS INSTRUMENTS

brass@geomag.gly.fsu.edu

Send message to: brass-request@geomag.gly.fsu.edu

All types of brass music are included in this list: trumpets, french horns, tubas, and trombones. The list focuses on performance issues and related topics.

C

CHAPMAN STICK

Stickwire list

Send message to: sticky request@cs.nott.ac.uk

Mailing list for player who play the Stick, a 10-12 string instrument that covers the range from a bass to a guitar. The mailing list covers technique, artists, and sources.

D

DOUBLEREED

Doublereed-L

Send message to: listproc@acc.wuacc.edu

Message body: Subscribe doublereed-l "your name"

A mailing list for discussion about bassoon and oboe music. Discussion includes dialogue about music, reed making, performances, instruments, and anything else concerning double reed instruments.

DRUMS

Send message to: drum-request@brandx.rain.com

Discussion about anything related to drums and percussion.

E

ELECTRONIC MUSIC

Netjam

Send message to: netjam-request@xcf.berkeley.edu

NetJam is a conduit for people to collaborate on musical compositions by sending MIDI files to each other and allowing others to make adjustments.

267

F

FLUTE PLAYERS

Send message to: Flute-M-request@unixg.ubc.ca

Flute playing, flute music, and anything related to the flute is fair game for this mailing list.

FRENCH HORN

Horn List

Send message to: mugreene@merlin.nlu.edu

Message body: Indicate that you want to subscribe.

Discusses all aspects of playing the French Horn.

G

GUITAR

The Digital Guitar List

Send message to: pvallado@waynesworld.ucsd.edu

Discussion of music technology for string instruments.

H

HAMMER DULCIMERS

Send request to: hammerd@mcs.com

List for players of hammered dulcimer, cymbaloms, yanq qin and related instruments.

HAMMOND ORGAN

Send request to: hammond-request@zk3.dec.com

Hammond organ players are represented on this list.

HANDBELLS

Send message to: Handbell-L@ringer.jpl.nasa.gov

Message body: place word "subscribe" in the subject field.

Players and directors of handbell choirs exchange information on this list.

HARMONICA

Harp-L

Send message to: mxserver@wkuvx1.wku.edu

List to discuss harmonica's - playing them, listening to them, discussing performers, and the instrument itself. The list is open to novices as well as experts.

HARPSICHORDS

Hpschd-l

Send message to: listserv@albany.bitnet

Message body: Subscribe hpschd-l

List is devoted to harpsichords and related instruments like the clavichord, fortepianos, and all similar instruments that came before the modern piano. Theory, construction, restoration, and playing technique are all discussed on this list.

HORNS

International Horn Society maillist

Send message to: majordomo@spock.nlu.edu

Message body: SUBSCRIBE HORN

This Internet discussion group is administered in the name of the International Horn Society, and its purpose is to provide a forum for electronic conversation about all things relating to the (French) horn. Topics include repertoire, teachers and students, pedagogy, workshop and festival announcements, alternate fingerings, the nasty business about whether stopping raises or lowers pitch, horn players versus conductors, horn humor and anecdotes, instrumental repair and technology, scholarly reports, orchestra or band music, chamber ensembles, relations with other brass instruments or anything else the subscribers may want to take on. Although the initial list was sponsored by the International Horn Society, list membership is open to all interested.

L

LUTE

Send message to: lute-request@cs.dartmouth.edu
List for lute researchers and players.

O

OBOE see Doublereed

P

PIANO

Piano-L

Send message to: piano-L-request@uamont.edu

Mailing list for pianists, students and piano teachers. Discussion on this list centers on all aspects of performance and instruction. Topics include: chamber music, practice techniques, history, theory, performance and anything else related to pianos.

PIPE ORGANS

Send message to: listserv@albany.edu

Message body: Subscribe piorg-l

Technical, historical, and musical aspects are discussed on this list. Discussion of performance techniques, recordings and job postings are also appropriate for this list.

T

TROMBONE

Send message to: listproc@showme.missouri.edu

Message body: sub "your name"

TRUMPET

Send message to: listserv@acad1.dana.edu

Message body: Subscribe trumpet

List that is devoted to anything related to the trumpet including performance, repair and instruction.

TUBA

Send message to: listserv@cmsvmb.missouri.edu

Message body: sub "your name"

V

VOCALIST

Send message to: majordomo@phoenix.oulu.fi

Vocalist is a list for singers and anyone interested in singing. Subscribers include students and experienced teachers of singing. Topics include technique, voice car, auditions, concerts, and anything else related to singing.

ACADEMIC and RESEARCH ORIENTED LISTS

AESTHETICS

Send message to: mailbase@mailbase.ac.uk

A discussion of problems, issues, and research into musical aesthetics.

EDUCATION

Library Association, Music

Send message to: listserv@iubvm.ucs.indiana.edu

Message body: SUBSCRIBE MLA-L "Your name"

Any topics related to music libraries or music librarianship.

MUSIC RESEARCH

Send message to: music-research-request@cattell.psych.upenn.edu

Discussion of the application of computers in music research. The list is for musicologists, music analysts, and computer scientists. The list is oriented to those who are interested in music representation systems, music analysis, and retrieval systems for musical scores. The list does not cover MIDI and electronic music.

PERFORMANCE

Send message to: listserv@smsuvmb.cmsu.edu

Academic list for discussion of music performance and instruction. Discussion includes performance practices, aesthetics, and repertoire as applied to music performance.

THEORY

Send message to: listproc@husc.harvard.edu

Articles and reviews targeted to the music profession in the area of music theory and related discussion.

Music Making Newsgroups

These are newsgroups for people interested in music making.

alt.guitar	alt.guitar.amps
alt.guitar.bass	alt.guitar.tab
alt.music.4-track	alt.music.harmonica
alt.music.lyrics	alt.music.makers.dj
alt.music.makers.electronic	alt.music.makers.woodwind
alt.music.midi	alt.music.producer

alt.music.synth.roland	rec.music.makers
rec.music.makers.bagpipe	rec.music.makers.bands
rec.music.makers.bass	rec.music.makers.bowed-strings
rec.music.makers.builders	rec.music.makers.classical.guitar
rec.music.makers.dulcimer	rec.music.makers.french-horn
rec.music.makers.guitar	rec.music.makers.guitar.acoustic
rec.music.makers.guitar.tablature	rec.music.makers.marketplace
rec.music.makers.percussion	rec.music.makers.piano
rec.music.makers.songwriting	rec.music.makers.synth
rec.music.makers.trumpet	

For Dreamers

The problem with the future is two fold:

1. In some ways it's already here, and we already are behind. Much of what we will experiment and create with over the next decade or so is already available. It's just that we've only begun understanding the possible uses. The World Wide Web, which even for most experienced users seems to be nothing short of a miracle, will improve exponentially as bandwidth increases and as modem speeds increase. (Most people on the Net remember 300, 1200, and 2400 BPS modems like they were yesterday. The jump to the current standard of 28,800 has happened in a heartbeat. With ISDN connections on the horizon, we'll be moving up to 58,600 BPS soon. The jump from 2400 to 128,000 is the same kind of jump you'd make if you suddenly could drive 2500 m.p.h. on the highway!)

2. As the Net grows and as information surges upon us, it's inevitable that we won't be able to control it to use it satisfactorily. It's

no wonder you picked up this book off a rack of about a jillion other Net books. People everywhere are panicked about keeping things under control. Well, we are, too obviously. That's why we wrote this book, in part to help ourselves keep things straight.

But no matter what we want. The future is already happening. Musicians are already composing online—sending their music zipping through cyberspace to collaborators, record companies, and fans. Aerosmith and the Rolling Stones have both experimented with live and recorded concerts online. Hard disk drive recording means the possible end of recording tape in studios worldwide. No loss of clarity, no tape error, nothing but perfect reproduction of sounds—the goal of nearly every musician and producer since music making began. And that's not even to mention the archival benefits. Committing rare and vintage LPs, 78s, and deteriorating tapes to disk means that we can maintain the work forever, even cleaning up the hisses, glitches, and scratches from years and years gone by.

As we see it, here are some things to watch:

VIDEO and CONCERTS LIVE on the NET

Live music and concerts on the Internet—a pipe dream? Not at all. You can receive live concerts with a piece of software called CU-SeeMe. (Zip over to Cornell University to download your free copy for either Windows or Mac; the address follows in the list of CU resources.)

CU-SeeMe is a video-conferencing system for Mac, Windows, and the PowerMac. It is being used to "broadcast" live concerts over the Internet. It was developed at Cornell University and is available free from the University. It provides either one-to-one conferencing or one to many conferencing by using a reflector. The reflector, as the name suggests, allows a video and audio signal to be "reflected" to all that log onto the reflector site.

CU-SeeMe allows users with a 14.4 or 28.8 modem, and a SLIP/PPP connection to receive live audio and video from anywhere in the world. Internet concerts are broadcast using a reflector. Here is a sampling of a few of the events and daily programs that have been broadcast using this technology.

Concerts

- A Benefit Concert for Oklahoma City
- SleazeFest: A 21 band music festival in Chapel Hill, NC
- Ongoing Broadcasts: KVR-InternetTV Internet TV Music all the time. http://www.utexas.edu.depts/output/www/tstv.html

Right now it is a bit jerky because it transmits far slower that the 30 frames per second we're used to on the television. However, you can still see the band and the picture live in glorious black and white. Today, there is a bandwidth problem—even at 28.8 kbps—transmitting audio and video; this technology is still in heavy development. However, in the near future, we may all be watching concerts and live shows on our computers.

Here are a few resources to help you out.

CU-SeeMe Event Guide

http://www.umich.edu/~johnlaue/cuseeme/events.htm

CU-SeeMe Software & the FAQs

http://cu-seeme.cornell.edu/

CU-SeeMe Unofficial Users Guide

http://www.indstate.edu/msattler/sci-tech/comp/CU-SeeMe/
   how-to.html

Eden Matrix

http://www.eden.com

Features live Internet concerts from time to time from groups like Machine Screw and Black Pearl, both from Austin, Texas.

One of the really exciting developments regarding music and the Net is the advent of live music feeds. Users can receive audio and video data from a live performance as it happens. I think this kind of service will become very popular in the future. Users can attend concerts electronically if they aren't able to do so in person. Maybe this idea could be extended to allow users to interact with a band's performance. This would allow each show to be unique, as the crowd could contribute to the performance in some way.

Shannon Lawson
lawson@sol-tx.sps.mot.com

CD LINK

http://www.voyagerco.com/cdlink/cdlink.html

Imagine reading an album review and when the reviewer mentions the incredible guitar work, you can instantly hear it. Well, that is the meat of CD Link, a web-based tool developed by Voyager, and is available for free download for Windows and Mac.

CD Link controls the CD ROM player built into your computer. At the Voyager site, you will find a list of CDs, many of which you probably already have in your collection. All you do is insert the music CD in your CD ROM and click on the album you want to interact with. As you can see on the next page, the "Wish" CD by the Cure is given the CD Link treatment. Initially a review or introduction to the artist comes up on the screen and different parts of the article are highlighted. These highlights link the text of the article to your CD ROM player. When you click on the underlined phrase, "sad melodies," Robert Smith's somber vocals come out of your speakers.

Netscape - [Voyager: WISH]

File   Edit   View   Go   Bookmarks   Options   Directory   Help

SPIN   VOYAGER
                                            CD LINK™

THE CURE

"WISH"
                    1992

by Jon Young

Sob, sob. Whimper, sniff. Sorry. I was just savoring the new Cure disc, which means
taking a headlong plunge into a deep, dark pit of despair, with no hope of relief. Or does
it? Fitting comfortably into the category of Another Cure Album, *Wish* makes it hard not
to stereotype Robert Smith and his band of "merry" men: The sad melodies and pathetic
subject matter, amplified by Smith's morbid vocals, offer the ultimate in exquisite pain.
They're so down it's almost funny.

This product promises some interesting interactive applications. Voyager has already teamed up with *Spin* magazine and has provided CD Linked reviews at its site.

Fans will probably start writing CD Link script for their favorite bands and begin posting them on their web sites to introduce newcomers to the bands or just to have more interactivity on the site.

Record companies will use this application and the emerging CD Plus technology to add liner notes and merge its products with the Internet. We imagine that the CDs will be marketed as "web ready" and will include everything from CD Link notes to connections to the band's official Internet page.

CD PLUS

http://www.eden.com/cdplus/

As you have seen in Plug In, the music industry and the computer industry are moving closer and closer together. One of the newest formats to emerge is CD Plus. Keep an eye on the Eden web site listed to keep current.

CD Plus was created by Sony, Microsoft, and Phillips Corporations. The technology allows CD Plus discs to play audio on traditional audio CD players, while adding the ability to play videos and display text and graphics on computer systems with multimedia (CD drive, sound card, and speakers). You can play a CD Plus discs in your existing home or car CD player, then pop the same disc into your PC or Mac and have a whole new multimedia experience. The engine that runs it is packaged right there in Microsoft's newest version of Windows and the CD Plus disks include the drivers for Windows 3.1 (you probably already have everything you need if you have a Mac). Here are the minimum requirements:

PC Minimum Requirements:

- 486SX 25 MHz or faster
- 8 megabytes RAM
- Microsoft Windows 3.1 or higher
- 640x480 screen resolution 256 colors (8-bit)
- Double speed or faster multi-session CD ROM drive
- 8 bit sound card

Mac Minimum Requirements:

- Mac LC III or higher
- 25 MHz 68030 or faster
- 8 Megabytes of RAM
- System 7.1 or later
- Quicktime 2.0 & Soundmanager 3.0 (included on disc)

The really cool thing in the latest version of Windows is that once you load in a CD Plus disc, all the drivers and software you need to take advantage of CD Plus are automatically loaded on your system and the disc plays automatically as well. Once you unload the disc, all the special drivers and libraries (DLLs) are unloaded from the system. It is nice and tidy.

Building on the performance and the digital audio, CD Plus allows the artists to express themselves through some really impressive video and graphical elements. CD Plus discs may include music videos, video interviews, behind the scenes audio, karaoke-style lyrics, biographies, discography—even a direct link to the plugged-in world online.

Artists like Michael Bolton, Mariah Carey, the Cranberries, Willie Nelson, Alice in Chains, Soundgarden, and Bob Dylan have kicked off the project with their own releases. Soon, all artists will have a CD Plus version issued with the audio only CD.

Dylan on CD Plus

For a cool example of how CD Plus will change the way we hear and see music, here's a sample of how Sony Music used the technology to spice up their CD Plus version of Bob Dylan's "Greatest Hits Volume 3."

There are all kinds of cool stuff on the two disk set; in addition to the audio tracks you get: sound samples from various albums, rare photos and "surprises of Bob Dylan." If that isn't enough, you also get 2 full length music videos, a biography of Bob Dylan, and a kind of karaoke that syncs a graphical display of the lyrics with the audio tracks from the "Greatest Hits Vol. 3" disc. The neatest thing is a nifty little Dylan discography viewer that lets you see all songs and liner notes from each album he's recorded, and hear a 15 second sound clip from every song on every album!

This simple application may be the package that finally combines both the computer and music for the home user. In the future, we can easily see the college student bringing a laptop with some great speakers as his only music system to the dorm room.

SMART SHOPPING

Bargain Finder

http://bf.cstar.ac.com/bf

Leave it to the folks at one of the big consulting companies, Andersen Consulting, to develop a CD comparison shopping agent for the world wide web called Bargain Finder.

We like to shop so we did. We typed in the name of one of our worn out vinyl favorites, "Blood on the Tracks" by Bob Dylan, and the agent went shopping at nine different Internet based CD stores. In less than a minute it came back with the results:

EMusic	$11.66
GEMM	Couldn't locate the CD, and suggested that we contact the store directly.
IMM	Couldn't locate and also suggested a direct connection.
CD Now	Blocked the Agent!
NetMarket	Blocked the Agent!
Music Connection	$11.05
CD Land	Blocked the Agent!

Now what about these blocks. Stores don't like to be shopped for price only; in some of the above cases, the stores installed another agent that recognizes the one from Andersen and literally won't let him in. As we all know, price isn't everything; shipping costs, processing time, service, and past experience are all important criteria to consider when shopping and the same thing holds true on the Net.

The Future

Imagine the implications. If it can work on CDs the same agent can find that bargain priced Fender guitar or a new Pioneer system for your home. Maybe this is just another step in the retailing trend of cutting out the middleman. Retailing has moved from small specialty stores to the department store to the warehouse store to super stores that specialize.

Maybe the future search will turn up with Sony offering it to us at wholesale cost just to move the unit.

MOVE INTO HIGH GEAR

Higher bandwidth. It's real and it's going to happen. The choking sound your computer makes as it struggles to take in the millions of bits and bytes will one day be replaced with a whoosh. Once you start moving around on the Net, downloading graphics, and listening to music, you will soon come to the conclusion that there has to be a faster way to cruise than at 28.8 kbps.

There is. It is called ISDN (Integrated Services Digital Network). The typical home phone line is analog; to transfer digital data between computers, a modem is required to turn digital information into analog information (that's what all the noise is when your modem connects).

ISDN is a true digital system that works on the phone lines that you currently have. In addition to the digital data communication, you will also get extremely clear voice communication.

Getting connected at high speed involves some cost and patience. First, you have to work closely with your local phone company to get connected. Some areas of the country are ready for ISDN and others are not. Each telephone system is different, but prices to get set up with ISDN range from free to over $500. The phone companies really are not ready for mass distribution of this network yet. However, the customers are.

You will also need a special ISDN modem and wiring for your computer to establish the connection. In addition, you will need to work with your access provider; they charge more for ISDN access.

ISDN rates are getting affordable as are the modems needed to take advantage of it. ISDN runs at about 128 kbps, quadrupling the 28.8 modem speed.

Before making the final decision to move to a high speed ISDN connection, weigh the combination of the cost of the line, the modem, and the access against the need to get data this fast. If you are happy with your current speed go with it, and wait for the next generation of fiber optics and cable connections to the Net.

The nature of computing will change as dramatically in the next 12-20 years as it has in the last 12-20. Memory and processing chips will shrink down to the molecular level, allowing computers of unprecedented speed, energy efficiency, and portability. Imagine the ultimate Walkman - a tiny, super high-quality speaker in your inner ear. You have a thin keypad the size of a saltine cracker from which you can order any song, and it is transmitted in burst-mode to the ear-unit, and stored there for later playback. (And the fidelity is excellent). This sort of stuff is not fantasy - it will happen, and it will not only change music, but our whole society in ways we cannot imagine.

Aaron Woodin
DeltaV@ix.netcom.com

INTERACTIVE FUN and GAMES

As you cruise around the Net, a lot of the sites you will run across are fairly passive, some information is fed to you and that is about it. Sites are being developed that provide information and make you want to come back for more.

Virtual Nashville

http://virtualnashville.com

Virtual Nashville is a music oriented game. You are in the role of an aspiring country singer who is in search of a recording contract. If you visit the right places and collect the right stuff you win the prize, a virtual recording contract.

You travel around Nashville and visit recording studios, clothing shops, music stores, the Grand Ole Opry, and see various sites around the city. As you travel, you are presented with screens of things to do, music to listen to, and some fairly unobtrusive advertising. In the following shot, you will see the famous Ryman Auditorium (the former home of the Grand Ole Opry) in virtual Nashville.

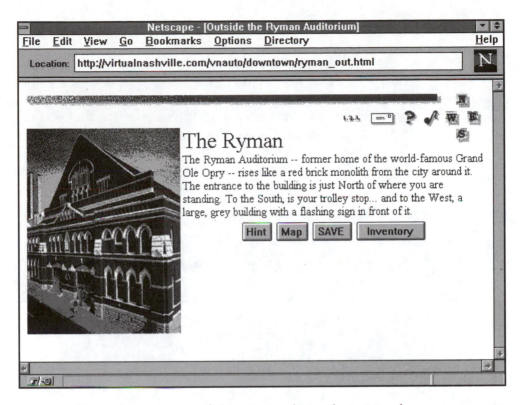

Now, the purpose of this site is obviously to introduce someone to the city and expose us to some advertising, but for the music fan there are a lot of goodies here.

The possibilities with this are endless. Imagine, using similar graphics and technology to let you take a virtual tour of the backstage area of a concert or in the inner workings of a recording session.

MUSIC RECOMMENDATION SERVICES

Do you ever get bored with you music collection and want to find something new and unusual. The Internet is the perfect vehicle to help you find new styles of music and new artists to listen to. With access available to huge databases there are tools that will recommend music to you based on your preferences.

Firefly

http://www.agents-inc.com/

This is a service in transition. It's been called Ringo, then HOMR; now it's Firefly. Regardless of the name, however, it's a cool service. After you gain access you are presented with a list of several artists and groups. You can then choose to rank the artists that you are familiar with or skip the band if you are unfamiliar. Once you have completed the rankings, you are given a list of recommended groups and groups to avoid. As you can see below, the service thought we should pick up some more R.E.M and Sex Pistols stuff.

Netscape - [Music]

File   Edit   View   Go   Bookmarks   Options   Directory   Help

Back   Forward   Home   Reload   Images   Open   Print   Find   Stop

Netsite: http://www.agents-inc.com/~25435/M1SwLbOOH5.:/CgiBin/MusicPage?Skip=2   N

people firefly music buzz

[PEOPLE]   [WELCOME]   [BUZZ]

bobhate, **You might like to try these artists.**

An asterisk indicates your current rating.

*7: the best   ± Sex Pistols
    Suggested ▤▨

*6: great stuff   ± R.E.M.
    Suggested ◧▤▨

Submit _Send More

ASCAP and BMI LICENSING CONCERNS

Regulation is creeping in on the Net. Copyrighted material is being protected.

As upstart music services create their home on the Internet, music licensing giants ASCAP and BMI are creating licensing agreements to extend the protection of their playlists on the World Wide Web and the Internet.

In the late summer of 1995, ASCAP issued its first performance license to Hajjar/Kaufman Advertising to license the computer transmission of music. Radio HK, http://www.hkweb.com/radio, is an audio-on-demand service that allows the user to choose music in a jukebox type format for play-back over the Real Audio player.

BMI and ASCAP both have secured an agreement with Music Previews, http://www.mpmusic.com/, to license all of their songs for downloading and previewing. Music Previews allows users to listen to 30 second clips of up to five songs from various CDs of new music, in addition CD covers and artist information is also available.

Both services are creating special agreements for radio stations and anyone that wants to put copyrighted sounds on the Net.

RADIO on DEMAND

So, do you feel limited by the same old radio stations in your listening area? Do you think there might be a format that is better than what the stations in your area are broadcasting? Are you missing out on some tunes that others around the country are listening to? Turn on the radio on the net.

Imagine clicking on a button on your web browser and hearing a radio station from anywhere in the US, or the world, coming from your PC's speakers. It seems like science fiction, but two different services have made it possible. These services offer a combination of live feeds and audio on-demand. Audio on-demand is a live download of pre-recorded material. A live feed is the same live radio broadcast that someone is listening to in their car in, for example, San Francisco. With audio on-demand, you can hear this live feed, in real time, anywhere in the world. The quality is 100% digital stereo just like a CD; in fact it is cleaner than the local radio since the conduit of the Net isn't affected by propagation (the influence of the atmosphere on a radio signals).

Stream Works from Xing Technology

http://www.xingtech.com/

Stream Works is our favorite. The station list is really good and it features one great standout, KPIG from Santa Cruz, California. KPIG has a diverse playlist featuring Dr. John, Stevie Ray Vaughan, Grateful Dead, Bob Dylan, the Allman Brothers Band, and many more. KPIG is what free form radio became when it disappeared.

If you have a PC, Unix system (SGI, Sun, Linux) or Mac, you can download client software from Xing's web site,

http://www.xingtech.com/,

as well as some mirror sites including

http://www.butterfly.net.

Here are some already active Internet-ready radio stations:

KPIG	Santa Cruz	http://www.kpig.com
KMPS Country	Seattle	http://www.kmps.com
CFRA	Canada	http://www.worldlink.ca
KZOK	Seattle	http://www.kzok.com
iRock Radio		http://www.irock.com
KWBR	Arroyo Grande	http://www.xingtech.com

All you only need is a sound card or built-in sound hardware; all compressed stream decoding is performed in software, though StreamWorks. Be sure once you get the software to check out the video feeds that are being experimented with.

Audio Net

http://www.audio.net.com/

Audio Net currently offers talk radio; they have a 24 hour sports station and one of our favorites, KLIF radio from Dallas, TX. Tuning in on KLIF, you can hear the talk shows live from one of the sports guys, or listen to some entertainment from Kevin McCarthy or to some politics from David Gold.

If you can't catch the live feed you can catch up on previous shows from the audio on demand menu. Audio Net uses the Real Audio software (http://www.realaudio.com) that we discussed in chapter two.

Both of these services give a glimpse of what the future brings to the plugged-in user of the net. These two are ready and waiting for the bandwidth to grow. Of course, as advertisers catch on, the medium will flourish and all of us will benefit by having radio stations only a mouse click away.

MUSIC on DEMAND

Click on the network and up comes a screen with a list of musical styles. You might be in the mood for some big band with guitar. So you click on Big Band and are presented with a list of artists and a search engine. Charlie Christian was a great guitar player with Benny Goodman's band, so you type in Goodman and Christian and you see a list of songs featuring Charlie's guitar with the Benny Goodman band. Click on one of these and music instantly fills the room.

Music on demand isn't a pipedream. The real hang-up in a system like the one described above is that music storage requires too much disk space; think about the last time you downloaded a song clip. A typical CD requires 600 to 700 Mbytes of storage. Researchers have been working on sonically pleasing music compression software for years and it seems that a couple of the labs have got it down.

The technology to compress music and re-expand it has been developed by both Bell Labs and Dolby. In fact, technology exists that will allow 15 hours of music to be placed on a typical CD that would then run through a compression decoder box for playback.

Once we are all wired for fiber optics in the home the next step would be to create a distribution system for music on demand. The music would be stored on a centralized system and made available for playback for a minimal fee. Our wired computer would access the main menu and the music will be routed to the stereo system.

Distribution of music in the next 10 years will change dramatically.

The 1994 Recording Industry Association of America's Annual Report.

"...The RIAA is dedicated to preserving... its existence in the midst of the digital revolution."

"A revolution that is everywhere: it the steady march of computers into homes... in the explosion of interest in the Internet... in the growth of online services... in the business alliances among entertainment, communications, cable, and computer companies. It is changing our business dramatically. The way consumers interact with the music they love. The way they receive it. And the way they pay for it. Our industry must continue to take advantage of this revolution. Otherwise, the revolution will take advantage of us.

Jay Berman
Chairman and CEO

Hilary Rosen
President and COO

Internet By Cable?

John Malone, CEO of TCI Cablevision (the country's largest cable provider), is pushing his corporate buddies at Hewlett-Packard and Motorola hard to come up with standards for a cable-modem. The plan is to provide music, video, TV, and the Internet through two way cable connections—like the ones in the back of your TV. At this time only about 40% of the cable subscribers in America have two way capability; for the other 60%, cable comes in on a one-way pipe. So, the technology has to be refined; homes nationwide have to be re-wired, but the forecast is good with TCI's massive monetary base. The speed of the cable-modem will likely hover around 10 million bits per second (10 megabits per second). That's about 1000 times faster than a 14.4 KPBS modem carries now. That kind of speed guarantees digital audio and video that has only been hinted at by current technology.

One of the few positive things I have to say about the inevitable commercialization of the Net by cable and telephone companies is that music is going to forge new channels of direct-to-the-people distribution. Although some bands now record their music for the Internet for free or limited distribution, there are few people who have the time and computer resources to take full advantage of this; with the advent of combined telecommunications, it should be feasible for any band to go digital and distribute music (free or for a price) through the Net, in whatever form the Net takes in the coming years. I only hope that the censorship of the Net which seems equally (and woefully) inevitable is defeated or limited before the amazing creativity and civil liberties of artists and fans alike is in jeopardy.

Peter DiFalco
pdifalco@ecst.csuchico.edu

KEEPING CURRENT

The Internet and its music resources are growing at a huge pace. Every six months the number of websites on the Net doubles. New users are plugging in with ease, thanks to connectivity software being built into newest Windows operating system. E-mail addresses are becoming as common of an identifier as a home telephone number. Bands, record labels, and fans are connecting like never before in the plugged in world of music.

With the exponential growth of the Net, Plug In the book is merely a starting point. There are a variety of ways to keep current with the world of music. Here are a few suggestions.

- Our collection of pointers to music resources is updated weekly at the Plug In web site, http://www.prenhall.com/~plugin. You can use this site as a starting point or just somewhere to check in occasionally.

- Use the Search Engines and detailed lists of lists that we pointed you to in Chapter One. One of the most helpful lists is the Yahoo list that updates sites daily. If you are looking for specific information use the Info Seek search engine. Both of these are linked in the Netscape package.

- Maintain your audio drivers. New sounds, recordings, and music are coming out with leaner and meaner drivers. Here's a great place to check out for Macintosh sound utilities http://www.wavenet.com/~axgrindr/quimby4.html or find more Mac and Windows utilities at http://www.cs.brown.edu/fun/bawp/sound_utilities.html.

- Subscribe to at least one Mailing List Group and become a regular in a couple of newsgroups that interest you. Announcements of new sites and general Net news usually turn up in these areas before they show up anywhere else.

- Find a couple of web sites you like and log into these weekly. If you're interested in popular and new music, check in with Addicted to Noise. If you are interested in Blues, go to The Blues Highway.

THE END

That's it for this edition. We aren't kidding ourselves. We know the Internet is a big fantastic world that we've only just begun exploring. But it's a start.

Just like music, the joy is in the discovery. The journey justifies itself.

Visit the PLUG IN Website!
http://www.prenhall.com/~plugin
If you find some neat stuff online, please let us know.
You can send us mail directly at!
Ted: tgurley@onramp.net
W.T.: bobhate@airmail.net

292

Plug Into
the Bonus CD ROM

As we put this book together we found a lot of sound tools and programs that helped us in our exploration of the Net and music. All of the software developers let us give you a version that is functional on the bonus CD ROM. These are evaluation versions meaning that you may not be able to save a file or the database may be limited, but in all other ways these work just like the full version. If you find one you like, register it!

On the CD ROM, you'll find sound editors, business management software, HTML editors, MIDI sequencers, music databases, music instruction and notation programs and some original songs in both *.MIDI and *.WAV formats to play with.

Any PC or MAC with a CD drive will read the CD. If you use or find some other software that we should know about, please let us know.

Enjoy!

Ted & W.T.

AUDIO EDITING/PLAYBACK SOFTWARE

Cool Edit [Digital Sound Editor/Player— Windows]

Syntrillium Software Corporation
PO Box 60274
Phoenix, AZ 85082
(602) 941-4327
(602) 941-8170 (fax)
e-mail: syntrill@aol.com

This is by far the best player/sound editor for Windows and your browser. Any *.WAV or *.AU file you can find is playable with this program. In fact we haven't found a soundfile we couldn't play through Cool Edit. It also allows a number of effects like reverb, echo, flanging, reverse play, etc. to modify the sounds. In many ways it's like a paint program for audio. Go to the COOL directory and run cool.exe. The price ranges from $25-100, depending on the level you register at; there are 3 different models— Lite, Regular and Preferred Wav Files.

We've included some music you can play with. In the "Samples" sub-directory, you'll find two files True.wav and Tina.wav. These are two acts managed by Moonguy Management. You can find more information about these fine people by checking out:

http://web2.airmail.net/bhate/moonguy.htm

True.wav
True Story "Face Down"
Stephen Thomas & Bob Hate 1996

True Story has been playing around Dallas over a year, logging a tremendous number of gigs. Their first CD came out in early 1996 and this cut comes from it.

They can be further researched at:

http://web2.airmail.net/bhate/band.htm

Tina.wav
Griffin Shawe "Tina"
Bob Hate 1995

Griffin is a terrific vocalist who is currently shopping for a record deal. This is a tune from her most recent recording sessions.

SAWPlus [Windows]

Software Audio Workshop
Innovative Quality Software (IQS)
2955 E. Russell Road
Las Vegas, NV 89120-2428
(702) 435-9077
(702) 435-9106 (fax)
(702) 435-7186 (BBS)

This is some very high end (but affordable at a list price of $599) hard disk recording software from IQS, a well respected and award winning corporation out of Vegas. If you have a band, radio station, or recording studio, this is for you. The trial version on the disc also comes with some utilities software that will allow you the kind of sound reinforcement and modification of a pro studio (compressors, equalizers, gates, etc.). Run the setup.exe from the SAW directory on the CD ROM and follow their instructions from then on.

BUSINESS MANAGEMENT SOFTWARE FOR DJs or AGENTS

BPM Counter [Windows]

e-mail: richie@i-max.co.nz

This is freeware written by a couple of guys in New Zealand. It's a tiny Windows program that allows you to count beats per minute by tapping the rhythm on your space or enter key. It's a very valuable little tool for DJs. There is an enhanced version of the program that you can get from the e-mail address above. Run BPMcount.exe from the BPM directory.

Info Manager 2.0
[Windows—Business Utility]

CustomWare Systems
1517 Livingston Drive
Plano, TX 75093
(817) 929-2800
e-mail: tweeks@pic.net / 74544.3200@compuserve.com
WWW: http://cwarenet.com

This is an evaluation version (the number of records in the database is limited) of Info Manager, a very useful database designed for the special needs of Mobile DJs for tracking business related data. However, it is easily adapted for bands, managers, booking agents, etc. It generates invoices, tracks employee data, generates bar code, prints CD and tape inserts, and much more. The cost for the full version is $225. Nice interface. It's in the INFOMAN directory. Run setup.exe from the subdirectory Disk 1.

Showbiz and Showdisc
[Windows—Business Utility/Music Database]

Entertainment Solutions
880 Joyce Road
Mayfield Village, OH 44143
(216) 473-2098

These are two different programs. Showbiz is an excellent database for DJs and performers. Comes with clipart (useful for making your own business promotional materials) and links to word processors with its mail merge feature. Showdisc is a music library database that features terrific list making capabilities. It's very useful for collectors and DJs alike. Showbiz is $249 and that price gets you a free copy of Showdisc. Showdisc by itself is $89.99. These are both in the SHOW directory. Run setup.exe out of subdirectory Disk 1 to get started.

HYPERTEXT MARK-UP LANGUAGE (HTML) EDITOR

Hot Dog [Windows—HTML Editor]

Sausage Software
PO Box 36
Briar Hill
Victoria 3088
Australia
WWW: http://www.sausage.com

Here's the software you can use to build your own page. This is a 30 day evaluation copy, but both of us bought the real thing shortly after trying it. It's simply the best HTML editor available, easy to use, friendly, and full of shortcuts around the sometimes tricky world of website creation. Run hdgsetup.exe from the HOTDOG directory on the CD ROM.

MIDI SQUENCERS

Cakewalk [Windows—MIDI]

Twelve Tone Systems
PO Box 760
Watertown, MA 02272
(800) 234-1171
(617) 924-6657 (fax)

This requires an installed MIDI Interface or soundcard (configured for MIDI). The demo is in the CAKE directory. Run setup.exe. The demo will allow you to do everything that this impressive and powerful MIDI software can do except save songs. As noted extensively in Chapter Three, this is the finest Windows MIDI software available.

MIDI Songs and Samples for Cakewalk

We've also included lots of *.WRK files on the CD ROM in the SONGS directory. You can play and modify these samples at will as you get used to the various software. All of these files are originals composed by Bob Hate of the "Eddy" band, "True Story," and owner of Moonguy Management in Dallas. In fact, once you get familiar with the product, you can run these song files in the background while you do other things. Make sure you check out PLUG.MID or PLUG.WRK first— it's the theme song for this book!

Jammer Professional (Windows)

Sound Trek
3408 Howell St., Suite F
Duluth, GA 30136
(770) 623-0879
(770) 632-3054 (fax)

Jammer contains a 256 Track MIDI sequencer. This is fun; you create a style and a chord progression, and Jammer cranks out a song for you. It includes over 200 styles of music. Jammer won the Editors' Choice award from Electronic Musician. Run Setup from the JAMPRO directory. Retail $199.

Jammer SongMaker (Windows)

With the Songmaker, you can create music ranging from current alternative sounds to classics. Enter the chord progression and the style and you are off and running. Run Setup from the JAMSONG directory. Retail $89.

Music Sculptor [Sequencer/Windows]

Aleph Omega Software
Box 61085
Kensington Postal Outlet
Calgary, Alberta
T2N 4S6
Canada
72613.3575@compuserve.com
403-257-2115

This is a basic music sequencer with some public domain files. This allows you to record, play and edit MIDI files and has a lot of instruments to play with. Run Music.exe from the SCULPT directory. This is a full shareware version. Registration includes manuals and a lot of additional files for $29.95.

Musicshop [Macintosh— Sequencing Software]

Opcode Sequencing Products
3950 Fabian Way, Suite 100
Palo Alto, CA 94303
http://www.opcode.com/index.html

Musicshop is Opcode's entry level sequencing software. With a MIDI interface and keyboard, you have the makings of a MIDI studio. The on-screen display uses familiar tape-deck-style controls allowing simple, quick recording, playback and MIDI editing. It has 16 tracks (one for each of the 16 MIDI channels) and its dual editing screens can toggle between standard music notation and graphic piano roll editing. The music notation is especially well presented, and can be used to print professional sheet music. Go to OPCODE and install the Musicshop demo.

Vision [Macintosh— Sequencing Software]

Opcode Sequencing Products

It may be simple to call this a souped up version of Musicshop, but essentially it is. It's a complete, professional software system for the recording, editing, and playback of MIDI-based music. This latest version boasts major new features such as music notation editing and printing, Track Overview, and Groove Quantize plus many other enhancements (including very sensitive note editing functions). Opcode's Open Music System is required to use the demo. Go to the OPCODE directory, and install the Vision demo.

MUSIC COLLECTORS AND DJs

Music Database [Windows & DOS—Music Database]

Stallion Software Systems
5227 Viceroy Dr. N.W.
Calgary, AB T3A 0V2
CANADA
(403) 286-9711
e-mail: 72624.1063@compuserve.com

This is an easy way to computerize your music collection. You can sort and store by tracks, artist name, album titles, or individual tracks. Fast search function. Good looking printout; perfect for collectors and DJs. The US price is $34.95. It's in the MDS directory with sub directories for both Windows and DOS. For the Windows version you'll have to run setup.exe. In DOS, look for install.bat.

MUSIC INSTRUCTION SOFTWARE

Chord (DOS & SPARC Utility)

Martin Leclerc
19 Browning
Dollard des Omeaux, QU H9G 2K5
CANADA

All over the Internet, you'll find files of chords for guitarist. Here's a simple utility program that converts the sometimes hard to read *.CRD files you'll download from FTP sites and turns them into easy to read sheet music/lyric sheets. Go to the CHORD362 directory. Read the .doc file in the DOC subdirectory. There are a couple of tricky routines to run the program, but they are explained in the document.

Claire [Macintosh - Music Instruction]

Opcode Sequencing Products
WWW: http://www.opcode.com/index.html

     Claire teaches fundamental music skills - ear training, sight reading, and music theory. You play and/or sing notes into your Mac's microphone, and Claire hears you. It provides customized instruction based on your own needs - acting as a teaching assistant that guides you through the curriculum. You can keep and print a log as you learn new lessons. The program is easy enough for kids, yet multi-faceted for more serious students. Go to the OPCODE directory and install Claire.

Guitar Workshop [Windows— Guitar Instruction]

Oberwerk Corporation
3997 N. Lakeshore Drive
Jamestown, OH 45335
(513) 675-6792
(513) 675-6793 (fax or BBS)
WWW: http://www.erinet.com/oberwerk/gws.html

     This is a very nice music instructional program that while dedicated to guitarists will also prove useful to composers and piano players. The full feature version with drop-in modules costs $59.95. (You can order the full version online at their BBS number above.) Run the setup.exe from the GWS directory on the CD ROM.

MiBAC Music Lessons Software
(Windows & Mac— Piano Instruction)

MiBAC
PO Box 468
Northfield, MN 55057
(507) 645-5851

     This is a good entry level piano instruction program that features ongoing progress reports, allowing a student to keep track of his or her progress. Its emphasis is on reading and understanding music, everything from major and minor scales, to the more obscure— but important— circle of fifths, jazz scales, etc. The full featured version is $119.95. This is in the MIBAC directory, with sub directories for Mac and Windows. We recommend copying the files to a new directory on your hard drive and then running the demo program.

Music Ace [DOS— The Fundamentals of Music Instruction]

Harmonic Vision
906 University Place
Evanston, IL 60201
(708) 467-2395
(708) 467-3008 (fax)

Don't be bothered by the DOS format. This a fantastic music instruction program that blows away most other programs of its type. It's graphical and fun to use and its ability to utilize not only Soundcards but full MIDI setups moves it ahead of competitors. The full version has 24 different lessons that "develop and reinforce fundamental music skills." It's in the ACE directory. Get out of Windows and then install. The price for this gem of a program is about $30, a terrific bargain.

Neon Notes [Windows— Piano Instruction]

P.O. Box 8727
La Jolla, CA 92038=09
(619) 587-1732
e-mail: neonnote@ix.netcom.com

This is a beginner level piano instruction program great for kids. It's loaded with colors and a handful of songs to begin with. The full feature version includes a easy to read 50 page book that will help the young student learn basic skills. It's in the NEON directory. Run setup.exe from there. The full version is $19.95.

Piano [Windows— Piano Instruction]

Musicware
8654 154th Avenue NE
Redmond, WA 98052
(206) 881-9797
(800) 99-PIANO
(206) 881-9664 (fax)
e-mail: 73122.3137@compuserve.com
WWW: http://www./halcyon.com/musicware/

This is a very powerful and interactive music instruction program for piano. It has multiple levels so beginners and advanced players can gain help. The full featured discs are sold separately at about $90 a pop. There are also song discs available (pop, rock, Christmas, folk, etc.) available to help in your training at about $40 a piece. The demo is in the PIANO directory. Run setup.exe from there.

Virtuax [Windows - Guitar Instruction and Practice]

Shannon Terry Software
2930 Addison Dr.
Grove City, OH 43123-2050

Virtuax is a neat program for guitar players and those that want to be. Go to the AXE directory on the CD ROM and run the install routine. You will be greeted by a spinning guitar and a hot rock lick. The program is a 30 day full function demo. All you do once you configure it for your sound card is select a chord and double click either on the scale, arpaggio or chord button and you will here to selection you made.

MUSIC NOTATION SOFTWARE

Master Tracks Pro [MIDI— Windows]

Passport Design
100 Stone Pine Road
Half Moon Bay, CA 94019
1-800-443-3210

Master Tracks Pro is a very powerful MIDI sequencing program. Passport is a terrific company with a wide range of products. The pricing information and availability of all the Passport stuff is also available at their 800 number. In the PASSPORT directory is a demo of their Master Tracks 6.0, their top of the line software. If you are installing in a Windows based system go to the PRO6DEMO subdirectory and run setup.exe.

Music Time [Music Notation— Mac and Windows]

Passport Design

Entry Level notation system. An easy and entertaining way to compose, play and learn music on your computer. To install for Windows systems run setup.exe from the MUZKDEMO subdirectory and for Macintosh. It is targeted to students, teachers, and hobbyists.

Encore [Music Notation— Mac and Windows]

Passport Design

Professional notation program. This demo allows you to do everything except save and print. Encore lets you compose and edit standard music notation. Run setup.exe from the ENC_DEMO directory for Windows and for Macintosh. It is a professional level product used by several studios.

MIDI Workshop [MIDI— Mac and Windows]

Passport Design

Complete MIDI sequencer and MIDI interface for your soundcard. An entry level program. Handles up to 64 tracks. To install for Windows go to the WKSDEMO sub-directory and run setup.exe.

Passport has also been kind to include a lot of MIDI songs in two different directories for you to play with. They range from jazz to rock to holiday songs, look in the QWKTUNES or the XMAS sub-directory for a bunch of *.MID songs.

Mozart [Windows— Music Composition]

David Webber
484 Warrington Rd.
Cylcheth
Warrington, WA3 5RA
UK

This is a music processor designed to work like a word processor. It is primarily used for producing printed music for instrumentalists. Once you have written the music you can play the tune if you have MIDI synthesis capability. You can easily edit errors, copy passages, and transpose written music to new keys. There are two versions of the registered one ranging from $42 to $49. Go to the MOZART directory and run setup.

PRO AUDIO MIXING SOFTWARE

SAMM
[Audio Mixing, Windows, Must have a Yamaha ProMix Mixer]
Software Audio Midi Mixer
Innovative Quality Software (IQS)
2955 E. Russell Road
Las Vegas, NV 89120-2428
(702) 435-9077
(702) 435-9106 (fax)
(702) 435-7186 (BBS)

This is a major step forward to computerizing audio mixing. The software is a mixer that interfaces with the Yamaha ProMix 01 Digital Mixing Console. It brings all the features of the mixer to your screen. Even if you don't have the Yamaha, try it out, the visuals are awesome. Go to the SAMM subdirectory and run setup.exe.

Index

Numerics

A

I

P

Q

R

Z